Practical Module Development for Prestashop 8

Create modern, customizable, and dynamic online stores using efficient modules

Louis AUTHIE

BIRMINGHAM—MUMBAI

Practical Module Development for Prestashop 8

Group Product Manager: Alok Dhuri

Publishing Product Manager: Himani Dewan

Content Development Editor: Rosal Colaco

Technical Editor: Jubit Pincy

Copy Editor: Safis Editing

Project Coordinator: Manisha Singh

Proofreader: Safis Editing

Indexer: Pratik Shirodkar

Production Designer: Alishon Mendonca

Developer Relations Marketing Executives: Deepak Kumar and Mayank Singh

First published: April 2023

Production reference: 1070423

Published by Packt Publishing Ltd.

Livery Place

35 Livery Street

Birmingham

B3 2PB, UK.

ISBN 978-1-83763-596-2

www.packtpub.com

To my honey, Alice, and my lovely boys, Tom and Noé.

– Louis AUTHIE

Contributors

About the author

Louis AUTHIE is a freelance full-stack developer with over 25 years of experience in PHP. He graduated from the ENAC, Toulouse, France in 2011 as an engineer and from the CNAM Paris, France as an analyst programmer in 2017.

Since 2012, he's developed and maintained modules and themes from various versions of PrestaShop. Becoming an associate for Label Naturel's bedding e-shop in 2016 improved his awareness of online sellers' challenges. In 2019, he started contributing to the PrestaShop open source project, first to the documentation, then to back-office migration and bug fixes. Louis co-founded Web-Helpers, a web agency, in 2020, and teaches professionals in PHP, WordPress, PrestaShop, and Symfony development as a consultant trainer.

I want to thank my girlfriend and our beloved boys who supported me during this writing adventure, even if they won't understand a word of this book! Thanks to my family for their good care. Thanks to all the Packt Publishing staff who guided me during the whole process, and special thanks to my amazing reviewers, Hervé Hennes and Franck Lefevre.

All the royalties of this book will be donated to the Friends of PrestaShop association, which constantly contributes to the PrestaShop Project and manages a very helpful Slack channel.

About the reviewers

Hervé Hennes, the lead developer at Advisa, is a senior PrestaShop developer, and Magento certified. His famous blog at h-hennes is a must-read for all PrestaShop and Magento developers.

Franck Lèfevre has been a self-made PHP developer for more than 15 years. Working as a freelance developer, he helps businesses to solve their technical problems. He is a big expert on PrestaShop and remains the main PrestaShop open source project contributor. He is also an indie maker and the creator of the *Skypaper* application.

Table of Contents

6

The Themes   61

Part 2 – How to Create Your Own Modules

7

What Are Modules? Let's Create a Hello World Module   71

8

A Reinsurance Block Module   81

9

A Customer Callback Request Module 95

10

Category Extension Module 139

11

A Simple Blogging Module — 165

12

A Cash Payment Module — 207

13

A Drive Delivery Module — 223

Part 3 – Customizing Your Theme

14

How to Create a Child Theme   245

15

Overriding Some Templates   251

16

Assets Compiling with Webpack   257

Preface

Since version 1.7, PrestaShop began its migration from the old legacy core to a brand new Symfony-based system, this has resulted in many changes for developers, from maintenance to module development, and that's what this book is all about.

The 16 chapters are grouped into 3 sections, each of which can be read individually. Feel free to go directly to what you need; there are no rules! However, it is best to read everything if you want to get the big picture of the system.

The first section explains how the legacy and the Symfony core work together and explores the main components of PrestaShop. There, we use many reverse engineering analyses. Even if it can be tough sometimes, the general idea is to show us how and where to search into the core objects so as to be able to find answers and go further.

The second section explains how to create various types of modules, with many hands-on examples. This practical approach will enable us to face most of our everyday requests from the simplest `Hello World!` to a full blogging module. Carrier and payment modules are also covered.

The third section provides the best practices and solutions to customize the themes and graphical parts of PrestaShop: child theme creation, module template and asset overrides, and asset bundling with Webpack.

As you can see, many aspects of PrestaShop are covered in this book, and our method is different from the general feature listings available in the developers' documentation. The main target is to provide a practical approach with examples, which is lacking on the web or in the multiple available sources of information.

I hope you will enjoy your journey into the PrestaShop development world and that this book will become a useful toolbox!

Who this book is for

If you are a PHP developer already using PrestaShop as a simple user wanting to know more or solve online sellers' problems by creating modules as a professional, either in a web agency or freelance, this book is definitely for you. In order to learn from this book, you should have a basic knowledge of the Symfony framework. This book will be a really good help for the module developers expecting to move from the old legacy environment to Symfony. Magento or WooCommerce developers can use this book as a tool to compare and move to PrestaShop.

What this book covers

Chapter 1, Quick Overview of the System, explores the structure of PrestaShop.

Chapter 2, Configuration and Initialization of PrestaShop, explains the initialization process of PrestaShop and how to configure it.

Chapter 3, The Front Office, shows how front office pages are generated in PrestaShop.

Chapter 4, The Back Office, shows how Symfony-based and legacy-based back office pages are processed.

Chapter 5, The Hooks, explains what Hooks are, and why they are so important for PrestaShop module developers.

Chapter 6, The Themes, covers the structure of a theme.

Chapter 7, What Are Modules? Let's Create a Hello World Module, shows you how to create your first simple module.

Chapter 8, A Reinsurance Block Module, shows you how to create a module to increase the rate of conversion for your shop.

Chapter 9, A Customer Callback Request Module, shows you how to create a modern module using Symfony and find a way to get customer details to increase the rate of purchase.

Chapter 10, Category Extension Module, shows you how to create a category extension module to add fields to your category page in the back office and provide them to the front office.

Chapter 11, A Simple Blogging Module, shows you how to create a simple blog module with posts and post categories to apply all the most useful pieces of knowledge in module development.

Chapter 12, A Cash Payment Module, shows you how to create a payment module with its specificities.

Chapter 13, A Drive Delivery Module, shows you how to create a carrier module with a pickup relay point choice in the checkout process.

Chapter 14, How To Create a Child Theme, explains how to extend an existing theme by creating a child theme.

Chapter 15, Overriding Some Templates, teaches you how to override module templates and assets to make them fit in a theme graphical context.

Chapter 16, Assets Compiling with Webpack, offers a simple guide to use the Webpack bundler.

To get the most out of this book

You will need to be an intermediate PHP developer, having a basic knowledge of Symfony and knowing how to use PrestaShop and its back office. You will also need an operational PrestaShop v1.7.x or 8.x version installed, functional, and accessible. All the code examples have been tested using PrestaShop 1.7.8.8 and 8.1.

If you are using the digital version of this book, we advise you to type the code yourself or access the code from the book's GitHub repository (a link is available in the next section). Doing so will help you avoid any potential errors related to the copying and pasting of code.

Download the example code files

You can download the example code files for this book from GitHub at `https://github.com/PacktPublishing/Practical-Module-Development-for-Prestashop-8`. If there's an update to the code, it will be updated in the GitHub repository.

We also have other code bundles from our rich catalog of books and videos available at `https://github.com/PacktPublishing/`. Check them out!

Download the color images

We also provide a PDF file that has color images of the screenshots and diagrams used in this book. You can download it here: `https://packt.link/9XyJg`

Conventions used

There are a number of text conventions used throughout this book.

`Code in text`: Indicates code words in text, database table names, folder names, filenames, file extensions, pathnames, dummy URLs, user input, and Twitter handles. Here is an example: "Usually, handling a form submission is done with the help of the `handle()` method of the `FormHandler` instance."

A block of code is set as follows:

```
$this->hookDispatcher->dispatchWithParameters('actionAfterCreate' .
Container::camelize($form->getName()) . 'FormHandler', [
    'id' => $id,
    'form_data' => &$data,
    ]);
```

Bold: Indicates a new term, an important word, or words that you see onscreen. For instance, words in menus or dialog boxes appear in **bold**. Here is an example: "Let's install the module by browsing the **Modules | Module Manager** page of the PrestaShop BO."

> **Tips or important notes**
> Appear like this.

Get in touch

Feedback from our readers is always welcome.

General feedback: If you have questions about any aspect of this book, email us at customercare@packtpub.com and mention the book title in the subject of your message.

Errata: Although we have taken every care to ensure the accuracy of our content, mistakes do happen. If you have found a mistake in this book, we would be grateful if you would report this to us. Please visit www.packtpub.com/support/errata and fill in the form.

Piracy: If you come across any illegal copies of our works in any form on the internet, we would be grateful if you would provide us with the location address or website name. Please contact us at copyright@packt.com with a link to the material.

If you are interested in becoming an author: If there is a topic that you have expertise in and you are interested in either writing or contributing to a book, please visit authors.packtpub.com.

Share Your Thoughts

Once you've read *Practical Module Development for Prestashop 8*, we'd love to hear your thoughts! Scan the QR code below to go straight to the Amazon review page for this book and share your feedback.

https://packt.link/r/1-837-63596-X

Your review is important to us and the tech community and will help us make sure we're delivering excellent quality content.

Download a free PDF copy of this book

Thanks for purchasing this book!

Do you like to read on the go but are unable to carry your print books everywhere?

Is your eBook purchase not compatible with the device of your choice?

Don't worry, now with every Packt book you get a DRM-free PDF version of that book at no cost.

Read anywhere, any place, on any device. Search, copy, and paste code from your favorite technical books directly into your application.

The perks don't stop there, you can get exclusive access to discounts, newsletters, and great free content in your inbox daily

Follow these simple steps to get the benefits:

1. Scan the QR code or visit the link below

https://packt.link/free-ebook/9781837635962

2. Submit your proof of purchase
3. That's it! We'll send your free PDF and other benefits to your email directly

Part 1 – Understanding How PrestaShop is Structured and How It Works

Mastering the mechanics of PrestaShop is a prerequisite for a good understanding of how modules are embedded in to the system. In this first part, we will explain the data structure and present the architecture of the whole system from the front-office to back-office controllers (migrated or not). Then, we will learn how Hooks work and enable modules to customize and improve the CMS. Finally, we will discover the themes, defining the graphical appearance of the front office.

This part has the following chapters:

- *Chapter 1, Quick Overview of The System*
- *Chapter 2, Configuration and Initialization of PrestaShop*
- *Chapter 3, The Front Office*
- *Chapter 4, The Back Office*
- *Chapter 5, The Hooks*
- *Chapter 6, The Themes*

Quick Overview of PrestaShop

Having set up **PrestaShop** (please see `https://devdocs.prestashop-project.org/1.7/basics/installation/`, if you haven't) and used it, you may know the two main parts of it. As with other **content management systems** (**CMSs**) such as **WordPress**, there's a public part unrestricted and visible by any visitor of your website named the **Front Office** (**FO**), and there's a restricted part, only visible by employees with email and password authentication, called the **Back Office** (**BO**).

In this chapter, we will explain quickly how everything is designed, from the database to the core structure of the FO and the BO, and how they are linked.

In this chapter, we will cover the following main topics:

- The data model—how and where data is stored
- The core classes—how the **Model-View-Controller** (**MVC**) works

By the end of this chapter, you will know how the database is built, the types of tables, and how the core manages and manipulates entities. You will understand, from a high-level point of view, the MVC structure of FO and BO pages and how some BO pages are being migrated from the legacy-based core to a Symfony-based one.

Technical requirements

As we will explore the environment of PrestaShop to understand how everything is articulated, you will have to use some tools to do mainly reverse engineering:

- **phpMyAdmin** or other MySQL database clients such as **Adminer**
- Any PHP code editor
- A (**Secure**) **File Transfer Protocol** ((**S**)**FTP**) client to browse your website files (only if you work on a remote server—not necessary if you work on a local server)

The data model–how and where data is stored

Let's start this journey into PrestaShop by presenting how data is stored.

Data is all mutable information stored on the server to make the shop work, such as product information, customer details, orders, category information, employee settings, and so on.

All this information is stored in a MySQL database on the server. You may already know this because you have been requested to provide the database details to access the MySQL database during the installation steps.

Let's browse the data to see how it works.

Browsing the data

To browse all the data stored in the PrestaShop database, please follow these steps:

1. Connect to the database created for your PrestaShop with your favorite database client such as `phpMyAdmin`.

2. Show all tables.

There, you will see a list of all tables, named following these patterns:

- `prefix_nameofentity` (for example, `ps_cms` and `ps_access`):

    All entities should use the `prefix_nameofentity` table name to store all non-localized data, without any restrictions on the number of columns. The first column for those tables is always the **unique ID** (**UID**) of each row, and its name always follows the same pattern: `id_nameofentity`. This is useful for creating relationships with other entities and makes data management easier.

- `prefix_nameofentity_lang` (for example, `ps_cms_lang` and `ps_carrier_lang`):

    If an entity has localizable data, you should use another table called `prefix_nameofentity_lang` to store fields depending on the user's language.

    It should represent a many-to-many relationship between the `prefix_nameofentity` table and `prefix_lang` table that contains all available languages in your PrestaShop platform. That's why you will always find an `id_nameofentity` column to represent the link with the `prefix_nameofentity` table and an `id_lang` column to represent the link with the `prefix_lang` table. These tables are not mandatory if you don't have localized data to store.

- `prefix_nameofentity_shop` (for example, `ps_cms_shop` and `ps_product_shop`):

    If an entity is shop-dependent (in the context of a multistore website, as PrestaShop makes this possible), you will find another table called `prefix_nameofentity_shop`. It represents a many-to-many relationship between the `prefix_nameofentity` table and the `ps_shop` table containing all available stores created in your PrestaShop platform. Exactly the same way as `_lang` tables do, you will always find an `id_nameofentity` column to represent the link with the `prefix_nameofentity` table and an `id_shop` column to represent the link with the `prefix_shop` table. These tables are only present if you want to make your entity multistore compliant.

What are prefix_ and nameofentity?

`prefix_` is a string that is set during the installation process, in the database details step, and by default, it's set to `ps_`, but you may have chosen a different one.

In the rest of the book, we will assume that you chose `ps_` as a prefix.

`nameofentity` stands for the name of the entity stored. For example, for products, the name of the entity is `product`; that's why you should find a `ps_product` table in the database!

Reverse engineering the contact entity

The `contact` entity contains all information about the recipients of contact queries done through the **Contact us** page of your store. You can put as many recipients of services as you need. Usually, there are two of them automatically set: one for technical queries and the other for customer/sales queries.

The best way to understand how things work is by doing reverse engineering. So, let's explore how the `contact` entity is built in the database. By browsing the tables list, considering that our prefix is set to `ps_`, you will find three tables corresponding to the `contact` entity:

- The `ps_contact` table:

Name	Type	Extra information
id_contact	Int(10)	Auto_increment
email	Varchar(255)	
customer_service	TinyInt(1)	
position	TinyInt(2)	

Table 1.1 – The ps_contact table

This table contains all universal, non-translatable fields about contact information: the email address, a flag (`true=1`/`false=0`) to inform the system if the recipient provides customer service, and the position for the display order on the contact form. Please note that there is always a key column following the `id_nameofentity` pattern in entities. It is auto-incrementing and set as the primary key. It enables us to identify and manipulate rows easily. It is also mandatory if we have to create a many-to-one relationship with this table.

- The `ps_contact_lang` table:

Name	Type	Extra information
`id_contact`	Int (10)	
`id_lang`	Int(10)	
`name`	Varchar(255)	
`description`	Text	

Table 1.2 – The ps_contact_lang table

This table contains all localizable data languages linked. It is used to provide translated content to the system. For the `contact` entity, there are only two fields requiring localization: the `name` field, designating the recipient of contact queries, and the `description` field, explaining the function of the recipient. This table materializes the many-to-one relationship with `ps_contact`, as there are many translations for only one contact. The `id_contact` column is used to map translations with the corresponding `ps_contact` rows. The `id_lang` column is used to map translations with the corresponding languages (1 for English, 2 for French, and so on, depending on your settings).

- The `ps_contact_shop` table:

Name	Type	Extra information
`id_contact`	Int(11)	
`id_shop`	Int(11)	

Table 1.3 – The ps_contact_shop table

This table represents the many-to-many relationship between the `ps_contact` entity and the `ps_shop` entity. It links contacts to the store in which they are available to customers/visitors. The `id_contact` column stands for the linked contact, and `id_shop` stands for the shop where the corresponding contact is available.

As you may have seen, the tables are not linked by foreign keys, which would be normal with a many-to-many relationship, but in PrestaShop, this is not the case yet.

You now know with this example how things are linked and stored together in the database.

> **Tip**
> If you want to inspect the whole structure and the links between tables, the structure is available during the installation process—that is, if you have not yet removed the `install` folder (which is recommended), at this path: `/install/data/db_structure.sql`.

Now that you know how and where data is stored in the database, let's see where and how entities are coded in PHP in order to manage them.

Manipulating data by extending the ObjectModel class

PrestaShop is a set of PHP files, templates, and assets (such as images, JavaScript, or style sheets) working together to generate an e-commerce system.

Specifically, inside the PHP files, in the `/classes/ObjectModel.php` folder, you will find the definition of the `ObjectModel` class, which implements the `EntityInterface` interface defined in the `/src/Code/Foundation/Database/EntityInterface.php` folder with these methods:

```
public static function getRepositoryClassName();
public function save();
public function delete();
public function hydrate(array $keyValueData);
```

Almost all entities of the system extend this `ObjectModel` class, which contains all the necessary tools to manipulate the entity.

Practically, all entities' definitions are PHP classes defined in `/classes/NameOfEntity.php`. Feel free to open some of the files to see how they work.

If you come back to the `ObjectModel` class, you will see that it contains a property named `$definition`. This is an array that will contain all metadata fields and properties of the entity. It has to follow this prototype:

```
public static $definition = [
    'table' => 'nameofentity',
    'primary' => 'id_nameofentity',
    'multilang' => true,//if not localizable set to false
    'multishop' => true,//if not multistore set to false
  //'multilang_shop' => true,
  //can replace both previous fields set to true
```

```
    'fields' => array(
        'id_nameofentity'  => ['type' => self::TYPE_INT,
            'validate' => 'isUnsignedInt'],
        'field_name'              => ['type' => ... ],
    ....)
];
```

Member variables have to be defined to represent each field that will be hydrated with their value. For example, if you have a field named `field_name` in the database, it has to be added to the entity class, like this:

```
public $field_name;
```

As seen before, to comply with the `EntityInterface` interface, we have to implement the three following methods:

- The `save()` method implements, in the database, the insertion or updates of the row represented by the current entity instance

- The `delete()` method removes the current row

- The `hydrate()` method sets the member variables of the current instance in order to be able to use the object

Practically, after having defined an entity with the creation of its class, everywhere in the code of PrestaShop, we will be able to create a new instance of it by using this:

```
//To create an empty instance of NameOfEntity
$entityInstance = new NameOfEntity();
```

If you want an entity to be instanced and hydrated with the values of the row with `id_nameofentity` equal to `$value_id_nameofentity`, you can use this code:

```
/* To create a hydrated instance of NameofEntity with id_
nameofentity=$value_id_nameofentity */
$entityInstanceHydrated = new NameOfEntity((int) $value_id_
nameofentity);
```

> **Try this**
> As a practical exercise, try to open one of the classes defined in the `/classes` folder.

Using the Db class

As you may have seen by opening some classes of the /classes folder, the ObjectModel child class uses the Db class defined in the /classes/db/Db.php file to work with the database's low-level actions, such as insert, update, and delete. We won't dive deeply into this class—you just have to remember that you can use this class anywhere with the following methods. In this method, we'll instantiate the Db class to use its functions:

```
/*Instantiate the Db class in order to be able use its functions*/
$db = \Db::get Instance();
```

The following are the SELECT methods:

```
/*To do a select query with _DB_PREFIX_ a constant that contains the
prefix for tables*/
$select_query = 'SELECT * FROM `' . _DB_PREFIX_ . 'nameofentity` WHERE
1';
$result = $db->executeS($select_query);
/*To get the first line of the results as an array */
$select_query = "SELECT `id_nameofentity`, `field_name` FROM `' . _DB_
PREFIX_ . 'nameofentity` WHERE 1";
$result = $db->getRow($request);
```

The following code can be used to insert, update, and delete and for custom query methods:

```
/*To insert row(s) with pSQL() a function to avoid SQL injections or
other threats*/
$result = $db->insert('nameofentity ',
    [
        //First row
        [
            'field_name' => pSQL('field_value'),
            'field_name' => pSQL('field_value'),
        ],
        //Second row
        [
            'field_name' => pSQL('field_value'),
            'field_name' => pSQL('field_value'),
        ]
    ]
);
/*To update row with id_nameofentity=2*/
$result = $db->update('nameofentity', [
    'field_name' => pSQL('field_value'),
    'field_name' => pSQL('field_value'),
], 'id_nameofentity = 2', 1, true);
/*To delete row with id_nameofentity=2*/
```

```
$result = $db->delete('nameofentity', 'id_nameofentity = 2');
/*To execute a raw custom query*/
$sql_query = "UPDATE `' . _DB_PREFIX_ . 'nameofentity`  SET ` field_
name `= 3 WHERE `id_nameofentity `=2";
$result = $db->execute($sql_query);
```

> **Important note**
>
> The way of managing data by using the `ObjectModel` extension is a bit old-fashioned. As PrestaShop is being migrated to a Symfony-based core, the target is to use the `Doctrine` library for all entities as soon as the migration is finished.

Currently, while the migration is still a work in progress, most entities are still using `ObjectModel` to manage the database interfaces, as illustrated in the following diagram:

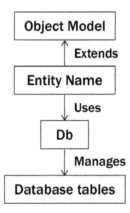

Figure 1.1 – The data management process in PrestaShop

Now that we know how the data is stored and can be manipulated, we need to understand how FO and BO pages are generated by PrestaShop.

The core classes – how the MVC works

Let's explore how pages are generated by PrestaShop. Don't worry if you think that we won't go deep enough into how everything works; we want to stay in a high-level point of view to get a full picture of the system. In *Chapters 3* and *4*, we will be more technical!

FO and BO pages are automatically generated by the core of PrestaShop. As with many existing CMSs, PrestaShop uses a custom PHP framework that was improved following the versions. This original framework built from the beginning to version *1.7.x.x* is called the **legacy core** by the developers of the PrestaShop community. It is still improving to cope with the immediate needs of users, but the choice was made by the core developers to move to a new framework based on Symfony.

As it is a strong and efficient framework, it can take care of all the main generic needs of the system, such as security, database handling, and forms generation, and all the most useful tools it provides. It should enable the PrestaShop community to focus on e-commerce-specific needs.

Presenting the legacy core MVC pattern

The legacy core is based on an MVC pattern. If you don't know this famous design pattern, just remember that each page is generated by a PHP **Controller**. It uses a **Model Object** to retrieve or modify data in the database and takes care of all computation and data processing to provide it to a **View** template. This View template is responsible for the graphical aspect of the page.

It enables the different actors of a project not to interfere. The developers can work on the controller while data managers can take care of the model and the integrators build the views. This way, you can also change each tier of the structure without changing others. Here is a diagram illustrating the same:

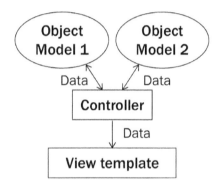

Figure 1.2 – The legacy core MVC design pattern

As presented in *Figure 1.2*, the **Controller** calls **Object Model(s)** to get or manipulate the data, processes it, and sends it to a **View template** to generate a final view.

> **\What is the legacy core?**
>
> As it is not obvious, the legacy core is a set of PHP classes that are part of the PrestaShop framework. They are mainly stored in the `/classes` and `/controllers` folders.

Discovering the core migration

As we have seen before, a migration from the old legacy core to a Symfony-based one is in progress. This migration started with the BO pages and will end with the FO pages. The FO migration will start when the BO has fully migrated. That's the reason why some BO pages are still using the legacy core MVC and some others use the new Symfony design. All FO pages still use the legacy core before and in the **v8.0** release.

You can discriminate which BO pages are migrated by watching their URLs: those containing `/index.php?controller=Admin` are not migrated yet, and those containing `/index.php/` are migrated.

The Symfony migrated pages also use an MVC structure, but they follow the Symfony way of coding by using a different templating engine. Even if Symfony is made to use Doctrine and its entities to manipulate the data, during the migration process, we will still use the `ObjectModel` child objects we have seen before. The new core of PrestaShop is being built into the `/src/` folder. We will see in *Chapter 4*, *The Back Office*, how this can be done.

In the following diagram, you will find a summary of how the different pages can be managed during the migration of PrestaShop from **Legacy Core** to **Symfony Core**:

During the Migration Process

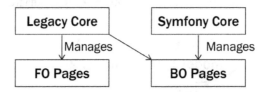

Figure 1.3 – How things work during the migration process

The aim of the migration process is to remove **Legacy Core** and make every page of PrestaShop generated by **Symfony Core**, as illustrated in the following diagram:

After the Migration Process

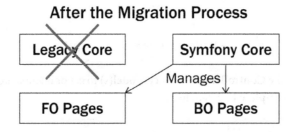

Figure 1.4 – How things will work after the migration process

Once everything is migrated, every page of the BO and FO will rely on the Symfony core and the full system will be able to use Doctrine entities. This process is likely to spend some years. The full PrestaShop open source project is working on it.

Summary

In this chapter, we learned that all data is stored in MySQL tables. There are three types of tables, depending on the localization and the multistore support of each entity. The entities of the core are still stored in the `/classes/` folder, and each entity class extends `ObjectModel`.

We also learned that the Db class must be used to manipulate the data in the database. The core is a set of classes generating the pages of the FO and the BO. The core is MVC pattern-based. The FO and some pages of the BO are using the legacy core. Some BO pages are using the Symfony-based core. The interface with the database is still managed by the ObjectModel child classes during the migration process.

We know now how data is managed, and the design of the core. From a high-level point of view, we know how pages are generated. In the next chapter, we will discover how PrestaShop is initialized both for the FO and the BO, how global variables are set, and how to manually set parameter variables to manage access to the database.

The Configuration and Initialization of PrestaShop

Knowing how data storage works and how the system is structured, we can dive into the initialization routines of **PrestaShop**. All this description of the CMS will enable us to master it, to understand how modules embed into the system, and how we will be able to use its components. By following the **initialization process**, we will see when and how the system is configured and how we can set some important constants to ease our development and change the database connection and cookies parameters.

In this chapter, we will cover the following main topics:

- The legacy **Front Office(FO)** controller initialization
- The legacy **Back Office (BO)** and Symfony admin controller initialization
- The most important constants to set as a developer
- The `Dispatcher` class

By the end of this chapter, you will know how an FO and a BO page initialize their controllers to generate the view even with a new Symfony-based one. You will understand how and when the main configuration and settings constants are set and how to manage them.

Technical requirements

As we will explore the environment of PrestaShop to understand how everything is articulated, you will have to use the following tools to do reverse engineering:

- Any PHP code editor
- An (S)FTP client to browse your website files (only if you work on a remote server, not necessary if you work on a local server)

The legacy FO controller initialization

Here, we will do reverse engineering of a legacy FO controller. As seen in *Chapter 1*, *Quick Overview of PrestaShop*, when you visit a public page of a PrestaShop website, it is managed by a controller using an `ObjectModel` child object for the database interactions and generating the view with a Smarty template (MVC pattern).

For this practical study, we will focus on how the system initializes and handles a front-page call from the URL request to the controller instantiation.

Let's do it with a product category page example. When you browse the FO, it's a product listing page. Indeed, in PrestaShop, a Category is the entity responsible for displaying groups of products.

Initializing a Category FO controller

By default, when **URL rewriting** is on, the category page URLs are structured like this: `https://www.urlofthewebsite.extension/categoryId-name`, with `categoryId` as an integer and `name` as the slug of the category name:

1. First, the web server handles the HTTP request, relying on the `.htaccess` file located at the root of your website to process the rewritten URL, and calls the `/index.php` file. Here are the steps for that: the `/index.php` file loads the `/config/config.inc.php` file, and if a `/config/defines_custom.inc.php` file exists, it loads it.

2. Then it includes the `/config/defines.inc.php` file, responsible for setting the constants that define the main behaviors of PrestaShop, such as the **debug mode** with `_PS_MODE_DEV_` or the **profiling mode** with `_PS_DEBUG_PROFILING_`. There you will also find all the directories' constants' definitions.

3. After that, `/config/autoload.php` is included; it defines some tool functions, such as `pSQL()`, and includes all the **legacy core objects** stored in `/classes` and in `/controllers/`.

4. Then the `/config/bootstrap.php` file is loaded. This is where the **database access variables** and the **cookies settings** are set. Those values are stored recursively inside the `/app/config/parameters.php` file. We will come back to this important file later in this chapter.

5. After some optional profiling tools loading, it initializes the `Context` object that provides important variables extracted from the **cookies** and the database. It stores the current customer details if we are logged in and the localization settings, such as the language displayed and the currency. The active **theme** name is stored in a constant, and some of the previously initialized `Context` object variables are hydrated.

6. When all those steps are done, back in the `/index.php` file, the `Dispatcher` object located in the `/classes/Dispatcher.php` file is instantiated and handles the URL request. It matches the URL (rewritten or not) with **routing rules and patterns** set by default or in the database for each controller of PrestaShop. In our case, the controller matched is `CategoryController` located in the `/controllers/front/listing/CategoryController.php` file, a new instance of it is created, and the `run()` method is called. It starts the initialization process of the controller.

Why are all the core objects named with the Core suffix?

Indeed, when we talk about classes such as the `Category` object defining category entities in the legacy core, we forget to add the `Core` suffix. The real name of the class located in the `/classes/Category.php` file is `CategoryCore`; it is a language shortcut we make. This is the same for the controller class located in `/controllers/front/listing/CategoryController.php`; the real name of the class is `CategoryControllerCore`. The reason why the core team decided to give that suffix is to point out that this class is the original class from the core of PrestaShop, and it enables developers to extend those classes by using the `Category` or `CategoryController` names. If you want to override functionalities to the core classes without changing their content, you can create new classes extending the core objects by using simple names.

Every FO controller extends the `/classes/controller/FrontController.php` file and is indirectly a child of `/classes/controller/Controller.php`.

How does an FO controller manage to generate an HTML view?

If you browse the `/classes/controller/Controller.php` class, you will note that the life cycle of an FO Controller is defined in the called `run()` method. It is calling successively `init()` | `setMedia()` | `postProcess()` | `initHeader()` | `initContent()` | `initFooter()` | `display()` (or `displayAjax()`).

The `display()` method can be overridden in each FO controller class and uses the Smarty templating library to generate the HTML code based on the defined templates fetched. It is done with the help of the `smartyOutputContent()` method.

By doing this reverse engineering, we know how everything works, from the request to the HTML code delivery for the FO controllers. Let's now understand how a legacy BO and a Symfony admin controller can be instantiated.

The legacy BO and Symfony admin controller initialization

As explained in the first chapter, all the old controllers of the BO rely on the legacy core of PrestaShop, while modern controllers use the Symfony framework. During the migration of the controllers from the old BO to Symfony, we need to access all of them.

We will now study this by reverse engineering the way both types are initialized.

The legacy BO controller initialization

After the PrestaShop setup, you are given the BO base URL, which is structured like this: `https://www.urlofthewebsite.extension/adminXXX`, with XXX as a random sequence of digits provided by the PrestaShop installation. It is different in every shop for security reasons.

If you browse the website folder structure, you will find the `/adminXXX/` folder.

Let's do reverse engineering of the login page of the BO. Its URL follows this pattern: `https://www.urlofthewebsite.extension/adminXXX/index.php?controller=AdminLogin`.

In fact, it acts exactly like an FO controller without URL rewriting in the `/adminXXX/` folder instead of the root folder, executed by the `/adminXXX/index.php` file.

Instead of directly calling `Dispatcher`, Symfony and its router are initialized by instantiating the `AppKernel` class located in the `/app/AppKernel.php` file.

If the Symfony router is not able to process the request, the `Dispatcher dispatch()` method is called exactly like for the FO controller initialization. The GET variable named `controller` is parsed, and for the login page, it equals `AdminLogin`. This triggers the instantiation of the `/controllers/admin/AdminLoginController.php` controller and acts the same way an FO does.

We know how everything works for a legacy core-based FO controller, but what if Symfony finds a route corresponding to the requested URL?

The Symfony BO controller initialization

Next, let us focus on a migrated controller from the legacy core to the Symfony core. Let us study the case of a standard **migrated** controller, such as the Admin Contact controller nested inside the Shop Parameters menu of the BO. You will note that the URL pattern changes, in our case, correspond to: `https://www.urlofthewebsite.extension/adminXXX/index.php/configure/shop/contacts/?_token=YYY`, with YYY a random token used for security.

An efficient way of discriminating a modern controller URL from a legacy one is to check whether it starts with `/index.php/`. If so, it is a modern controller; if not, the URL is likely to start with `index.php?controller=`.

What are the versions of Symfony used by PrestaShop?

You can find that out if you open the /composer.json file that contains all the libraries available. In the **v1.7** of PrestaShop, the version of Symfony is **3.4**, and in the **v8.0+** versions, the version of Symfony is **4.4**.

As seen before, in the /adminXXX/index.php file, Symfony is loaded, and the router checks whether the route described by the URL requested exists and leads to an existing controller.

The routes of the BO are all declared in /src/PrestaShopBundle/Resources/config/routing/admin.yml and successively in the /src/PrestaShopBundle/Resources/config/routing/admin/ subfolders.

In our case, the route is defined in /src/PrestaShopBundle/Resources/config/routing/admin/configure/shop_parameters/contacts.yml with this code:

```
admin_contacts_index:
    path: /
    methods: GET
    defaults:
        _controller: 'PrestaShopBundle:Admin\Configure\ShopParameters
        \Contacts:index'
        _legacy_controller: AdminContacts
        _legacy_link: AdminContacts
```

It will directly instantiate the ContactsController controller whose namespace is PrestaShopBundle\Controller\Admin\Configure\ShopParameters.

As you can see in the /composer.json file, the PrestaShopBundle namespace root is mapped with /src/PrestaShopBundle/.

After that, the indexAction() method of the /src/PrestaShopBundle/Controller/Admin/Configure/ShopParameters/ContactsController.php file is called. Then the call of the render() function enables the generation of the HTML output with the help of the **Twig** rendering library.

We have now mastered the initialization process of PrestaShop for both legacy and Symfony core objects. As a developer, it is not mandatory to know all of that, but it is a real advantage to understand how everything works. It enables us to know where to find any constant definition and where to set our custom constants and all the settings of the shop.

The most important constants to set as a developer

Earlier, we saw in the initialization process that all the constants are defined in /config/config.inc.php. This file includes /config/defines_custom.inc.php if it exists.

If you need to set custom constants, `/config/defines_custom.inc.php` is a good place to put their definitions.

We also saw that the `/config/defines.inc.php` file was also included in the `/config/config.inc.php` file. Two very useful constants to set are the following:

- `_PS_MODE_DEV_`: If you set it to `true`, it will enable the debug mode for the whole shop. Inside Symfony controllers, you can use the awesome profiler.

> **Important note**
>
> All warnings, notices, and errors will be displayed. *Do not use the debug mode in production* if you want to keep your user experience safe. *It is useful for developers but not for your customers!* If you want to disable it, you have to set it to `false`.

- `_PS_DEBUG_PROFILING_`: If you set it to `true`, you will get a full profiling of the memory uses and timings for the components of the page displayed and for the SQL queries.

> **Important note**
>
> Do not use the profiling mode in production because it will decrease the user experience quality, and people will not understand the presence of profiling!

If you want to change your database access, you can update the database connection credentials inside the `/app/config/parameters.php` file. Specifically, you will find the following keys inside the `Array` parameters returned by the `parameters.php` file:

- `database_host`: This is the host of the database (IP or domain name)
- `database_port`: This is the port used by the database server (if blank, it will use the 3306 port for MYSQL databases)
- `database_name`: This is the name of the database storing the data
- `database_user`: This is the username of the database storing the data
- `database_password`: This is the password of the database storing the data
- `database_prefix`: This is the prefix used in the table names (as presented in *Chapter 1, Quick Overview of PrestaShop*), by default set to `ps_`.

These constants or parameters are the most important to know to enable you to debug, profile, or manage your database credentials. Feel free to test them in your test shops.

We now know how to set the most important constants and variables for our development tasks and how everything is articulated in the initialization steps. Let's go a bit further inside the details of matching the URL rewriting rules and the controllers to instantiate with the `Dispatcher` class presentation.

The Dispatcher class

As seen in the previous reverse engineering example, there are two main tools to manage the controller's routing: for the legacy FO and BO core classes, it is the `Dispatcher` class, and for the Symfony migrated controllers, it is the Symfony router.

As Symfony routing is already well documented on the Symfony website at the following address: `https://symfony.com/doc/4.4/routing.html`, we will not provide more explanations about it. Even if it is going to sadly disappear once the migration is finished, the `Dispatcher` routing class requires more explanation.

Let's continue the reverse engineering, with the **product category** front controller already presented at the beginning of the chapter.

We will now focus on the use of `Dispatcher::getInstance()->dispatch();` in `/index.php`.

The `getInstance()` static function instantiates the `Dispatcher` object with the `request` information injected as an argument.

The `_construct()` method checks whether the `_PS_ADMIN_DIR_` constant exists; if it exists, it is a **BO controller** that is being called (it is initialized inside the `/adminXXX/index.php` file only); if the `$_GET` array contains an `fc` key, it is a **module controller** that is being called. Else, it is a **FO controller** that is being called, and that is the case with the `Category` front controller.

Then the URL to be routed is cleaned of the domain name and the language string (en, fr, es, and so on) with the help of `$this->setRequestUri()`. For example, `https://www.urlofthewebsite.extension/en/categoryId-name` will be cleaned, and we will get the following value: `/categoryId-name` into `$request_uri`.

Next, the `loadRoutes()` call preprocesses and puts into `$routes` the **URL rewriting rules** to make it possible for PHP to match them with `$request_uri`. For our example, by default, the URL of a product category front controller is to follow the `{id}-{rewrite}` rule. That enables the use of the `dispatch()` method.

It calls the `getController()` method that checks whether the `controller` GET variable is set, and if so, it will use its value for instantiation (it is the case in the legacy BO controllers).

If the URL rewriting is activated, all the preprocessed URL rewriting rules in `$routes` are checked for a match with the requested URI. If a rule matches, then all the items of the rule are stored in the `$_GET` array. In our case, the found `{id}` is stored in the `id_category` GET key, and the category controller type is stored in the `controller` GET key.

Back to the `dispatch()` method, the lowercase controller name found is stored in the `$controller_class` variable, and an instance of the `Category` object defined in `/controllers/front/listing/CategoryController.php` is created. Finally, its `run()` method is called.

Summary

In this chapter, we got deeper inside the controller's instantiation process for FO and BO.

We saw that for FO and BO controllers, many constants were initialized inside `/config/config.inc.php` and `/config/defines.inc.php`. Some custom constants can be set inside `/config/defines_custom.inc.php`, depending on your needs. All the database access and cookies parameters can be updated in `/app/config/parameters.php`.

For legacy BO and FO core controllers, routing is managed by the `Dispatcher` class located in `/classes/Dispatcher.php`, whereas for Symfony-based controllers, the Symfony routing component manages it.

It is now time to jump into the FO controller mechanics and see how an FO controller works, retrieves data, uses ObjectModel-based objects, and displays data with the templating engine, which is the topic of the next chapter.

3
The Front Office

We know how the system acts from the HTTP request to the controller instantiation, both for **front office** (**FO**) and **back office** (**BO**) controllers. Understanding the behavior of a front controller will make things easier to understand when we have to create our own modules also containing some kinds of front controllers.

We will follow this process to discover how things are done:

- Discovering how an FO controller works
- Using the model
- Using the views from the theme

By the end of this chapter, we will have mastered how a front controller works and the details of its life cycle, how object model child objects are manipulated, how theme templates are called, and how objects are assigned to Smarty views.

Let's see how things work from the FO instantiation to the view display on the browser.

Technical requirements

As we will explore the environment of **PrestaShop,** to understand how everything is articulated, you will have to use some of the following tools to do reverse engineering:

- Any PHP code editor
- An (s)FTP client to browse your website files (only if you work on a remote server; not necessary if you work on a local server)

Discovering how an FO controller works

As seen in the previous chapter, the best way to understand how things work is by studying a practical example. Why not continue our explanation with the reverse engineering of the **content management system (CMS)** front controller displaying the content of CMS pages or categories? Those pages can be used, for example, for legal notices or information pages.

This FO controller is called `CmsControllerCore` and is defined in the `/controllers/front/CmsController.php` file.

The front controllers still rely on the legacy core because the migration to Symfony has not started yet for FO objects. That's why routing is managed by `Dispatcher`, which matches URL rewriting rules with FO controllers.

In our example, when a CMS page URL is called, the `CmsControllerCore` class is instantiated. The first method to be called by `Dispatcher` is `run()`.

First, when browsing the `/controllers/front/CmsController.php` file, we can see that the `CmsControllerCore` class extends the `FrontController` class.

All the FO controllers are child classes of `FrontControllerCore`, which is the base object for the front pages. If you want to look at `FrontControllerCore`, it is defined in the `/classes/controller/FrontController.php` file.

The `FrontControllerCore` class extends the `Controller` class defined in `/classes/controller/Controller.php`, which is the same root for both FO and BO legacy core controllers. The following diagram sums up this workflow:

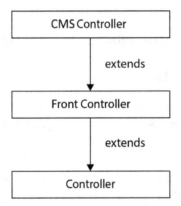

Figure 3.1 – The legacy FO workflow

Let's start our presentation of FO controllers by studying the structure of a `ControllerCore` object, continuing with the `FrontControllerCore` object, and finishing with our `CmsControllerCore` class.

Discovering the ControllerCore object

Located in the `/classes/controller/Controller.php` file, this is the root abstract class defining the behavior of all BO and FO legacy-based controllers in PrestaShop.

Everything starts from the `__construct()` function. This constructor mainly initializes the `Context` object and the translator service responsible for string localization.

Following our example, as it is not overridden in the `CmsControllerCore` class, the `run()` method is called by `Dispatcher`. For non-ajax front controller usage, it defines the life cycle of the `Controller` child classes following this method's execution sequence:

1. `init()`: This method is responsible for the initialization routines of the page. By default, if not already existing, the `_PS_BASE_URL` and `_PS_BASE_URL_SSL` constants are defined and `$this->container` is filled with a light version of the Symfony Container for legacy front controllers. Then `$this->context->currentLocale` is filled with a **Current Locale Data Repository (CLDR)**.

2. `setMedia()`: This is an abstract method that needs to be defined by child classes. This is where you will have to prepare the assets (`.js` or `.css` files) to display on your page.

3. `postProcess()`: This is an abstract method that needs to be defined by child classes. This is where you will be able to handle POST requests such as input processing.

4. `initHeader()`: This is an abstract method that needs to be defined by child classes. This is where you will have to assign variables to the Smarty header template for the current page.

5. `initContent()`: This is an abstract method that needs to be defined by child classes. This is where you will have to assign variables to the Smarty main content template for the current page.

6. `initFooter()`: This is an abstract method that needs to be defined by child classes. This is where you will have to assign variables to the Smarty footer template for the current page.

7. `display()`: This is an abstract method that needs to be defined by child classes. This is where you will be able to display the page view.

> **What is Smarty?**
>
> We have talked many times about it, but if you still do not know, Smarty is a PHP templating engine that enables the generation of views from template files written in HTML and contains some variables to display and some tool functions. The values of the variables to display inside the templates are assigned by the controllers. This enables us to take care of the views apart from the controllers in the MVC pattern. An integrator will be able to update the views by working on the Smarty templates without accessing the controllers or the model. Feel free to read the documentation from the official website at this URL: `https://www.smarty.net/documentation`.

You may have noticed the css_files and js_files variables. Just keep in mind these variables are the arrays containing the lists of .css and .js files to be added to the displayed page.

As our FO controller extends FrontController, let's dive into its definition. We will be able to see what makes a FrontController object different from a simple Controller.

Discovering the FrontControllerCore object

Located in the /classes/controller/FrontController.php file, the FrontControllerCore object extends the Controller class. It implements the FO-specific behavior in the legacy core. As seen in the last paragraph, the ControllerCore class is abstract, so some of the abstract methods need to be implemented by the child classes.

> **What are deprecated variables or methods?**
>
> You may have seen that there are many variables or methods with a comment containing @deprecated or deprecated before their definition. This means that the community has decided to remove them or change their name or usage. So if you meet one of them, please don't use it anymore.

Let's follow the life cycle overrides in our FrontController object and see how it impacts the behavior of Controller. As a reminder, the sequence of methods of the Controller life cycle is as follows:

1. __construct()
2. init()
3. setMedia()
4. postProcess()
5. initHeader()
6. initContent()
7. initFooter()
8. display()

We will now see what is going on inside each of them.

The __construct() method

First, the __construct() method sets the $controller_type variable to "front", executes the parent constructor, and sets the $ssl flag variable and the global $useSSL depending on the activation of the **Secure Socket Layer (SSL)** mode in your configuration.

Then, the $objectPresenter and $cart_presenter variables are set with the corresponding Presenters.

> **What are Presenter objects?**
>
> From **version 1.7** of PrestaShop, the Presenter classes appeared; they implement `PresenterInterface` defined in the `/src/Adapter/Presenter/PresenterInterface.php` file, which consists of defining a `present($object)` method. This method will output an `Array` or a `LazyArray` (a sort of array that loads on demand to save resources). More concretely, it helps to present the data from an object to an array in a safe way.

The `$templateFinder` variable is filled with the `TemplateFinder` object, which is responsible for finding the best template in Smarty.

The `$stylesheetManager` and `$javascriptManager` variables contain classes extending the `AbstactAssetManager` class defined in `/classes/assets/AbstractAssetManager.php`. Their general behavior is to manage the stack of assets in a good order to deliver them to the view without repeats.

Finally, the `$cccReducer` variable is filled with an instance of `CccReducer` defined in the `/classes/assets/CccReducer.php` file. The `CccReducer` class is a tool to combine, compress, and cache the assets to reduce the loading time of the pages with a smart cache for CSS and JS assets and a possible Apache server optimization.

> **The Configuration object**
>
> You may have noticed the use of the `Configuration` object in the `__construct()` method. This is a very useful object extending `ObjectModel`, used to manage the configuration settings of your shop in the database. It is now a bit outdated but is still used in the legacy environment. Just remember the following:
>
> - To retrieve the value for the configuration key named `$configKeyName`, you should use `Configuration::get(string $configKeyName);`
> - To update the value of the configuration key named `$configKeyName` with the `$value` value, you should use `Configuration::updateValue(string $configKeyName, mixed $value);`

To sum up, the `__construct()` method prepares the necessary tool objects and puts them into their variables to enable the `FrontController` object to work and prepare the front content and view.

Let's now jump to the `init()` method. As it is a long definition, we will sum it up. It initializes the data and sets some variables and properties, and redirects if needed.

The init() method

First, the `init()` method calls the `init()` parent and tests whether the SSL mode is active, and if `true`, redirects to the SSL URL if the HTTPS URL was not called. Then, it instantiates a `Link` object responsible for generating the URLs to call for other controllers and stores it in the `Context` object inside `$this->context->link`.

It takes care of the geolocation business, depending on the mode in the configuration. The geolocation can be found with the IP, the customer address, or the language called in the URL of the shop, and makes the cart taxes, currencies, and localized content fit with those constraints.

If there is a logout request, or a cart retrieval request in the `GET` variables, it handles and impacts the cookie session with it. If no cart exists, it initializes it.

To follow the sequence in the life cycle of the `FrontController` object, let's see how the `setMedia()` method is implemented.

The setMedia() method

In fact, it is a short sequence; it is a list of registrations of CSS and JS assets from the theme. It loads the `theme.css` and `custom.css` files (and the `rtl.css` file if the language is right to left), from the `assets/css/` folder of the activated theme, and the `core.js`, `theme.js`, and `custom.js` files from the `assets/js/` folder of the activated theme. Specific assets issued from the `theme.yml` file of the theme are loaded if required.

The postProcess(), initHeader(), and initFooter() methods

You will find that the `postProcess()` function is implemented but left empty. This is the same for `initHeader()` and `initFooter()` but not for `initContent()`.

Let's see what happens in `initContent()`.

The initContent() method

The `initContent()` method starts by assigning general- purpose variables to Smarty in order to give the views all the information necessary for the e-commerce functionality (customer, cart, language, and so on).

Then a `prestashop` JavaScript variable is created by using `Media::addJsDef(['prestashop'=> $this->buildFrontEndObject($templateVars)])`.

This `prestashop` object contains all the general-purpose variables necessary for e-commerce, to give the same information to the JavaScript layer.

> **What is the Media object?**
>
> The `Media` object defined in the `/classes/Media.php` file does not extend `ObjectModel`. It is a class is a class responsible for handling the registration of JavaScript variables, and inline scripts of various minifications. We will give further explanations about it later in this book.

To finish the definition of the methods composing the life cycle, the last function to study is `display()`.

The display() method

The `display()` method assigns some important variables necessary for the Smarty template to set up the view:

- `layout`: This variable enables the Smarty template to know what layout type to use (one single column, two, or three, depending on the settings for the current controller)

- `stylesheets`: This is the list of stylesheet files to include in the view

- `javascript`: This is the list of JavaScript files to include in the view

- `js_custom_vars`: This is the array of JavaScript variables to set in the view

- `notifications`: This is the array of error, success, info, and warning notifications to display inside the view

The generation of the view is done with the help of the `fetch()` function in Smarty.

We saw how the life cycle of the Controller was impacted in a `FrontController` object. In fact, it adds all the e-commerce data to the view and handles the business part, such as the cart, and the localization parameters, such as taxes and currencies, in order to make everything functional for sales. Let's see a practical implementation of a `FrontController` object by reverse engineering our `CmsController` definition.

Discovering the implementation of CmsController

Getting back to `CmsController`, located in the `/controllers/front/CmsController.php` file; let's study how the life cycle is finally overridden.

Our first method of the life cycle is `init()`. It starts with the retrieval of the data to display from the database for this CMS page or category by instantiating a `CMS` or `CMSCategory` object extending `ObjectModel`. Just remember that it is the Model layer part, and we will get back to it later, in the *Using the model* section of this chapter. This data is stored in the `$cms` and `$cms_category` class variables.

It calls the `parent::init()` function, inheriting the `init()` method actions.

This method also takes care of potential redirections.

The `setMedia()`, `postProcess()`, `initHeader()`, and `initFooter()` functions are not overridden, so this controller follows the behavior defined by the parent class.

The `initContent()` function is set and overrides the standard behavior. In fact, it only checks whether the current requested CMS element is a CMS page or a CMS category and then assigns the data to display to the Smarty template.

Then it calls `parent::initContent()` to inherit the standard actions.

A call to `$this->setTemplate(...)` is done and defines the name of the template file to call inside the theme depending on the type of CMS page or category to display.

> **What are the Hook::exec() calls in the methods?**
>
> You may have seen many `Hook::exec()` calls during the exploration of the classes. They are very important, but please refer to *Chapter 5*, *Hooks*, where you will get a full explanation of them!

Finally, we saw that `CmsController` added the data retrieval from the database and assigned it to the template, and chose which Smarty template to display.

Let's get deeper into the usage of the model with data retrieval. It will show us a real-life example of an `ObjectModel` subclass presented in *Chapter 1*, *A Quick Overview of PrestaShop*.

Using the model

While exploring `CmsController`, we saw that the `init()` method contained this portion of code:

```
if ($id_cms = (int) Tools::getValue('id_cms')) {
  $this->cms = new CMS($id_cms,
    $this->context->language->id,
    $this->context->shop->id);
}
```

This code is important because it selects data from the database for the CMS page with `id_cms` equaling the `id_cms` GET variable value. It is a good example for us to review:

```
if ($id_cms = (int) Tools::getValue('id_cms')) {
}
```

This code is storing the value of the `id_cms` GET variable retrieved with the help of `Tools::getValue('id_cms')`. If the `id_cms` GET variable doesn't exist, it won't work. Feel free to inspect the `/classes/Tools.php` file if you want to know more about the `Tools::getValue(key, $default_value = false)` definition.

The following code stores in the $cms variable the CMS object instance extending ObjectModel, with its class variables hydrated with the row values corresponding to the id_cms GET value:

```
$this->cms = new CMS($id_cms, $this->context->language->id,
    $this->context->shop->id);
```

As a reminder, we saw in *Chapter 1, A Quick Overview of PrestaShop*, that the constructor of ObjectModel child classes was directly instantiating the object by hydrating it. It enables us to directly use the object.

Now you know how to make a simple row selection by using an ObjectModel child class inside a controller. Let's now see how the controller uses the theme and sets which template to display.

Using the views from the theme

As PrestaShop uses the MVC pattern, it uses views, and the list of views of the FO is stored in what we call a **theme**. In PrestaShop, you can have one or multiple themes for the FO. Only one is used at a time in the FO; it is the active theme, and the activation can be configured in the BO of your shop. A theme is a folder following a standard architecture and is stored inside the /themes/ folder. We will further study the structure of a theme in *Chapter 6, The Themes*, but just remember that a theme folder contains a subfolder named templates following this /themes/themeName/ templates/ path with themeName as the chosen theme name. In this subfolder, you will find many .tpl files, which are the Smarty view templates composed of HTML and variables between brackets in the Smarty syntax (the Smarty documentation is available at https://www.smarty. net/documentation).

Every FO controller must display content in a view, following a Smarty template stored in this subfolder. To understand how the system chooses the right template file for the corresponding FO controller, let's get back to our initContent() function in the CmsController class. It contains an example of the template choice for the CMS pages:

```
$this->setTemplate(
    'cms/page',
    ['entity' => 'cms', 'id' => $this->cms->id]
);
```

This setTemplate($template, $params = [], $locale = null) function can take three arguments. In our case, we provide only the name of the template, 'cms/page', and the params named 'entity' and 'id'. It sets the variable template of the class and Smarty can fetch it. In this example, the template file is cms/page.tpl.

Now PrestaShop knows that it must display the HTML processed by Smarty based on the content in the /themes/themeName/templates/cms/page.tpl file.

Summary

In this chapter, we saw that all FO pages are generated by controllers located in the `/controllers/front/` folder. All those controllers are child classes of the `FrontController` class defined in the `/classes/controller/FrontController.php` file. The `FrontController` class is a child of the `Controller` class defined in the `/classes/controller/Controller.php` file.

While `Controller` defines the generic life cycle of both BO and FO controllers, `FrontController` prepares all the general e-commerce data for the views and makes sales possible.

Finally, we saw in the `CmsController` example that FO controllers can manipulate the database with the help of the `ObjectModel` child classes. They can define which template to use to generate the view with Smarty.

This explanation can be tough for beginners, but even if you don't need to know all of that to create a module, it is interesting to master the whole process behind FO controllers. In the next chapter, we will jump into the BO and see how it works for both migrated and legacy-based controllers.

4

The Back Office

Now that we know how a legacy-based **front office** (**FO**) controller is initialized, its specificities, and how it uses the model and the views from Smarty, let's have a look at the **back office** (**BO**) controllers by doing a comparison between the legacy-based controllers and the Symfony-based migrated controllers.

Our journey into the BO controllers will go through the following topics:

- Discovering how a legacy-based BO controller works
- The most useful tool for recurrent HTML generation – the helper classes
- Studying how a migrated Symfony BO controller works
- Using the Symfony Forms
- The CQRS design pattern inside modern controllers
- Generating table views by using the `Grid` component

By the end of this chapter, we will have mastered how the BO works for both generations of controllers, from legacy-based to Symfony-migrated ones. You will know how the legacy `Helper` class works, as well as new concepts, such as the **command query responsibility segregation** (**CQRS**) design applied to PrestaShop, and the use of Symfony Forms and PrestaShop Grids. Let's discover together how migration works and how it can make PrestaShop a modern CMS.

Technical requirements

As we will explore the BO of PrestaShop to understand how it works, you will have to use some of the following tools to perform reverse engineering:

- Any PHP code editor
- An (s)FTP client to browse your website files (only if you work on a remote server, not necessary if you work on a local server)

Discovering how a legacy-based BO controller works

We learned in *Chapter 3*, *The Front Office*, that all the controllers were children of the `Controller` class and studied the features added by the `FrontController` class. For BO controllers, we will follow the same steps, but as we know the life cycle of a `Controller` class, we won't repeat the explanation, and instead, we will dive directly inside the specificities of BO controllers.

We will use a practical example by exploring the `AdminCart` controller, which is accessible in the BO of PrestaShop inside the Orders Menu , from the Shopping Carts link. The URL structure of this controller uses the following pattern: `https://www.domainname.ext/adminXXX/index.php?controller=AdminCarts&token=abcdef1234`.

As we saw in *Chapter 2*, *Configuration and Initialization of PrestaShop*, the legacy-based BO controllers are instantiated by the `Dispatcher` if no routes are found by the Symfony router. In that case, `Dispatcher` manages the initialization and instantiates the `AdminCartsControllerCore` class defined in the `/controllers/admin/AdminCartsController.php` file. All the old legacy-based controllers are stored inside the `/controllers/admin/` folder.

Like every legacy-base BO controller, it extends the `AdminController` class, which is stored inside `/classes/controller/AdminController.php`, a child class of the already-known `Controller` class. The following is a summary of the BO legacy controller workflow:

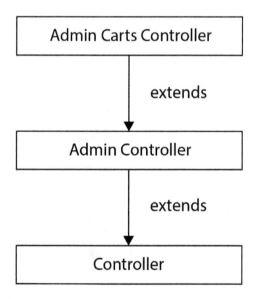

Figure 4.1 – The legacy BO controller workflow

The first function to be called is the `run()` function, and as it is not overridden inside the `AdminController` class or the `AdminCartsController` class, the life cycle will be the same as in the FO controllers.

First, let's have a look at the features provided by `AdminController` to our BO controllers and see how `AdminCartsController` uses them. By having a general idea of how it works, you will be more likely to master how the BO works.

Discovering the AdminController features

Let's open the `/classes/controller/AdminController.php` file and go through the controller's life cycle, function by function:

1. `__construct()`: This sets the `controller_type` and `controller_name` by removing possible suffixes, and sets the themes variables depending on the employee settings. It also sets the BO theme templates path in Smarty.

2. `init()`: This executes the `parent::init()` function and handles the logout if requested by a `get` variable or if the cookie lifetime is exceeded. It calls `initProcess()`, which sets the `$display`, `$action`, `$boxes`, and `$identifier` variables depending on the GET variables provided. It translates the URLs requested in order to give instructions to the CMS. Then, `initMultiStoreHeader()` is called to manage the display of the multistore header, which is displayed if the multistore mode is active. The `InitBreadCrumbs()` method fetches the data and assigns it to Smarty for further display. The `InitModal()` method also assigns modal-linked data to Smarty and `initToolbarFlags()` generates the content provided to Smarty to generate the toolbar (title, buttons, and so on). `initNotifications()` provides Smarty with the settings necessary for displaying, or not displaying, new orders, new customers, or new customer message notifications at the top-right corner of the screen. To sum up, it gives all the important data to Smarty to generate the frame of a generic BO controller view.

3. `setMedia()`: This is overridden by a `$isNewTheme` variable set to `false` by default. As you may have noticed, some old views use the former theme created in **version 1.6** of PrestaShop and others use the new theme. Depending on which theme is used by the controller, it loads different CSS and JS with the use of `addJS()`, `addJQueryPlugin()`, and `addCSS()`. Both themes are stored in the `/adminXXX/themes/` folder of PrestaShop, the new one is stored in `/adminXXX/themes/new-theme/`, and the old theme is in `/adminXXX/themes/default/`. The old default theme can be duplicated and renamed to create a customized theme, but we won't go deeper than this because it is not often used. Whatever BO theme is used, `setMedia()` assigns the JavaScript-required variables.

4. `postProcess()`: This mainly handles list filtering.

5. `initHeader()`: This assigns to Smarty all the elements necessary for a good display of the header and settings values for the rest of the page.

6. `initContent()`: This is a kind of dispatcher, which generates the CRUD, depending on the value of the `$display` variable processed, as seen in the `init()` method. If `$display` equals `edit` or `add`, it calls `renderForm()` to generate the form for the creation or edition of the current object. If `$display` equals `view`, then `renderView()` is called to show the view (not editable) of the current object and if `$display` equals `details`, then `renderDetails()` generates the table containing a list of objects of a required type. The output of the `renderView()`, `renderDetails()`, or `renderForm()` methods is stored in the `$content` variable and assigned to Smarty to display it inside the view. We will see in the next section how `renderView()`, `renderDetails()`, and `renderForm()` use the `Helper` objects to generate a form, a list table, or a view, by providing some key elements only.

7. `initFooter()`: This assigns the lists of CSS and JavaScript files, generated in the `setMedia()` method that can be overridden in all the child classes, to Smarty. Then it assigns modal views.

8. `display()`: This assigns to Smarty the display settings and calls the `smartyOutContent()` method to display the layout of the BO view. It looks for any overrides, and, if there are some present inside the `/override/controllers/admin/templates/` folder, it uses them instead.

We now know how the `AdminController` class adds the necessary features for a nicely displayed BO page. How about continuing our journey by exploring the `AdminCartsController` class?

Exploring the AdminCartsController class

Now, we can open the `/controllers/admin/AdminCartsController.php` file and study its content. It will help us understand how it generates our view by following the usual life cycle:

- `__construct()`: It sets all the variables necessary for the display of a list with the help of the `HelperList` class, such as `$fields_list`, `$_select`, `$_allow_export`, `$_orderWay`, or `$bulk_actions`. Please refer to the *The most useful tools for recurrent HTML generation – the Helper classes* section if you want to know more about the `Helper` classes.

- `init()`: This is not overridden, so it just follows the parent behavior.

- `setMedia()`: This is not overridden, so it just follows the parent behavior.

- `postProcess()`: This is not overridden, so it just follows the parent behavior. It seems normal as it is not a controller made to process or display a form.

- `initHeader()`: This is not overridden, so it just follows the parent behavior.

- `initContent()`: This is not overridden, so it just follows the parent behavior but as you can see, `renderKpis()`, `renderView()`, and `renderList()` are overridden to respectively display the **key performance indicators (KPIs)**, the view of specific cart information, and the table listing the existing carts.

- `initFooter()`: This is not overridden, so it just follows the parent behavior.
- `display()`: This is not overridden, so it just follows the parent behavior.

> **What are all the ajaxProcessXXX() methods available in AdminCartsController?**
>
> We haven't explored in detail the behavior of `AdminController` in case of an **AJAX** call. If you go back to the `/classes/controller/AdminController.php` file, in `postProcess()`, you will see that if `$this->ajax` is `true`; then if `$action` (equals to the action GET variable) is not empty, it checks whether an `'ajaxProcess'` . `Tools::toCamelCase($action)` named method exists. If it is `true`, then it executes it to return its output. If not, it checks whether `ajaxProcess()` exists and returns its output.
>
> You can also find the `processXXX()` methods in the case of non-AJAX calls, if `$action` is not empty, and if a method named `'process'` . `ucfirst(Tools::toCamelCase($this->action))` exists, then the controller returns the output of this function.

This simple BO controller is a good example of a controller using Helper classes to generate HTML views used to assign it inside its `$content` variable to Smarty. Let's have a look at the `Helper` classes to see how they can be used to generate some useful generic views.

The most useful tools for recurrent HTML generation: the Helper classes

The `Helper` classes are defined in the `/classes/helper/` folder and enable us to generate useful recurrent BO views, such as edition forms with `HelperForm`, or entity elements listing tables with `HelperList`. Other `Helper` classes exist, such as `HelperCalendar`, `HelperImageUploader`, `HelperKpi`, `HelperKpiRow`, `HelperOptions`, and so on, but we won't cover all of them because the aim of this book is to show you the way to understand how everything is articulated and to be able to create your own modules following those design patterns.

The parent class for all the `Helper` objects is defined in the `/classes/helper/Helper.php` file by the `HelperCore` object. The final aim will be to use the `generate()` method to return the HTML content requested.

Generating an edition form with HelperForm

The `HelperForm` object is a child object of `Helper`, and it is used to generate an HTML form by calling its `generateForm($fields_form)` method, providing an array argument containing all the required information describing the requested form.

$ fields_form is an associative array containing one key per form section (or fieldset) requested. Each section value is also an associative array that must contain a 'form' key. The following example sums it up:

```
$fields_form = [

'section1' => ['form'=>$firstFormDefinition],

'section2' => ['form'=>$secondFormDefinition]

]
```

Each section form, such as $firstFormDefinition, has to be an associative array containing three required keys named legend, input, and submit:

```
$firstFormDefinition = [
  'legend' => [
    'title' => $this->l('This is the dislayed title'),
    'icon' => 'icon-cogs'
  ],
  'input' => [
    ['type' => 'text',
    'name' => 'first_field_name'],
    ['type' => 'textarea',
      'name' => 'second_field_name']
  ],
  'submit' => [
    'title' => $this->l('Title of the button'),
    'class' => 'btn btn-default pull-right'
  ],
];
```

The legend key value has to be a dictionary composed of a minimum of two keys:

- title: This contains the heading title
- icon: This contains the class corresponding to a **FontAwesome** icon

The input key value has to be a list of input fields, and each one has to be described by an associative array composed of a minimum of two keys:

- type: This contains the type of the input field; it can take the following values: text, select, textarea, radio, checkbox, file, shop, asso_shop, free, or color.
- name: This contains the name of the input (the value of the attribute name of the input element).

The `submit` key value has to be a dictionary composed of a minimum of two keys:

- `title`: This contains the text on the **Submit** button

- `class`: This contains the classes to append to the class attribute of the **Submit** button

In `AdminController`, inside `renderForm()`, you have an example of the use of `HelperForm` to generate a form:

```
$helper = new HelperForm();
$this->setHelperDisplay($helper);
$helper->fields_value = $fields_value;
$helper->submit_action = $this->submit_action;
$helper->tpl_vars = $this->getTemplateFormVars();
$helper->show_cancel_button =
(isset($this->show_form_cancel_button)) ? $this->show_form_cancel_
button : ($this->display == 'add' || $this->display == 'edit');
...
$form = $helper->generateForm($this->fields_form);
```

As you can see, we can set the `$fields_value` field to provide the existing values to the form.

If you want to get more documentation on all the optional keys available to customize your form, feel free to visit the official documentation at `https://devdocs.prestashop-project.org/8/development/components/helpers/helperform/`.

Generating an element list table with HelperList

The `HelperList` object is also a child object of `Helper`; it is used to create an HTML table composed of a list of rows and columns already provided by the controller by calling the `generateList($list, $fields_display)` method.

`$list` is an array containing all the rows to display and `$fields_display` is an associative array containing all the columns and their display settings.

Let's see an example of a `$fields_display` associative array:

```
$fields_list = [
  'id_gender' => [
    'title' => $this->trans('ID', [], 'Admin.Global')
  ],
  'name' => [
    'title' => $this->trans('Social title', [],
      'Admin.Shopparameters.Feature')
  ]
];
```

The previous example is simple and shows that we will generate a list composed of two columns titled ID and Social title by using the trans() function responsible for automatically localizing the text.

Now let's see an example of the $list array, even if it is very often used with a SELECT result from the database with the help of the Db class:

```
$list = [
    ['id_gender' => 1, 'name' => 'Gender item 1'],
    ['id_gender' => 2, 'name' => 'Gender item 2'],
    ['id_gender' => 3, 'name' => 'Gender item 3'],
    ['id_gender' => 4, 'name' => 'Gender item 4'],
    ['id_gender' => 5, 'name' => 'Gender item 5'],
];
```

And here is an example of how to instantiate a HelperList object:

```
$anotherHelperList = new HelperList();
$anotherHelperList->shopLinkType = '';
$anotherHelperList->simple_header = true;
// Actions to be displayed in the "Actions" column
$anotherHelperList->actions = array('view', 'edit',
    'delete');
$anotherHelperList->identifier = 'id_gender';
$anotherHelperList->show_toolbar = true;
$anotherHelperList->table = 'genders';
$anotherHelperList->title = 'Test HelperList Genders';
$anotherHelperList->currentIndex =
    AdminController::$currentIndex;
$listGenerated = $anotherHelperList->generateList($list,
    $fields_list);
```

If you want to get more details about the optional keys available to customize your list, please visit the official developer documentation at https://devdocs.prestashop-project.org/8/development/components/helpers/helperlist/.

It was important to look at those Helper child classes, which were very often used in the old legacy-based BO controllers. They are about to disappear and be replaced by the Symfony Form and Grid components used in the migrated controllers, but if you want to understand how PrestaShop works, you need to know the full story. Let's move on to the new generation of migrated controllers that rely on Symfony.

Discovering how a migrated Symfony-based BO controller works

Understanding the legacy is important for a good understanding of the full system, but as the BO controller's migration is in progress, it is far more important to know how a Symfony BO controller works.

Let's consider the already-migrated `General` parameter's controller, visible from the BO Menu via **Shop Parameters | General** at the following URL – `https://www.domainname.extension/adminXXX/index.php/configure/shop/preferences/preferences?_token=abcdef123` – with `adminXXX` as the variable corresponding to your shop and `abcdef123` as the generated token.

In *Chapter 2, Configuration and Initialization of PrestaShop*, we saw that the Symfony kernel was loaded in the `/adminXXX/index.php` file. In our example, the router checks the routing configuration files located in the `/src/PrestaShopBundle/Resources/config/routing/admin/` folder and particularly inside the `/src/PrestaShopBundle/Resources/config/routing/admin/configure/shop_parameters/preferences.yml` file, and finds the route defined by the following YAML:

```
admin_preferences:
  path: preferences
  methods: [ GET ]
  defaults:
    _controller: 'PrestaShopBundle\Controller\Admin\Configure\
ShopParameters\PreferencesController::indexAction'
    _legacy_controller: AdminPreferences
    _legacy_link: AdminPreferences
```

As a reminder, the route name is `admin_preferences`, the request methods covered are only the `GET` ones, the controller instantiated namespace is `PrestaShopBundle\Controller\Admin\Configure\ShopParameters\PreferencesController`, and the called method is `indexAction()`.

Let's proceed to this controller definition and see how it works. So, let's browse to the `/src/PrestaShopBundle/Controller/Admin/Configure/ShopParameters/PreferencesController.php` file. First, we see that the class is called `PreferencesController` and extends `FrameworkBundleAdminController`.

We will see how `FrameworkBundleAdminController` works and get back to the `PreferencesController` child class.

This Symfony admin base controller is located in the `/src/PrestaShopBundle/Controller/Admin/FrameworkBundleAdminController.php` file. It extends the well-known Symfony base controller called `AbstractController`, defined in the framework.

The constructor `__construct()` function is the first called. It instantiates the `Configuration` class in the `$configuration` variable of the class. It is issued with the `PrestaShop\PrestaShop\Adapter\Configuration` namespace. It is the class defined in the `/src/Adapter/Configuration.php` file. This is an example of the use of an `Adapter` class.

What are the Adapter classes?

Usually, in Symfony, when we want to deal with the database and its tables, we use the `Doctrine` library. It uses the Doctrine entities directly. In the case of PrestaShop, if we create Doctrine entities directly even during the migration process, we have to maintain the Legacy `ObjectModel` child object for the legacy-based controllers and the new Doctrine entity.

Then, when all the controllers use the Doctrine entity, we will be able to delete the Legacy `ObjectModel` child object. It would take a long time and a huge amount of work to maintain all of that. To make it easier during the migration process, the `Adapter` classes are used. They are used by Symfony directly and use the old Legacy `ObjectModel`-based objects to create the interface between the Legacy objects and Symfony. At the end of the transition, they will be replaced by the Doctrine entities, implementing the same functions and containing the same variables. Every time you have to manipulate Legacy objects in a class, this class has to be placed in the `/src/Adapater/` subfolders. It will have to be deleted and replaced by a new class manipulating non-legacy objects once the migration is done.

This class contains many tool functions necessary for admin. Feel free to explore them further.

Getting back to `PreferencesController`, the call function is `indexAction(Request $request, FormInterface $form = null);` it uses Symfony auto-injection to instantiate `Request $request` and `FormInterface $form`.

It stores the result of `$this->get('prestashop.adapter.preferences.form_handler')->getForm();` in `$form`. In fact, `$this->get('nameOfTheService')` enables us to load a service named `'nameOfTheService'` from the Symfony service container.

To get the definition of the `prestashop.adapter.preferences.form_handler` service, let's get to the `/src/PrestaShopBundle/Resources/config/services/bundle/form/form_handler.yml` file.

What if I can't find my service definition?

If you can't easily find a definition of a service, you can use a search tool to find the service name in `/src/PrestaShopBundle/Resources/config/services/`.

The service is defined by the following YAML code:

```yaml
prestashop.adapter.preferences.form_handler:
  class: 'PrestaShop\PrestaShop\Core\Form\Handler'
  arguments:
    - '@form.factory'
    - '@prestashop.core.hook.dispatcher'
    - '@prestashop.adapter.preferences.form_provider'
    -'PrestaShopBundle\Form\Admin\Configure\ShopParameters\General\
      PreferencesType'
    - 'GeneralPage'
```

It instantiates the class defined in the `/src/Core/Form/Handler.php` file with the `form.factory`, `prestashop.core.hook.dispatcher`, and `prestashop.adapter.preferences.form_provider` services instances, and instance of the class defined in the `/src/PrestaShopBundle/Form/Admin/Configure/ShopParameters/General/PreferencesType.php` file an the `'GeneralPage'` string. All those objects are stored in member variables and the `getForm()` function is called. It uses the **Symfony Form component** to generate a custom form. First, it gets the form **factory** to create a builder following the pattern defined by `PreferencesType.php`. It sets the data to fill in the form and then it gets the corresponding form object.

The `renderForm(Request $request, FormInterface $form)` function is called to return the output view containing the generated form. If you go to the bottom of the file defining the `PreferencesController` class, you will find the `renderForm()` definition.

It loads the `prestashop.adapter.tools` service in `$toolsAdapter`, generates the SSL URI in `$sslUri`, and then calls `render('pathOftheTwigTempate.twig', $arrayOfData)`. This function uses the **Twig** templating engine used by Symfony. It will replace Smarty in PrestaShop when the migration is done. In this case, it will use the template located in `/src/PrestaShopBundle/Resources/views/Admin/Configure/ShopParameters/preferences.html.twig` and assign the variables with the following array :

```php
[
'layoutHeaderToolbarBtn' => [],
'layoutTitle' => $this->trans('Preferences',
  'Admin.Navigation.Menu'),
'requireBulkActions' => false,
'showContentHeader' => true,
'enableSidebar' => true,
'help_link' =>
  $this->generateSidebarLink('AdminPreferences'),
'requireFilterStatus' => false,
'generalForm' => $form->createView(),
```

```
'isSslEnabled' =>
  $this->configuration->get('PS_SSL_ENABLED'),
'sslUri' => $sslUri,
]
```

The generalForm key is filled with the $form->createView() value, which is the generated form HTML code. It is the real content of the view; the rest of the keys are meta values.

We now know how the BO controller displays the form. As you can see, the Symfony Form component used here replaces HelperForm and provides a nice alternative!

Let's have a look at how the form is handled by PrestaShop and Symfony.

Handling the form submission

If you go back to the /src/PrestaShopBundle/Resources/config/routing/admin/ configure/shop_parameters/preferences.yml file containing the routes for the Symfony router, you will find the second route covering the form validation:

```
admin_preferences_save:
  path: preferences
  methods: [ POST ]
  defaults:
    _controller: 'PrestaShopBundle\Controller\Admin\Configure\
    ShopParameters\PreferencesController::processFormAction'
    _legacy_controller: AdminPreferences
    _legacy_link: AdminPreferences:update
```

The route name covering the form validation path is admin_preferences_save, the form sending methods are POST, the controller namespace to instantiate is PrestaShopBundle\ Controller\Admin\Configure\ShopParameters\PreferencesController, and the called method is processFormAction().

As the PrestaShopBundle\Controller\Admin\Configure\ShopParameters\ PreferencesController namespace designates the /src/PrestaShopBundle/ Controller/Admin/Configure/ShopParameters/PreferencesController. php file, let's look at it and study the processFormAction(Request $request) method with the auto-injection of a Request object.

The form object is loaded just like in the indexAction() studied earlier in this chapter by instantiating a service. With the help of the Symfony Form component, handleRequest() is called to handle all the POST and GET data sent.

If the form is submitted and the data is valid, the data is retrieved and stored inside the $data variable.

The save process is handled by the `save()` method located in the `prestashop.adapter.preferences.form_handler` service, and managed by the class defined in the `/src/Core/Form/Handler.php` file.

The definition of `save()` is as follows:

```
public function save(array $data)
{
$errors = $this->formDataProvider->setData($data);
$this->hookDispatcher->dispatchWithParameters(
"action{$this->hookName}Save",
[
'errors' => &$errors,
'form_data' => &$data,
]
);
return $errors;
}
```

The main action of this method is `$this->formDataProvider->setData($data);` and `formDataProvider` is an instance of the `prestashop.adapter.preferences.form_provider` service. Let's jump to its definition to see what `setData($data)` does.

The `prestashop.adapter.preferences.form_provider` service is defined in the `/src/PrestaShopBundle/Resources/config/services/bundle/form/form_data_provider.yml` file by the following code:

```
prestashop.adapter.preferences.form_provider:
  class: 'PrestaShopBundle\Form\Admin\Configure\ShopParameters\
  General\PreferencesFormDataProvider'
  arguments:
    - '@prestashop.adapter.preferences.configuration'
```

If we look at the `/src/PrestaShopBundle/Form/Admin/Configure/ShopParameters/General/PreferencesFormDataProvider.php` file, we see that `setData()` is defined by the following:

```
public function setData(array $data)
{
return $this->preferencesConfiguration->updateConfiguration($data);
}
```

And `$this->preferencesConfiguration->updateConfiguration($data)` is defined in the `/src/Adapter/Preferences/PreferencesConfiguration.php` file. It is a function responsible for saving the data given by the form via an array with the help of `$this->configuration->set($key, $value);`.

Once saved, this code is executed:

```
$this->getCommandBus()->handle(
new UpdateTabStatusByClassNameCommand(
'AdminShopGroup',
$this->configuration->get('PS_MULTISHOP_FEATURE_ACTIVE')
)
);
$this->addFlash('success', $this->trans('Successful
  update', 'Admin.Notifications.Success'));
return $this->redirectToRoute('admin_preferences');
```

This code is made up of three blocks:

- The execution of an `UpdateTabStatusByClassNameCommand` command via the **CommandBus**:

```
$this->getCommandBus()->handle(
new UpdateTabStatusByClassNameCommand(
'AdminShopGroup',
$this->configuration
  ->get('PS_MULTISHOP_FEATURE_ACTIVE')
)
);
```

- The addition of a success message to the template with `addFlash()`, which is a function provided by the Symfony framework:

```
$this->addFlash('success', $this->trans('Successful
  update', 'Admin.Notifications.Success'));
```

- The redirection to the route named `admin_preferences` with `redirectToRoute()`, which is a function provided by the Symfony framework that redirects the view to the route given in the first argument:

```
$this->redirectToRoute('admin_preferences');
```

You may wonder about the `UpdateTabStatusByClassNameCommand` command used in the first part of the previous code. It is a part of the **CQRS design pattern**. We will see in the next section how it applies to PrestaShop modern controllers.

Using the CQRS design pattern

In the Legacy core, all the controllers use the `ObjectModel` child classes to manage the interactions with the database for reading and writing. Whereas in the Symfony modern controller, the core uses the CQRS design pattern with the `Command` and `Query` objects.

Using a Command object and its CommandHandler class in the CommandBus

If you have to do an UPDATE, DELETE, or INSERT action in the database, you mustn't directly call Doctrine and handle it directly inside the controller. Instead, you should use a Command object that contains the necessary data for your action to be done. Every type of Command object has a linked CommandHandler class containing a handle() method responsible for executing the desired action.

Prestashop uses a CommandBus, managed by a library called Tactician, which is like a big pipe in which you can put your Commands, and it processes them one by one, matching each Command object with its CommandHandler and executing the corresponding handle() method. This way, you can easily change the way you handle a Command object without having to change the controller.

As Prestashop is migrating, we saw that during the migration process, the database business is still done by the Legacy ObjectModel child objects, via the Adapter classes for Symfony-based controllers. The good point is that when CommandHandler has to stop using Adapter to manipulate the database, we will only have to change the CommandHandler definition instead of having to update our freshly migrated Symfony-based controllers another time.

> **The bank example**
>
> If you don't understand the Command concept, imagine a simple real-life situation: you want to send a bank wire to a friend of yours. The bank employee responsible for your account asks you to fill out a little paper form with the amount to be transferred, the IBAN of the receiving account, and the IBAN of the sending account. You don't care about the transfer business as it is managed by the bank.
>
> To make the comparison, consider that you are equivalent to the Controller, the paper form is equivalent to the Command object, and the bank employee is equivalent to the CommandBus, sending the paper form (Command) to their colleague handling the money transfer who is equivalent to the CommandHandler.

Using a Query and its QueryHandler in the QueryBus

Queries work exactly like commands, but instead of dealing with database modifications, they are used to manage data retrievals (SELECT). This means that if you have to do a SELECT action in the database, you mustn't call for Doctrine repositories directly in the controller. You should use a Query object containing all the necessary data for your retrieval. Every type of Query has a linked QueryHandler class containing a handle() method responsible for executing the data retrieval.

Like the CommandBus with Commands, Prestashop uses a QueryBus, taking Queries as inputs, and outputs a **data transfer object (DTO)**, which is an object containing the retrieved data ready for further processing.

It protects and enables you to optimize the maintenance in the controllers exactly like for commands.

> **A fast-food restaurant example**
>
> As a real-life example is easier to understand, imagine that you want to order food from your favorite fast-food restaurant. You go to the front desk and order a meal with a burger and potatoes and a soft drink. The restaurant employee takes the order and sends it to the chef. 10 minutes later, he comes back to you and gives you a food bag with the order inside it.
>
> To keep up with the comparisons, imagine that you are equivalent to the `Controller`, the message you passed to the restaurant employee with the content of the order is equivalent to a `Query` object, the restaurant employee transmitting the order to the chef is equivalent to a `QueryBus`, and the chef is equivalent to the `QueryHandler class`. Finally, the food bag containing the meal is equivalent to a DTO.

It is important to understand this design pattern to know how everything works. We will not illustrate it directly, but you will get some command examples in the chapters where we will build modern modules together.

We saw in the legacy-based BO controllers that most of them use `HelperList` to generate list tables automatically. In Symfony-based controllers, we will use a component called `Grid`. As we did not have the chance to find a **Grid** example in the previous `PreferencesController`, let's find one now!

Generating table views by using Grid components

To find a good example of the use of a **Grid component**, please go to `https://www.domainname.ext/adminXXX/backoffice/index.php/configure/shop/contacts/?_token=abcdef1234` with `adminXXX` replaced by your admin folder name or via the BO menu in **Shop Parameters** | **Contact**.

It displays the list of the existing contact recipients available to your customers via the contact front controller. We will focus on how the table can be created with the help of a Grid component.

The definition of the controller managing this view is in the `/src/PrestaShopBundle/Controller/Admin/Configure/ShopParameters/ContactsController.php` file. We can open it and look at the `indexAction(Request $request, ContactFilters $filters)` definition:

```php
public function indexAction(Request $request, ContactFilters $filters)
    {
    $contactGridFactory = $this
        ->get('prestashop.core.grid.factory.contacts');
    $contactGrid = $contactGridFactory->getGrid($filters);

    return $this->render(
        '@PrestaShop/Admin/Configure/ShopParameters/Contact/Contacts/
        index.html.twig',
        [
```

```
                    'help_link' => $this->
                        generateSidebarLink($request->attributes->
                        get('_legacy_controller')),
                    'enableSidebar' => true,
                    'layoutTitle' => $this->trans('Contacts',
                        'Admin.Navigation.Menu'),
                     'layoutHeaderToolbarBtn' => [
                        'add' => [
                            'desc' => $this->trans('Add new
                          contact', 'Admin.Shopparameters.Feature'),
                            'icon' => 'add_circle_outline',
                            'href' => $this->
                              generateUrl('admin_contacts_create'),
                        ],
                    ],
                'contactGrid' => $this->presentGrid($contactGrid),
                ]
            );
    }
```

We see that an instance of the service named `prestashop.core.grid.factory` is stored in `$contactGridFactory`. This service is defined following this YAML, located in the `/src/PrestaShopBundle/Resources/config/services/core/grid/grid_factory.yml` file:

```
prestashop.core.grid.factory.contacts:
  class: 'PrestaShop\PrestaShop\Core\Grid\GridFactory'
  arguments:
    - '@prestashop.core.grid.definition.factory.contacts'
    - '@prestashop.core.grid.data_provider.contacts'
    - '@prestashop.core.grid.filter.form_factory'
    - '@prestashop.core.hook.dispatcher'
```

This generated instance of `GridFactory` is like an instance of `HelperList`, to make a comparison with the legacy core. It is the object responsible for generating the table view.

It takes four arguments:

- An instance of the `prestashop.core.grid.definition.factory.contacts` service:

  This argument is the object defining the structure of the table, it is equivalent to the `$fields_list` in `HelperList`. If you open the class defining the grid structure in the `/src/Core/Grid/Definition/Factory/ContactGridDefinitionFactory.php` file, you will see that you have to set some mandatory information via the getter function:

  - `getId()`: This returns a string, which is the unique ID of this grid. It is like its unique alias.

- getName(): This returns a string, which is the display name for the table.

- getColumns(): This returns a ColumnCollection() function, which is the list of columns for the table.

- getFilters(): This returns a FilterCollection() function, which is the list of filters supported by the table.

- getBulkActions(): This returns a BulkActionCollection() function, which is the list of actions available if you bulk-select multiple rows from the table.

- getGridActions(): This returns a GridActionCollection() function, which is the list of actions available for the whole table (such as export or show SQL query, for example).

- An instance of prestashop.core.grid.data_provider.contacts:

  This argument is a data_provider object, which is the object that defines the data to show in the table rows. It is equivalent to $list in HelperList. The generic data_provider is based all the time on an instance of the /src/Core/Grid/Data/Factory/DoctrineGridDataFactory.php file and instantiates it. You have to provide a DoctrineQueryBuilderInterface child class, which defines how to retrieve the data to display. For our contact list grid, this class is defined in the /src/Core/Grid/Query/ContactQueryBuilder.php file. If you study its content, you will see that those classes must implement some methods, such as the following:

  - getSearchQueryBuilder(): This returns the query builder object to manage the data selection considering the filtering with the search input values.

  - getQueryBuilder(): This returns the query builder object to select the rows of the table with or without any filtering.

  - getCountQueryBuilder(): This returns the query builder containing the query to count the results number.

- An instance of prestashop.core.grid.filter.form_factory

- An instance of prestashop.core.hook.dispatcher

Coming back to the indexAction() method of our BO controller displaying the contacts grid, now that we have $contactGridFactory filled with the freshly-created GridFactory, we can generate a Grid object by applying the getGrid($filters) method to $contactGridFactory. It will return a Grid object considering the potential filtering requests:

```
$contactGrid = $contactGridFactory->getGrid($filters);
```

The $filters argument has to be an instance of SearchCriteria. As we don't want to study all the details of the Grid components, feel free to go to the official documentation article located at https://devdocs.prestashop-project.org/1.7/development/components/grid/#search-criteria if you want to know more about the use of SearchCriteria.

Finally, the render() function uses a Twig template to generate the view. It is located in the /src/PrestaShopBundle/Resources/views/Admin/Configure/ShopParameters/Contact/Contacts/index.html.twig file.

If you look at it, you will see that the Grid component is displayed with this code:

```
{% include '@PrestaShop/Admin/Common/Grid/grid_panel.html.twig' with
{'grid': contactGrid} %}
```

Twig works a bit like Smarty does, but it sometimes uses different syntax. Feel free to read the Twig documentation at https://twig.symfony.com/.

If you don't yet know Twig, to display the table generated by the Grid component, this code includes a subtemplate located in /src/PrestaShopBundle/Resources/views/Admin/Common/Grid/grid_panel.html.twig and it assigns the content of contactGrid to the variable named grid.

Then everything is automatically managed by the grid_panel.html.twig file to display the table.

The grids are very often used in the BO controller; they are made to replace the HelperList found in the legacy-based controllers. Even if it can take longer to create all the definition services and data providers, we will see in the module creation chapters that Grids are easier to extend in modules than HelperList.

Summary

In this chapter, we saw that all the old legacy-based BO pages are generated by controllers located in the /controllers/front/ folder. All those old BO controllers are child classes of the AdminController class defined in the /classes/controller/AdminController.php file. AdminController is a child of the Controller class defined in the /classes/controller/Controller.php file.

AdminController prepares all the data for the setup of the frame of the back office. All the AdminController child classes managing the old BO views rely on useful classes extending the Helper class to generate recurrent HTML views such as editing forms or list tables with HelperForm or HelperList.

Since **v1.7** of PrestaShop, the migration from the old legacy-based controllers to the Symfony modern controllers has been ongoing. New Symfony BO controllers extend the `FrameworkBundleAdminController` class. All Symfony controllers now benefit from the possibilities offered by the Symfony framework. The forms are now using the Symfony Form component instead of using `HelperForm` and the list tables are now based on the Grid component instead of using `HelperList`.

All database inserts, updates, and deletes are not directly managed inside controllers anymore, we have to send `Commands` via the `CommandBus` component to handle them. Also, data queries cannot be made directly inside controllers anymore, we have to send `Queries` via the `QueryBus` to retrieve DTOs containing all the requested data. This new method of database management follows the CQRS pattern.

Knowing the way controllers are migrated is important to understand how to design our modules to fit with the core patterns. By creating our modules, we will extend the core behaviors, and we will have some time to get back to the core to make the best coding choices.

In the next chapter, we will present Hooks, as they will enable us to modify some core behaviors or data retrievals in the controllers, and also insert HTML data inside views for both BO and FO controllers and views. They are maybe the objects most by modules to enable shop customization.

5

The Hooks

We now have a broader view of how **PrestaShop** works, from the FO to the BO. Let's now focus on hooks, the most important objects for module developers.

If you look at all the best CMSs around, such as **WordPress**, their success is highly correlated with their customization ability. As WordPress extensions enable you to add as many behaviors as you want to your blog, PrestaShop modules do the same. If you know about actions and filters in WordPress, you will understand exactly what hooks are in PrestaShop.

Our trip through the hooks world will be structured like this:

- Quick presentation of a hook
- Discovering the hook `ObjectModel` child class
- Presenting the two types of hooks
- Registering/unregistering a module to a hook and implementing a module's behavior on a hook execution
- Executing a hook

By the end of this chapter, you will know what hooks are, their types of use, how to use them, and their relationship with modules. You will understand why they are one of the most important items to enable a good customization ability for PrestaShop.

Technical requirements

As we will explore the core and the templates of PrestaShop to understand how it works, you will have to use some tools to consult the files:

- Any PHP code editor
- An (S)FTP client to browse your website files (only if you work on a remote server, not necessary if you work on a local server)

Quick presentation of a hook

Before diving deep into the details, let's describe quickly what hooks are. Hooks are like events that can be triggered from anywhere in the code and are mainly defined by a name. They can be placed anywhere in the controllers' code of PrestaShop and in the **Smarty** or **Twig** templating code of the themes.

Modules are a kind of plugin, just like WordPress extensions. They can be attached to as many hooks as you want. The attachment of a module to a hook is called a **registration**. When you define a hook. Each hook execution can contain parameters provided to registered modules as a payload of information to transmit the necessary information.

Even if many hooks are pre-delivered in PrestaShop Core, you can also create your own hooks and use them from your modules. As hooks are `ObjectModel` child objects, let's see how hook features are stored inside the database.

Discovering the hook ObjectModel child object

Hooks are referenced in the database and are represented in the core via the `Hook` class defined in the `/classes/Hook.php` file.

The fields describing a hook in the `prefix_hook` table are as follows:

- The `name` column is used in the code as the string identifying the hook; it must be unique.

- The `title` column is the short text describing the hook.

- The `description` column is the longer text to define what the hook does.

- The `position` column is a Boolean always equal to `true`. It is not used anymore but stays in the code.

- The `active` column is a Boolean equal to `false` if the hook is not active, and equal to `true` if the hook is active.

As hook names can become long and hard to remember, a `prefix_hook_alias` table enables you to add an alias string to a hook in a one-to-one relationship between a hook and an alias.

Also, hooks have a many-to-many relationship with the `Module` object. This relationship is materialized by the `prefix_hook_module` table.

This relationship is very important and describes how modules can be triggered by hooks to customize the appearance or the behavior of PrestaShop.

Before learning how to register a module with a hook and how to define the module behavior as soon as it's triggered by the hook, let's have a glance through the two types of hook in PrestaShop.

Presenting the two types of hook

If you connect to your database and select all the rows of the table named `prefix_hook`, you may see that the name values almost always follow the same pattern. The `name` column is always in camelCase and sometimes starts with `action` or `display`. There we are: we found the two main types of hooks used by PrestaShop!

The `display` hooks are visual and are executed in one, or sometimes many, **Smarty** or **Twig** templates arbitrarily, and they trigger the registered module(s) to insert custom HTML. Some parameters can be retrieved by the called modules. They run like `actions` in WordPress, if you know them. For example, if you want a module to add a block of text inside a page, you can use a `display` hook.

The `action` hooks are invisible because they only have an effect on the payload data transmitted as referenced parameters. To continue with the WordPress comparison, they can be compared to WordPress filters. For example, if you have an array of products to display, transmitted as a parameter of an executed `action` hook, you can register a module to remove some products of this array to filter all the products of a specified supplier only.

You may wonder, if more than one module is registered to the same hook, how can we decide the triggering order of the registered modules? In fact, it is simple; as you have seen in the description of the `Hook` object in the previous section, there is a many-to-many relationship between `Hook` and `Module` entities. This relationship is defined with a `position` variable. The ascending order is used to define the triggering order. All this information may become a bit too abstract, and we need some code examples to see how to register a module to a hook.

Registering/unregistering a module to a hook and implementing a module's behavior on a hook execution

Even if we will study deeply the modules' definitions later in this book, please consider that a module will be defined by a class extending the `Module` class defined in the `/classes/module/Module.php` file.

When we install our module in the PrestaShop BO UI, it runs the `install()` method of our `Module` class. And this is precisely where we want to register our module to the hooks. It can be done with the help of the `registerHook($hook_name, $shop_list = null)` method of the parent `Module` class, where `$hook_name` has to be the string name of the hook to register with, and `$shop_list` has to be the integer array of shop IDs in the case of a multistore.

For example, if we want to register to the `displayTop` hook (which enables us to display HTML content at the top of our FO pages in the header), we will simply define our `install` method as follows:

```
public function install()
{
    if(parent::install() &&
```

```
        $this->registerHook('displayTop'))
    {
        return true;
    }
    return false;
}
```

When we uninstall our module in the PrestaShop BO UI, it runs the uninstall() method of our Module class. If you go to the Module class definition, in the uninstall() method, all the hooks registered by the module are automatically unregistered with the unregister($nameofthehook) method. Let's see now how to define the behavior of a module as soon as it is triggered by a hook execution.

To continue with our displayTop hook, we can imagine that we want to display a "Welcome dear customer!" string at the top of the page in our FO pages. First, let's suppose that we have registered to the hook via the install method, as explained before. Then we must define a public method (non-static) that is named with the hook prefix and followed in camelCase by the name of the hook. For us, it should be the hookDisplayTop($params) public function. This function will be triggered for all the modules registered to this hook and it will receive an array as an argument that is often named $params. This array is filled with objects during the execution. The expected behavior of the module will have to be defined inside the function. Getting back to our very simple example, it could be defined like this:

```
public function hookDisplayTop($params)
{
    return "Welcome dear customer!";
}
```

We decided to take the example of a display hook, but if you want to register to an action hook, it is the same. Just replace the hook name with your action hook name. For example, you can do the same with the actionCategoryAdd hook by defining the hookActionCategoryAdd($params) public function like this:

```
public function hookActionCategoryAdd($params)
{
    //Do something with your $params array…
    return true;
}
```

We have now mastered the registration process of modules to hooks, and we know how to define the behavior of our modules when they are triggered by the hook execution. Next, we need to know how to execute a hook from anywhere in the code.

Executing a hook

As we explained before, we can use hooks to customize our shop and we can register modules to them to trigger our customized behavior. We know how to register, unregister, and define the custom behavior inside the module definition. To get the full scope, we now need to see how to execute a hook in the shop, making the module triggers possible.

Hooks can be executed anywhere in the code of PrestaShop, from **legacy** to **Symfony** controllers, and from Smarty to Twig themed templates.

Executing a hook from a legacy controller

Any legacy controller can use the `static` method named `exec()` from the `Hook` object. You can find its definition in the `/classes/Hook.php` file. We commonly use it as follows:

```
Hook::exec($hook_name, $params = array())
```

This includes `$hook_name` (the string name of the hook to execute) and `$params` (an array containing the necessary objects for good use of the hook).

For example, if you go to the `/classes/controller/Controller.php` legacy controller file, you will find many examples of hook executions, including this one:

```
Hook::exec(
    'actionControllerInitBefore',
    [
        'controller' => $this,
    ]
);
```

Then, let's see how to execute a hook from a Symfony controller.

Executing a hook from a Symfony controller

While legacy controllers use the `Hook` object directly, **Symfony** controllers that extend the `FrameworkBundleAdminController` class can use the `dispatchHook()` method as follows:

```
$this->dispatchHook($hook_name, $params = array())
```

This includes the same arguments as defined in the `exec()` function shown before.

For example, if you go to the `/src/PrestaShopBundle/Controller/Admin/Sell/Order/OrderController.php` file, you will find this one:

```
$this->dispatchHook(
    'actionGetAdminOrderButtons',
    [
```

```
            'controller' => $this,
            'id_order' => $orderId,
            'actions_bar_buttons_collection' =>
                $backOfficeOrderButtons,
    ]
    );
```

We're now done with the executions from controllers, so let's jump into templates, starting with Smarty views.

Executing a hook from a Smarty template

If you want to insert a hook execution to display the output of the module triggers, just insert, in your .tpl files, the following code if you do that from a core legacy controller template:

```
{hook h='hookName'}
```

Here, 'hookName' is the name of the hook (displayTop, for example).

If you execute a hook from a module template (as it will be presented later in the modules chapters) the code is as follows:

```
{hook h='hookName' mod='moduleName'}
```

Here, moduleName is the name of the module responsible for the execution of the hook.

As Smarty is not used anymore in Symfony-based controllers, you will see now how things work in Twig templates.

Executing a hook from a Twig template

If you use Symfony controllers to generate a view, you will have to use **Twig** as a templating library. Inside PrestaShop, Twig can use the renderHook function as follows:

```
{{ renderHook('hookName', { params }) }}
```

Here, 'hookName' is the name of the hook and params is an array of objects to send to the registered modules. Now, you know everything about hook executions in all contexts.

Summary

In this chapter, we discovered what hooks are and their important link with modules. We saw how they were stored in the database with the hook ObjectModel child class.

Then, we listed the two types of hooks in PrestaShop: the display and action hooks, which can display HTML and filter/update data, respectively.

Modules can register and unregister to multiple hooks in order to be triggered as soon as those hooks are executed from anywhere in the code. The `Modules` classes will contain functions named `hookNameOfTheHook($params)` defining how to behave. Then, we showed how to execute hooks from any type of file in the code.

Hooks are easy to use and enable everyone to customize the shop without having to edit the core files. This way, you can have the core code of PrestaShop on one side and the modules on the other side. If you need to update your core files, you won't have to change your modules all the time, and that is very important. Hooks also enable one module to be used on multiple PrestaShop websites, and that's an important feature that leads a CMS to get a large user community with various applications.

We will see the real power of hooks in the module creation chapters!

In the next chapter, we will discover themes – their definition, structure, and main components. This will be the last step of our PrestaShop discovery before getting into the modules part.

6

The Themes

In previous chapters, we saw how the core of PrestaShop works and how it has evolved, as well as the added values of hooks. This will enable us to understand how modules will embed in the PrestaShop system. As modules can modify the graphical appearance of a shop, we need to understand what a PrestaShop theme is.

We will learn about themes by exploring these topics:

- Understanding what a theme is and its structure
- The FO Smarty templates
- The most used Smarty constants
- CSS/JS assets

By the end of this chapter, we will clearly understand what a theme is and where it has to be stored and structured. We will also know about the best constants and how assets are managed.

Technical requirements

As we will explore themes and their files, we will have to use some tools:

- Any code editor to discover the components of a theme
- An (S)FTP client to browse your website files (only if you work on a remote server – not necessary if you work on a local server)

Understanding what a theme is and its structure

First, you have to know what a theme represents. It is a folder located in the `/themes/` directory, and it contains all the necessary elements and a specified structure to provide a graphical appearance to the FO of PrestaShop.

If you are familiar with WordPress, you should already know about themes; they are the exact equivalent of PrestaShop themes. Even if you can have multiple themes stored in your /themes/ folder, only one can be activated at a time per shop. You always must have one theme activated.

If your website is multistore, you must have one theme activated per shop. PrestaShop stores the active theme name in the Shop ObjectModel class; you can verify that if you check the /classes/shop/Shop.php file, where you should note the presence of a variable called $theme_name. It's a string containing the theme name that corresponds to the folder name of the theme activated.

The theme is retrieved via the Shop object and stored in the Context singleton initialized in the /config/config.inc.php file, as seen in *Chapter 2, Configuration and Initialization of PrestaShop*. At any time, we can retrieve the active theme name by calling the $context->shop->theme->getName() function.

By default, PrestaShop is delivered with the classic theme, which is the base theme. To illustrate the structure of a theme and see what is mandatory, we will browse the content of the classic theme. Go to the /themes/classic/ folder so that we can discuss the folders' structure, which is organized as follows:

- _dev/: Contains the source files of the SCSS/JS and image assets ready to compile. We usually use webpack to compile and process the assets, with the assets/ folder as the output folder for production use. This folder is not mandatory and is sometimes not provided in commercial versions.

- assets/: Contains the assets for production, no matter whether they are the output of a compilation from _dev/ or not. In this folder, the mandatory files for a valid theme are assets/js/theme.js and assets/css/theme.css.

- config/: Contains the /config/theme.yml containing the metadata about the current theme, which is mandatory.

- modules/: This doesn't always exist and is not required. It contains subfolders that have module names and overrides some module template views, in order to adapt them to fit with the current theme. We will get back to this topic later, in *Chapter 7* to *Chapter 13* of this book.

- plugins/: This contains some custom Smarty plugins used in the view templates for the current theme (please go to https://www.smarty.net/docsv2/en/plugins.tpl for more information).

- templates/: This is the folder containing all the Smarty template files with the .tpl extension. As we saw in *Chapter 3, The Front Office*, the core FO controllers fetch the templates in this folder. The required files for a valid theme are listed in the developer documentation at https://devdocs.prestashop-project.org/8/themes/distribution/testing/; feel free to have a look at the full list.

We also need to discuss the preview.png file, which is required to enable PrestaShop to display a preview of the theme in the **Improve | Design | Theme & Logo BO controller**.

Inside the mandatory files listed in the subfolders of the theme, we have to focus a bit more on the `/config/theme.yml` file. It's a YAML file containing all the metadata to describe the theme and provide information to PrestaShop, in terms of compatibility and settings.

We will just focus on the main fields to provide because we are mainly module developers!

For the general description part, we have in the `classic` theme the following code:

```
name: classic
display_name: Classic
version: 2.0.6
```

Let's explain what each field stands for in the general description part:

- `name`: This is a string and has to be the same as the theme folder's name.
- `display_name`: This is a string; it is the pretty name displayed in the BO theme settings controller. It can be different from the theme folder name.
- `version`: This is a float equal to the version number.

For the `author` metadata part, we have the following code:

```
author:
  name: "PrestaShop SA and Contributors"
  email: "contact@prestashop.com"
  url: https://www.prestashop-project.org
```

Similarly, we can describe each field:

- `name`: This is a string describing the name(s) of the author(s)
- `email`: This is a string giving the email contact of the author
- `url`: This is a string equal to the website URL of the creator

Then, you can set several variables to change the settings for each theme. Everything is well explained in the developer documentation at this URL: `https://devdocs.prestashop-project.org/8/themes/getting-started/theme-yml/`.

If I change the theme.yml file from an existing theme, nothing happens. Why?

This is a recurrent issue reported by users! This `theme.yml` file is cached in the `/config/themes/theme_name/shopIdShop.json` file, with `theme_name` replaced by the theme name and `shopIdShop` replaced by the shop string, followed by the IDs of the active shops. If you want to update the theme manually, don't forget to delete all the `shop*.json` files in the `/config/themes/theme_name/` folder!

We know what a theme is, its folder structure, and how to set the general metadata and settings for a good setup. However, as the theme is the place where we have full control over the appearance of the website, we need to focus on where and how the template files are built. This will enable you to control the HTML content of the views and all the display parts. Let's see how the Smarty templates work.

The FO Smarty templates

We saw in *Chapter 3, The Front Office*, that the initContent() method of the front controllers was fetching the Smarty template of the active theme, with this code in the CMS FO controller example:

```
$this->setTemplate(
    'cms/page',
    ['entity' => 'cms', 'id' => $this->cms->id]
);
```

In this example, the code will fetch the /themes/classic/templates/cms/page.tpl file to generate the HTML view for the CMS page FO controller.

Remember that if you are not familiar with Smarty, you can go to the official documentation website via this URL: https://www.smarty.net/documentation.

Let's study the code of this template example:

```
{extends file='page.tpl'}
```

This line tells Smarty that this view is a child of the /themes/classic/templates/page.tpl file (the parent view). The following lines in this child template override the parent view:

```
{block name='page_title'}
  {$cms.meta_title}
{/block}
```

This code overrides the Smarty block named 'page_title' and replaces it with {$cms.meta_title}, which is the value of the meta_title key of the $cms variable that is assigned in the CMSController class. The next block does an equivalent thing, so we don't need to cover it.

If you're wondering about where the 'page_title' block is defined, you can find out where by going to the /themes/classic/templates/page.tpl file. In the /themes/classic/templates/page.tpl file, you will see that it also extends another file with the first code line:

```
{extends file=$layout}
```

`$layout` is part of the general settings of the theme; it is a variable set by the `getLayout()` method of the `/classes/controller/FrontController.php` file. Each FO controller can use one of the layouts available with the theme for each shop. Those settings are stored in the `/config/themes/theme_name/shopIdShop.json` files.

Usually, all the layout root templates are in the `/themes/classic/templates/layouts/` folder. They are the root views of the templates.

This example taken from `CMSController` can be generalized to all the FO controllers in the theme. Every file in `/themes/classic/templates/` is used by an FO controller.

If you look through all the templates, you will find hook executions, as seen in the last chapter. This is a nice way to make a link to the modules! If you want to try and create a new theme, it is highly recommended that you take the `classic` theme as an example. One good method is to duplicate it and change the name, settings, and your templates.

As you may have noticed, FO controllers have still not migrated to Symfony; they will be migrated when all the BO controllers are completed in Symfony. As soon as they migrate, the theme is likely to migrate to Twig instead of Smarty.

It is likely that it won't happen for many months, so we can keep going and discover the most useful constants used by Smarty.

The most used Smarty constants

Sometimes, in the Smarty files of your theme or in your module's templates, you will have to insert images or links to files. If you use WordPress, you may be familiar with constants such as TEMPLATEPATH to get the absolute path of the template files of the current theme. PrestaShop provides many constants, just like WordPress does.

The most important constants are assigned to Smarty in the `assignGeneralPurposeVariables()` method of the `/classes/controller/FrontController.php` file. The following constants are the most useful (if you want to get them all, feel free to reverse-engineer the `FrontController` class):

Constant	Content of the constant
`$urls.img_ps_url`	PrestaShop `/img/` directory
`$urls.img_cat_url`	PrestaShop `/img/c/` category images directory
`$urls.img_lang_url`	PrestaShop `/img/l/` lang images directory
`$urls.img_prod_url`	PrestaShop `/img/p/` product images directory
`$urls.img_manu_url`	PrestaShop `/img/m/` manufacturer images directory
`$urls.img_sup_url`	PrestaShop `/img/su/` supplier images directory
`$urls.img_ship_url`	PrestaShop `/img/s/` shipping method images directory
`$urls.img_store_url`	PrestaShop `/img/st/` store images directory

`$urls.img_url`	Active theme `/themes/theme_name/assets/img/` images directory
`$urls.css_url`	Active theme `/themes/theme_name/assets/css/` CSS files directory
`$urls.js_url`	Active theme `/themes/theme_name/assets/js/` JavaScript files directory
`$urls.pic_url`	`/upload/` directory
`$urls.theme_assets`	Active theme `/themes/theme_name/assets/` assets directory

Table 6.1 – Useful Smarty constants

If you monitor the templates' content, you are likely to meet those constants or others. Feel free to dump them by using the `var_dump` function, like this:

```
{$variable|var_dump}
```

A better way to dump a variable in the Symfony dumper mode is to use the `dump()` function, like this:

```
{dump($variable)}
```

To complete dumps, be aware that you can also display the **Smarty debug** window to show all the assigned variables by your FO controllers, by adding `{debug}` at the top of the `templates/_partials/header.tpl` file of your theme. It will add a pop-up window on your web browser when you visit any FO page (please deactivate your pop-up blocker if necessary).

The only FO theme topic we didn't cover yet is asset management. We will see how assets are compiled and managed in the themes.

The CSS/JS assets

If you go to the layout templates of the `classic` theme, by following `include` in the Smarty files, you will easily find that all the CSS and JavaScript file inclusions are managed in the `/themes/classic/templates/_partials/head.tpl` file with the following:

```
{block name='stylesheets'}
  {include file="_partials/stylesheets.tpl" stylesheets=$stylesheets}
{/block}
{block name='javascript_head'}
  {include file="_partials/javascript.tpl" javascript=$javascript.head
  vars=$js_custom_vars}
{/block}
```

Those two blocks include templates managing the CSS and JavaScript embeddings. Let's study the CSS part.

Embedding the CSS

Let's go to the `/themes/classic/templates/_partials/stylesheets.tpl` file, which contains the following code for the `stylesheets` file embedding:

```
{foreach $stylesheets.external as $stylesheet}
  <link rel="stylesheet" href="{$stylesheet.uri}" type="text/css"
  media="{$stylesheet.media}">
{/foreach}
```

As you can see, Smarty uses a `foreach` loop on the `$stylesheets.external` variable and adds links to all the style sheets included in it. That's it for the external style sheets. The template file also contains the following code for the inline styles:

```
{foreach $stylesheets.inline as $stylesheet}
  <style>
    {$stylesheet.content}
  </style>
{/foreach}
```

By looping on the `$stylesheets.inline` variable, it includes inline CSS code directly inside the HTML content.

We now know all about CSS embeddings; let's focus now on JavaScript inclusions.

Embedding the JavaScript

If we go to the `/themes/classic/templates/_partials/javascript.tpl` file, we can see that it contains the following code for the JavaScript file embedding:

```
{foreach $javascript.external as $js}
  <script type="text/javascript" src="{$js.uri}" {$js.attribute}>
  </script>
{/foreach}
```

With a `foreach` loop on the `$javascript.external` variable, all the JavaScript external files are included there.

The following code inserts the inline JavaScript code to embed in the page:

```
{foreach $javascript.inline as $js}
  <script type="text/javascript">
    {$js.content nofilter}
  </script>
{/foreach}
```

Finally, the following code declares all the JavaScript variables defined in the $vars dictionary:

```
{if isset($vars) && $vars|@count}
  <script type="text/javascript">
    {foreach from=$vars key=var_name item=var_value}
    var {$var_name} = {$var_value|json_encode nofilter};
    {/foreach}
  </script>
{/if}
```

Is it possible to use SCSS and Node.js compilation?

Sometimes, assets can be created with SCSS and Node.js. You are free to compile the CSS and JavaScript with your favorite tool, but you need to know that the PrestaShop classic theme is compiled with the help of webpack, which enables you to compile everything quickly and efficiently. All the webpack config files are in the /themes/classic/_dev/ folder in the webpack.config.js file, and the NPM business is defined inside the package.json file.

Now, you have mastered all the JavaScript embeddings inside FO templates.

Summary

The chapter enabled us to understand what a theme is physically and what it represents. We discovered that themes are structured folders located in the /themes/ directory, containing all the required files to provide nice graphical interfaces to the FO controllers.

All the necessary template files are in the templates folder inside the theme, and useful constants are provided by the FO controllers for Smarty to make media asset embedding easier.

We finally saw that raw or compiled CSS and JavaScript assets can be automatically inserted inside templates.

By covering themes, we are now aware of how the view layer of the FO's MVC pattern is managed. You should now have the necessary knowledge to understand how modules embed inside the PrestaShop system. Let's go and discover together what modules are and how we can create and use them.

Part 2 – How to Create Your Own Modules

In this second part, we will dive into the creation of seven useful modules. We will take a practical and progressive approach by explaining the structure of a module, hook registration, and the creation of front-office controllers and Symfony back-office controllers in a modern way by using Doctrine entities, services, grids, and forms. We will finish with payment and carrier modules.

This part has the following chapters:

7

What Are Modules? Let's Create a Hello World Module

In the first part of this book, we discovered how PrestaShop is structured, how it works, and the way it is being moved to a Symfony-based system. Even if it was sometimes a bit technical and abstract, it is important to have good knowledge of the full environment for what we will now work on, the modules.

As a PHP developer, your customers will ask you to modify the behavior of PrestaShop and add features. You could try to solve those tasks by finding the responsible files (controllers, views, or object models) and modifying them directly from the core, but you would have to ensure that your software can follow the updates cycle. In the case of PrestaShop, if you modify one of the files of the PrestaShop core manually so as to customize your shop, it will work, but your changes will be erased by the next update as new versions of the modified files are likely to replace your old ones.

Just as with other CMSes such as WordPress, the best way to customize or enhance the functionalities of PrestaShop is to use **modules**. They are independent from core updates even if they do require compatibility with the overall version, and they won't be erased. They can also be used on any other compatible PrestaShop platform, exactly like WordPress plugins.

In this chapter, we will see how to create a module by following these steps:

- Defining a module
- Creating our first hello world module
- Installing our first module

By the end of this chapter, we will know what a module is, where to find them, and how they work.

Technical requirements

You will need the following tools to create your first hello world module:

- Any PHP editor to code your module

- An (S)FTP client to browse your module files and folders (note that this is only necessary if you are working on a remote server, not a local server)

- A web browser in order to install and test your module

- A working PrestaShop installation (v1.7.x or above)

You can find the code used in this chapter here: `https://github.com/PacktPublishing/Practical-Module-Development-for-Prestashop-8/tree/main/Chapter%207`

Defining a module

Before creating our first module, let's define it. All the modules have a public name in regular language, such as `"Hello Word"`, as well as a technical name that must be written without spaces and contain only lowercase alphanumerical characters.

> **How do we choose the technical name for our module?**
>
> Even if the only constraint for the technical name is that it must contain only lowercase alphanumeric characters, we need to choose a meaningful one and find a solution to make it unique, as we don't want two modules to have the same technical name.
>
> One nice solution to ensure uniqueness is to prefix the technical name with the initials of the author company (so for Web Helpers, the prefix could be wh). This prefix is then followed by the main words of the module's regular name.

For our example `"Hello World"` module, we will use the `"whhelloworld"` technical name.

Technically, a module is a PHP file containing a class extending the `Module` class or one of its child classes (such as `PaymentModule` or `CarrierModule`). This main file has to use the technical name followed by the `.php` extension, and must be stored inside a folder also named with the technical name, itself inside the `/modules/` folder. The `/modules/` folder contains all the modules available for the current shop. So, in our example, the module class will be stored in the `/modules/whhelloworld/whhelloworld.php` file.

Creating our first hello world module

While theory is interesting, we can discover more by actually coding our `whhelloword` module. A practical example is better than thousands of explanations!

In the `/modules/whhelloworld/whhelloworld.php` file, let's define the module class:

- The first mandatory point is that the module class must use the technical name. But as PHP class names often start with a capital letter, the class name can use a camelcased version of the technical name with a capital letter for the second one. The camelcased version often improves the meaning of objects' names.

  We will create the `WHHelloWorld` class for our module.

- The second mandatory point is that this module class must extend the `Module` class or one of its child classes. As `PaymentModule` and `CarrierModule` are both child classes of `Module`, our module could extend one of them too.

Taking into account these constraints, let's declare our `Module` class. It should be coded like this:

```php
<?php
class WHHelloWorld extends Module
{
}
```

It is recommended that you add a little test to check that the module is loaded from PrestaShop and not from outside the system by adding the following condition at the beginning of the file:

```php
<?php
if (!defined('_PS_VERSION_')) {
    exit;
}
```

This code tests whether the `_PS_VERSION_` constant exists. If the module is called by the FO core, it is initialized in the `/config/autoload.php` file, so it is always `true`.

Let's add a constructor override to set some class attributes to define some variables necessary for the good use of the parent `Module` class. The required class variables to set are the following:

- `name`: This has to be a string holding the technical name of the module. For us, it will be `whhelloworld`.
- `tab`: This has to be a string and is used to assign the category under which the module will be listed in the BO at **Modules | Module Manager** in the category dropdown. Some default values are given in the following list:

  - `administration`
  - `front_office_features`
  - `pricing_promotion`
  - `payments_gateways`

- `shipping_logistics`

- `checkout`

- `advertising_marketing`

- `others`

- `theme_modules`, etc

You can also add custom categories that will be added to the category list automatically. But we will set our module to be listed in the `front_office_features` tab.

- `version`: This has to be a string. It is the version number and has to follow the **Semantic Versioning standard**. Our module version will be `1.0.0`.

- `author`: This has to be a string. It contains the name of the company or developer that authored this module.

The following are optional attributes. Some will have to be localized, but others won't:

- `dependencies`: This is an array and contains a list of strings. Those strings have to be the technical names of the other modules required by the main module. It is empty by default and the installation of the module will return a failure if at least one of the dependencies is not checked. For our module, it will be empty.

- `need_instance`: This has to be an integer, `0` or `1`. If it equals `0`, the module class won't be instantiated while visiting the BO controller in **Modules | Module Manager**. If it equals `1`, it will be instantiated. By default, it is set to `1` with the aim that you can tell a module to check for something (for example, updates) and send a notification in the **Module Manager** BO controller. For our module, it can stay equal to `0`.

- `ps_versions_compliancy`: This has to be an array with two keys (`min` and `max`) where each value must be strings defining the minimum and maximum versions compatible with the module.

  In our example it could be `[ 'min' => '1.7.0',  'max' => '8.99.99'];`

- `bootstrap`: This must be a boolean. If set to `true` for legacy BO configuration templates, it will include the Bootstrap CSS library and wrap all the helper HTML output with Bootstrap classes. If set to `false`, it won't use Bootstrap for those templates. It won't have any effect on Symfony templates. We can set it to `true` for our module.

- `confirmUninstall`: This is a string containing the message to display for the module uninstall confirmation. It can be localized if you want to cover many languages.

- description: This is a string describing the module. The text will be displayed in the modules list in the **Modules | Module Manager** BO controller. It can be localized if you want to cover many languages.

- displayName: This is a string containing the display name of the module in the **Modules | Module Manager** BO controller. It can be localized if you want to cover many languages.

How do I localize a string to make it multilingual-compliant?

For localized attributes, the Module class located in the /classes/module/Module.php file contains the l($string, $specific = false, $locale = null) method. You can use it with the first argument filled with the string to make localized. Usually, the reference text is in English. You can provide translated text for any active language via the BO menu in **International | Translations**.

If we want to use this l() method, we need to call the module parent constructor via the parent::__construct() method. It triggers many actions and just needs the name attribute variable to be filled.

With all these variables to set, let's apply this to our module. The whhelloworld.php file is added a constructor definition this way:

```php
public function __construct()
{
    //Required attributes
    $this->name = 'whhelloworld';
    $this->tab = 'front_office_features';
    $this->version = '1.0.0';
    $this->author = 'Web Helpers';
    //Optional non-localized attributes
    $this->need_instance = 0;
    $this->ps_versions_compliancy = [
        'min' => '1.7.0',
        'max' => '8.99.99',
    ];
    $this->bootstrap = true;
    parent::__construct();
    //Optional localizable attributes
    $this->confirmUninstall = $this->l('Do you still you
        want to uninstall the Hello World module?');
    $this->description = $this->l('This is a simple hello
        world module.');
    $this->displayName = $this->l('Hello World');
}
```

The preceding function first defined the mandatory attribute variables, then the optional ones that don't require any initialization from the parent object of the module. After that, we call the parent constructor function to set up the l () function and take care of all the module business. Finally, we set the localizable variables.

> **Reminder – where can we download the example code from?**
>
> It is recommended that you type all the code yourself to make sure that you properly learn about the things we cover. But, if you do want to download directly the code examples used in this book, you can find them on Packt's public GitHub repository at this URL: `https://github.com/PacktPublishing/Practical-Module-Development-for-Prestashop-8`.

Now that we know how to set the general attributes of our module, let's manage the installation and uninstallation processes.

Overriding the install() and uninstall() methods

In a module, you also have to implement overrides of the `install()` and `uninstall()` methods of the parent `Module` class. The `install()` function manages the installation process for the modules used in your shop. The `uninstall()` function likewise handles the uninstallation process. You may also need to carry out database interactions in those functions, such as adding or deleting specific tables, which can be done here, along with (un)registering the module with Hooks using the `$this->registerHook($nameofthehook)` function.

Let's say that we want our module to be displayed in the body of the home page of the FO. Let's register our module to the `displayHome` Hook in the `install()` function as follows:

```
public function install()
{
    return parent::install() &&
        $this->registerHook('displayHome');
}
```

This way, we can inherit from the parent `Module` class behavior and register the module with our Hook. The `uninstall()` function is done the same way, as follows:

```
public function uninstall()
{
    return parent::uninstall();
}
```

Even if this function does nothing special and could be deleted, it's worth keeping it in our development pattern as it will become useful when we need to complete some tasks on uninstall events.

Our module is now ready to install and provides the required information, and there's only one thing missing: the hookDisplayHome($params) method that will be triggered by the hook execution on the FO page. If we don't define this function, the installation won't succeed, and nothing will happen.

Defining the hookDisplayHome($params) function

The aim of our module is to display a Hello World! message in our home page body. As we saw in *Chapter 5*, *The Hooks*, when a module is registered to a hook, it must implement a hookNameOfTheHook($params) function with NameOfTheHook, the hook name. For us, it is hookDisplayHome because our hook is displayHome.

This is a display Hook and outputs a string with or without HTML. Even though we will use templates in the following chapters to tidy things up, in this example, we will see how to display a localized text. Let's use the following: "Hello World! I now know how to code a simple module!". We will implement localization by reusing the l() function of the parent Module class.

The following is our function:

```
public function hookDisplayHome($params)
{
    return $this->l("Hello World! I know now how to code a
        simple module!");
}
```

Now, our module contains all the most important things it needs to work well. Let's add a logo to the module for the listings in the BO.

Providing the module logo

Every module has a logo to help us recognize it easily. We define our logo by providing a **32 px by 32 px** PNG image called logo.png inside the /modules/whhelloworld/ folder. This logo will be visible in the **Modules | Module Manager** page listing in the BO.

Adding an index.php file for security

Just in case your web server doesn't handle the directory listings correctly, you should add a /modules/whhelloworld/index.php file. The template to use is provided by the PrestaShop community as follows – just copy/paste it into the body of the index.php file as provided at https://devdocs.prestashop-project.org/8/modules/creation/tutorial/#keeping-things-secure:

```
<?php
header('Expires: Mon, 26 Jul 1997 05:00:00 GMT');
header('Last-Modified: ' . gmdate('D, d M Y H:i:s') . '
    GMT');
```

```
header('Cache-Control: no-store, no-cache, must-
    revalidate');
header('Cache-Control: post-check=0, pre-check=0', false);
header('Pragma: no-cache');
header('Location: ../');
exit;
```

Once that is done, let's test our module!

Installing our first module

Our module is ready to be installed! It contains our module class, the logo, and the `index.php` file. Let's log in to our BO and click on the **Improve** section in the navigation menu, then **Modules | Module Manager**. You should see a listing of modules on the screen. If you scroll to the **Design & Navigation** subsection (because we defined the `$tab` attribute variable as `front_office_features`), you should get the following screen:

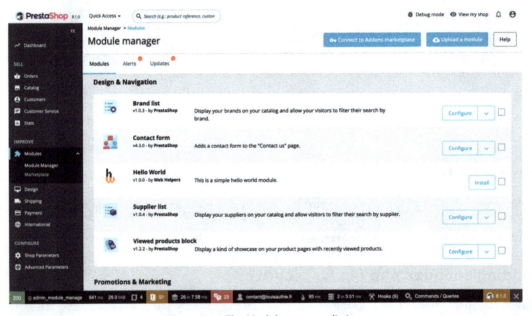

Figure 7.1 – The Module manager listing

As the third entry, we see our **Hello World** module. *TaS da!!!* Well done! You should be able to see all the different attribute values you set in the class.

Please click on the **Install** button, which will execute the `install` function of our module class. It will show a success message. Then test the module by visiting the FO index URL of your shop. If you scroll to the end of the body part, you should find your module output generated via the `hookDisplayHome($params)` function. Here is the output you should find:

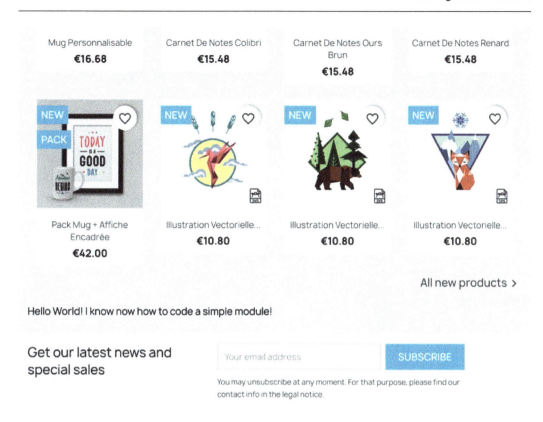

Figure 7.2 – The Hello World module displayed in the homepage content

If you want, navigate back to the BO **Module Manager** controller and click on the drop-down menu on the right side of the module entry on the list, then click the **Uninstall** button to trigger the `uninstall` function of our module, as shown in the following screenshot:

Figure 7.3 – Uninstall the Hello World module

Then you should get a success message confirmation. Please check that your module has disappeared from the FO home page to make sure.

Exercises

If you want to practice your skills yourself, you can try and change the content of the output of the `hookDisplayHome($params)` function to customize your message. Then you can try and register to another Hook such as `displayTop` and see how it works.

How can we install and uninstall modules via the command line?

While we can easily install and uninstall the modules via the graphical interface, we can also use the command line to do it via scripts.

For example, to install a module called whmodule, we can execute the following command from the root of our shop: `php bin/console prestashop:module install whmodule`

We can then uninstall it via the following command: `php bin/console prestashop:module uninstall whmodule`.

Summary

In this chapter, we discovered that a module is a class defined in the `/modules/` folder following certain rules on naming.

This class has to extend the `Module` class or one of its children classes. Every `Module` class must implement a `__construct()` method to set some required attributes, provide `install()` and `uninstall()` functions, and if the module registers with some Hooks, then it must implement the `hookNameOfTheHook($params)` function with `NameOfTheHook` replaced by the real hook name.

We also saw how to add a logo to our module listing, secure the folder, install/uninstall our module in practice, and finally tested it.

In the next chapter, we will create another module, displaying reinsurance blocks on the FO. This will be a nice way to further improve our knowledge of modules!

8
A Reinsurance Block Module

We got our first contact with the PrestaShop modules by creating a simple `Hello World!` module on the index. We know how to set the main variables and how to deal with the install and uninstall process by registering to hooks. Let's now go a little bit further by applying our knowledge to a new reinsurance module.

On many websites, merchants need to display information that reinsures customers to boost their rate of conversion. It can be very simple but powerful for online sales. This new example will enable us to learn how to code our module view in a separate Smarty template file and add some clean CSS styles.

The following process will lead us to an efficient working reinsurance block module:

- Defining our module design
- Creating the module's initial structure
- Adding a Smarty template view
- Adding CSS styles to our module
- Testing our module

By the end of this chapter, we will have mastered a simple module creation, hooked to the **front office (FO)**, using a Smarty template and a separate CSS file.

Technical requirements

You will need the following tools to create this reinsurance module:

- Any PHP editor to code your module
- An (S)FTP client to browse your module files and folders (only if you work on a remote server; not necessary if you work on a local server)
- A web browser in order to install and test your module
- A working PrestaShop installation (**v1.7**.x minimum)

You'll find the complete code used in this chapter here: `https://github.com/PacktPublishing/` `Practical-Module-Development-for-Prestashop-8/tree/main/Chapter%208/` `whreinsurance`

Defining our module design

Now that we're creating a useful module, as professional developers, we need to make sure that we exactly know what we want to obtain. Usually, customers expose their needs to the project management, and we are provided a mockup of what we need to deliver.

Let's imagine that we receive this ticket from our manager:

Please create a reinsurance module composed of three static blocks. No configuration interface is needed yet. It must be displayed on every front office page, in the footer. Please find attached the mockup:

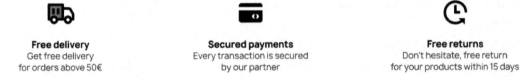

Figure 8.1 – The reinsurance block module mockup

This desktop layout will need to be adapted for mobile displays. The project manager told us to put each block in rows instead of columns for mobile after a little discussion. Before starting our development, we need to set some information; that's why you need to make sure that you have all the following details:

1. **Display name**: `Reinsurance block`

2. **Technical name**: `whreinsurance`

3. **Tab**: `front_office_features`

4. `need_instance` **value**: 0

5. **Description text**: `This is a reinsurance module for your front office.`

6. **Uninstall confirmation text**: `Do you still want to uninstall this module?`

7. **Hooks to register**: `displayFooterBefore` and `actionFrontControllerSetMedia` (we will explain how to choose hooks in the *Choosing our hooks* section that appears later in this chapter)

8. **Configuration page needed**: No

By completing the previous checklist, you will save much time creating your module structure. Now that we know where to go, let's jump to the module structure creation.

Creating the module's initial structure

Knowing our technical name (`whreinsurance`), we can now create our `/modules/whreinsurance` module folder. As explained in the previous chapter, we need to create a `/modules/whreinsurance/whreinsurance.php` file containing the module class definition, the `/modules/whreinsurance/index.php` file for security reasons, and the logo in the `/modules/whreinsurance/logo.png` file.

The `/modules/whreinsurance/index.php` file can be filled with the usual security content, as explained in the last chapter.

In the previous `Hello World!` module, we only defined a little text as an output sent to the hook. Now, we want to create a more elaborate module; that's why we want to generate HTML via a Smarty template. We also want to use a style sheet to define the CSS styles.

> **Where do we store the CSS and the Smarty template files?**
>
> For all the view templates and assets (such as images, `.css` files, and `.js` files), we store them inside the `views/` folder. This folder will contain a `templates/` subfolder for the Smarty templates, a `css/` subfolder for style sheets, a `js/` subfolder for JavaScript files, and an `img/` subfolder for image assets.

So, we can create a `/modules/whreinsurance/views/` folder. For security reasons, you can add a `/modules/whreinsurance/views/index.php` file, containing the same content as the module root `index.php` file.

Then, let's create the following subfolders:

- `/modules/whreinsurance/views/templates/`: This will contain all the template files
- `/modules/whreinsurance/views/templates/hook/`: All the templates used by display hook calls will be stored in the `hook/` subfolder
- `/modules/whreinsurance/views/css/`
- `/modules/whreinsurance/views/img/`

Please make sure to add an `index.php` file with the generic security content to all those folders and subfolders.

Defining the module class

Now, we have a nice folder structure, so let's code our module main class in the `/modules/whreinsurance/whreinsurance.php` file.

We can create the class, and its constructor function, as follows:

```php
<?php
if (!defined('_PS_VERSION_')) {
    exit;
}

class WHReinsurance extends Module{
    public function __construct()
    {
        //Required attributes
        $this->name = 'whreinsurance';
        $this->tab = 'front_office_features';
        $this->version = '1.0.0';
        $this->author = 'Web Helpers';

        //Optional non-localized attributes
        $this->need_instance = 0;
        $this->ps_versions_compliancy = [
            'min' => '1.7.0',
            'max' => '8.99.99',
        ];
        $this->bootstrap = false;

        parent::__construct();

        //Optional localizable attributes
        $this->confirmUninstall = $this->l('Do you still
            you want to uninstall this module?');
        $this->description = $this->l('This is a
            reinsurance module for your front office.');
        $this->displayName = $this->l('Reinsurance block');
    }
}
```

For this __construct function, you should understand everything; it follows the same structure as the previous Hello world! module.

Choosing our hooks

Before coding the `install()` and `uninstall()` methods, let's make sure that we choose the right hooks to register our module so as to complete our task.

How do we decide which display or action hook(s) to register?

It is very important to take enough time to target the appropriate hooks for your module.

For display hooks, every time you have to add content to an existing page, you will have to find or create a display hook to complete your task. The best way to find the appropriate hook to solve your problem is to do reverse engineering on the active theme. If you have to add content to the header, you can look at the `/themes/classic/templates/_partials/header.tpl` file if the classic theme is active, for example. In the same way, you can watch the `/themes/classic/templates/_partials/footer.tpl` file if you need to add something to the footer. If you need to add something to an existing core controller page, you can get to the corresponding controller view. By reading the content of those templates, you should find the best hook execution (`{hook h='displayNameOfTheHook' ...}` is the execution code) to see which hook would give you the best position on the page. If you want to add content in a place where no hooks are available, you will be able to create a child theme of the active one and create your own hook. Please refer to *Chapter 14, How to Create a Child Theme*, to know more about this topic.

When you need to modify or filter data assigned to a Smarty view template or inside a controller process (legacy or Symfony), you will have to find the corresponding action hook enabling this. For action hooks, the best way to locate the one you want to use is also to do reverse engineering to the good FO or **back office** (**BO**) controller, getting to the place where data is processed until you find the good action hook execution and the corresponding hook name and sent parameters.

The more you use views and controllers, the more you will know the most useful hooks and how they work. If you want to get a full list of the available hooks, please go to this URL: `https://devdocs.prestashop-project.org/8/modules/concepts/hooks/list-of-hooks/`.

In the previous section, *Defining our module design*, we decided to hook our module to the `displayFooterBefore` and the `actionFrontControllerSetMedia` hooks.

Initially, as a developer, we are not supposed to know directly which hook will be the best to solve our problem. Let's do reverse engineering together to show you an example.

First, our aim is to add a block to the footer. Let's see which hooks are available in the footer Smarty template of our active theme (the `classic` theme). Use the inspector of your favorite web browser (Firefox for me) and locate the place where you want to put your module's content, like this:

Figure 8.2 – Using the inspector to locate where to put the content

If you go to the active theme Smarty template files, as the root template of every view is the `/themes/classic/templates/layouts/layout-both-columns.tpl` file for the `classic` theme. You can locate the following code matching the code we found for the block we inspected via the web browser:

```
<footer id="footer" class="js-footer">
    {block name="footer"}
        {include file="_partials/footer.tpl"}
    {/block}
</footer>
```

In the footer block, the included template is the `/themes/classic/templates/_partials/footer.tpl` file. If you open it, you will see that our interesting block for the inclusion of our module is this one:

```
<div class="container">
  <div class="row">
    {block name='hook_footer_before'}
      {hook h='displayFooterBefore'}
    {/block}
  </div>
</div>
```

There, we find a very interesting hook execution:

```
{hook h='displayFooterBefore'}
```

Therefore, we want to register our module to the `displayFooterBefore` hook!

Then, our idea is to use a CSS style sheet to apply styles to our module block. First, let's locate where our CSS style sheets are included in the active theme templates; from there, we will get to the best hook enabling us to add a module custom style sheet. If you get back to the `/themes/classic/templates/layouts/layout-both-columns.tpl` file, you can locate the head tag there:

```
<head>
    {block name='head'}
        {include file='_partials/head.tpl'}
    {/block}
</head>
```

This leads us to open the included `/themes/classic/templates/_partials/head.tpl` file. There, we can see this interesting code:

```
{block name='stylesheets'}
   {include file="_partials/stylesheets.tpl"
     stylesheets=$stylesheets}
{/block}
```

And in the included `/themes/classic/templates/_partials/stylesheets.tpl` file, where the `$stylesheets` variable is sent, we can locate the style sheet's `link` tag responsible for the CSS loading:

```
{foreach $stylesheets.external as $stylesheet}
   <link rel="stylesheet" href="{$stylesheet.uri}"
     type="text/css" media="{$stylesheet.media}">
{/foreach}
```

We found that the `$stylesheets` variable is responsible for the style sheet's inclusion. Let's get to the controller responsible for the `$stylesheets` variable assignation to Smarty and see if there is an available action hook to add a style sheet from our module.

If we open the `/classes/controller/FrontController.php` file, in the `display()` method, we locate the `$stylesheets` assignation:

```
public function display()
{
    $this->context->smarty->assign([
        'layout' => $this->getLayout(),
        'stylesheets' => $this->getStylesheets(),
        'javascript' => $this->getJavascript(),
        'js_custom_vars' => Media::getJsDef(),
        'notifications' => $this->prepareNotifications(),
    ]);

    $this->smartyOutputContent($this->template);
```

```
    return true;
}
```

From there, we need to get to the `getStylesheets()` method definition:

```
public function getStylesheets()
{
    $cssFileList = $this->stylesheetManager->getList();

    if (Configuration::get('PS_CSS_THEME_CACHE')) {
        $cssFileList = $this->cccReducer
            ->reduceCss($cssFileList);
    }

    return $cssFileList;
}
```

If you get to the `stylesheetManager` variable definition, you will see that its type is `StylesheetManager`, and if you read the `/classes/assets/StylesheetManager.php` file and go to the `getList()` method definition, you won't find any hook execution! Too bad! What can we do?

Please leave it, and get back to the `FrontController` class definition in the `/classes/controller/FrontController.php` file! As we saw in *Chapter 3, The Front Controller*, the method responsible for managing the assets (CSS and JavaScript) is the `setMedia()` one. Let's get there and see what we can do:

```
public function setMedia()
{
    $this->registerStylesheet('theme-main',
        '/assets/css/theme.css', ['media' => 'all',
        'priority' => 50]);
    $this->registerStylesheet('theme-custom',
        '/assets/css/custom.css', ['media' => 'all',
        'priority' => 1000]);

    if ($this->context->language->is_rtl) {
        $this->registerStylesheet('theme-rtl',
            '/assets/css/rtl.css', ['media' => 'all',
            'priority' => 900]);
    }
...

    // Execute Hook FrontController SetMedia
    Hook::exec('actionFrontControllerSetMedia', []);
```

```
    return true;
  }
```

Focusing on the style sheet assets' registration, we see that everything is done by using the `registerStylesheet($id, $relativePath, $params = [])` method, and there is a hook execution via the `Hook::exec('actionFrontControllerSetMedia', [])`; code. Let's use this hook in our module. We will see that the `Context` singleton will enable us to retrieve the current controller instance and use the `registerStylesheet($id, $relativePath, $params = [])` method.

Those examples of reverse engineering show you how to behave in this kind of situation. Now that we've got our hook names, we can code our `install()` and `uninstall()` methods.

Defining the install() and uninstall() methods

Let's add the `install()` method to our `/modules/whreinsurance/whreinsurance.php` module definition file. Inside the `WHReinsurance` class, please add the following method:

```
public function install()
{
  return parent::install() &&
    $this->registerHook('displayFooterBefore') &&
    $this->registerHook('actionFrontControllerSetMedia');
}
```

This simply executes the parent `install()` method and registers the module to the two chosen hooks.

In the same way, we can code the `uninstall()` method this way:

```
public function uninstall()
{
return parent::uninstall();
}
```

This executes the parent `uninstall()` method and unregisters the module to the chosen hooks. Even if it is not mandatory, I suggest we keep it in our coding pattern as it can become useful later. Feel free to clean it if you prefer.

Now that all the modules are registered and unregistered, we need to add all the corresponding `hookNameOfTheHook($params)` methods to the module class to define how the module will handle each hook execution.

Defining the hook execution handlers

Let's add to our `WHReinsurance` class inside the `/modules/whreinsurance/whreinsurance.php` file the two handlers required to define the module behavior on the corresponding hooks' executions.

First, let's simply define the `hookDisplayFooterBefore($params)` and `hookActionFrontControllerSetMedia($params)` methods, like this:

```
public function hookDisplayFooterBefore($params)
{
}
public function hookActionFrontControllerSetMedia($params)
{
}
```

We will leave both empty now and will come back to each of them in the next two sections. We now have a sufficient module structure to register to the appropriate hooks and ready to handle any hook call. Let's now focus on the generation of the HTML to display, on the `displayFooterBefore` hook execution.

Adding a Smarty template view

Even if we could directly return the raw HTML code to display in the `hookDisplayFooterBefore($params)` function, we will do this by respecting the **model-view-controller** (**MVC**) concept. We will now use Smarty to generate the HTML view. First, we need to create a Smarty template that will be fetched by the module to return the right HTML output. We will now create a `/modules/whreinsurance/views/templates/hook/whreinsurance.tpl` file containing the HTML code of the module output. As we saw before, all the Smarty templates used inside the display hook calls must be stored inside the `/modules/whreinsurance/views/templates/hook/` folder. If you plan to have multiple display hook calls, you can call the `.tpl` file by the name of the hook calling. If you plan to use only one display hook, it is recommended by the PrestaShop developer documentation to call the `.tpl` file by the technical name of the module. It is not mandatory; it is just good practice.

One example of HTML code for our template could be the following:

```
<div id="whreinsurance_container">
  <div>
    <img src="{$module_img_dir}wh1.png"/>
    <span>{l s="Free delivery" mod="whreinsurance"}</span>
    <p>{l s="Get free delivery" mod="whreinsurance"}
        <br/>{l s="for orders above 50€"
        mod="whreinsurance"}</p>
  </div>
  <div>
    <img src="{$module_img_dir}wh2.png"/>
    <span>{l s="Secured payments"
        mod="whreinsurance"}</span>
    <p>{l s="Every transaction is secured"
        mod="whreinsurance"}<br/>{l s="by our partner"
        mod="whreinsurance"}</p>
```

```
      </div>
      <div>
        <img src="{$module_img_dir}wh3.png"/>
        <span>{l s="Free returns" mod="whreinsurance"}</span>
        <p>{l s="Don't hesitate, free return"
            mod="whreinsurance"}<br/>{l s="for your products
            within 15 days" mod="whreinsurance"}</p>
      </div>
    </div>
```

In the preceding code, we display one `div` container, containing one `div` tag per column. It is very simple.

As you can see, Smarty enables us to embed assigned variables by using the variable name between braces, such as in `{$module_img_dir}` embedding the `module_img_dir` variable content. This variable contains the path to find image assets in the module folder. Following the best practices, we will store the images inside the `/modules/whreinsurance/views/img/` folder with the following files: `wh1.png`, `wh2.png`, and `wh3.png`.

Then, you can also find the `l()` localization function call with `{l s="Free returns" mod="whreinsurance"}`, having `s` (the string to translate in the active language) and `mod` (the technical name of the module calling this function).

New translation system

Since PrestaShop *v1.7.6*, you can use the new translation system. For compatibility reasons in our examples, we prefer to use the old one, but it is easy to switch to the new system by using the `l()` function in Smarty, with the `s` variable providing the string to translate and the `d` variable providing a domain instead of `mod`. Our module could be translated with this code: `{l s="Free returns" d="Modules.Whreinsurance.Shop"}`.

The domain should follow these rules: for modules, it should start with `Modules` followed by a period. Then, we need to put the technical name of the module with an uppercase first letter, containing only letters without any underscores or other special characters. Then, we need a period, and to finish, we have the specific part that should be equal to `Shop` for FO-displayed strings and `Admin` for BO-displayed strings. Be aware that using this new system, from *v1.7.8* and above, you can export all the localized strings for your module into an XLF file so as to make it easy to manage localizations. To make this possible, you should add the following method to your module inside the main module class:

```
public function isUsingNewTranslationSystem()
{

    return true;

}
```

Once our template is complete, we need to fetch the generated HTML and return it in the `hookDisplayFooterBefore($params)` function so as to display our generated output. The following code will do the trick:

```
public function hookDisplayFooterBefore($params)
{
    $this->context->smarty->assign([
        'module_img_dir' => $this->_path . 'views/img/',
    ]);
    return $this->display(__FILE__, 'whreinsurance.tpl');
}
```

In this code, we execute the `$this->context->smarty->assign($arrayToAssign)` function that assigns the content of `$arrayToAssign` to the Smarty view displayed. `$arrayToAssign` can be an associative array; all the keys will become variable names, and the associated values will be stored respectively in each of them. In our example, it will store the value of `$this->_path . 'views/img/'` inside the `$module_img_dir` Smarty variable.

Finally, we return the output of `$this->display(__FILE__, 'whreinsurance.tpl')`, the view template we created before.

Smarty will return the generated HTML via the view template we created. If we leave the module like this, it will display the content but without any styles, and we would like to add some beautiful CSS styles to get the appearance requested by our customers. We will now see how to add external CSS style sheets to all the pages of our shop.

Adding CSS styles to our module

We decided to use the `actionFrontControllerSetMedia` hook execution to manage the insertion of our CSS style sheet into all the website pages. As `$params` is an empty array, in that case, there is no way to act on any variable.

The solution is to use `$this->context`, the instantiation of the `Context` singleton. It contains the `controller` variable, an instance of the current `controller` object, and a child class of `FrontController`. Then, we can use `registerStylesheet($id, $relativePath, $params = [])`, available in all instances of `FrontController`. Let's see how to do it for real:

```
public function hookActionFrontControllerSetMedia($params)
{
    $this->context->controller->registerStylesheet(
        'whreinsurance-style',
        $this->_path.'views/css/whreinsurance.css',
        [
            'media' => 'all',
```

```
                'priority' => 999,
        ]
    );
}
```

In this example, the first argument, $id, is set to 'whreinsurance-style'; it must be a unique string that will be used as a key in the associative array listing all the CSS assets to include in the page. The second argument, $relativePath, is set to $this->_path. 'views/css/whreinsurance. css' and provides the relative path to the CSS style sheet to include. Then, the last $params argument is set to ['media' => 'all', 'priority' => 999]. To sum it up, the media attribute of our link HTML tag including the style sheet will be set to 'all', and the priority is set to 999. It can go from 0 to 999, and the lower it is, the higher up the style sheet link will be included in the DOM of your page. You can get all the specifications for this array at this URL: https://devdocs. prestashop-project.org/8/themes/getting-started/asset-management/.

As it is an action hook, actionFrontControllerSetMedia doesn't return anything. Let's now install the created module and test it.

Testing our module

Our module is now ready for testing. If you want to download it, it is still available on the GitHub repository of the book at this URL: https://github.com/PacktPublishing/Practical-Module-Development-for-Prestashop-8/tree/main/Chapter%208/whreinsurance.

Let's install the module by browsing to the **Modules | Module Manager** page of your PrestaShop BO. Search for your Reinsurance block module inside the **Design & Navigation** section and click on the **Install** button. After the success toast message appears, go to any page of the FO of your PrestaShop, and you should see your new module in the footer. This is exactly what we wanted.

Keep in mind that a module is installed by default at the last position in the list of modules registered to a hook. That's why you should find your module at the bottom of the hookDisplayFooterBefore hooked modules. If you want to change the order of the modules triggered by a hook, just browse to the **Design | Positions** BO page and modify the order of the hooked modules for your hook.

We now have a working module ready for quick customer delivery!

Summary

We learned in this chapter how to create an FO hooked module, using a display and an action hook. We discovered how to find the best hooks to fit our needs. We went further into the folder structure of a module and saw where to store assets and hook view templates, with the best practices to choose template names.

Then, we coded our first Smarty template and fetched it into a hook call with a variable assignation. Finally, we saw how to embed CSS style sheets into our FO pages by using an action hook.

In the next chapter, we will create a new module by using our knowledge and learning how to create BO controllers with grids and entity management. It will be also time for us to create a module BO configuration page to manage settings.

9

A Customer Callback Request Module

The last chapter provided us with the opportunity to reapply all the processes of the module folder and class creation, and to learn new knowledge, such as the use of the Smarty templating library and new display hooks. Even if it was a great first use-case example, we will now discover many new useful features with the creation of a new module: a customer callback request module, hooked in the footer of our FO pages. This module will present a customer details form, enabling a visitor to receive a callback from customer services. It will send an email to customer services whenever a request is sent and archive the requests in a BO controller presented as a paginated and filtered list.

We will follow this process to code our new module:

- Define our module design
- Create the module's initial structure
- Implement the display hook and GDPR compliance
- Create the callback request entity
- Handle inserting a callback request into the database and send a notification email
- Create a modern BO controller containing a grid to list all the requests
- Add the delete action with the CQRS pattern
- Add the BO controller to the BO menu tabs
- Create a configuration page for our module and add a Symfony form

By the end of this chapter, you will know how to create a Symfony-based BO controller for your module, a grid component and its JavaScript components, a configuration page for your module, a Symfony form, and commands and queries following the CQRS design pattern, as well as how to send emails via PrestaShop.

Technical requirements

You will need the following tools to create this new module:

- Any PHP editor to code your module

- An (S)FTP client to browse your module files and folders (only if you work on a remote server; not necessary if you work on a local server)

- A web browser to install and test your module

- Terminal access to your web server with Composer, Node.js (v14.x or 16.x), and npm (v7.x or 8.x) installed and functional

- A working PrestaShop installation (v1.7.x minimum)

- The final code of the module, which is available in the GitHub repository at `https://github.com/PacktPublishing/Practical-Module-Development-for-Prestashop-8/tree/main/Chapter%209/whcallback`

Defining our module design

As we learned in *Chapter 8*, *Reinsurance Block Module*, we need to make sure that before we do any coding, we know exactly what we want to create.

As mentioned in the introduction, we want to create a module enabling customers to send their first name, last name, and phone number to customer services to receive a phone call back. We want customer services to be able to set the maximum number of hours before a callback via a configuration form inside the BO. Customer services will receive all the request notifications by email and will be able to find all of them as a list on a BO page, as well as being able to delete any request manually.

A mockup of the form we want to present in the footer of the FO pages could look as follows:

Any question? We can call you back!
Please leave us your details and we call you back in less than 2hour(s)

Firstname [   ]   Lastname [   ]   Phone number [   ]

☐ I accept that my personal information is saved and used by this shop for phone callbacks

SEND

Figure 9.1 – A simple mockup of a callback form

A mockup of the configuration form in the BO for our module could look as follows:

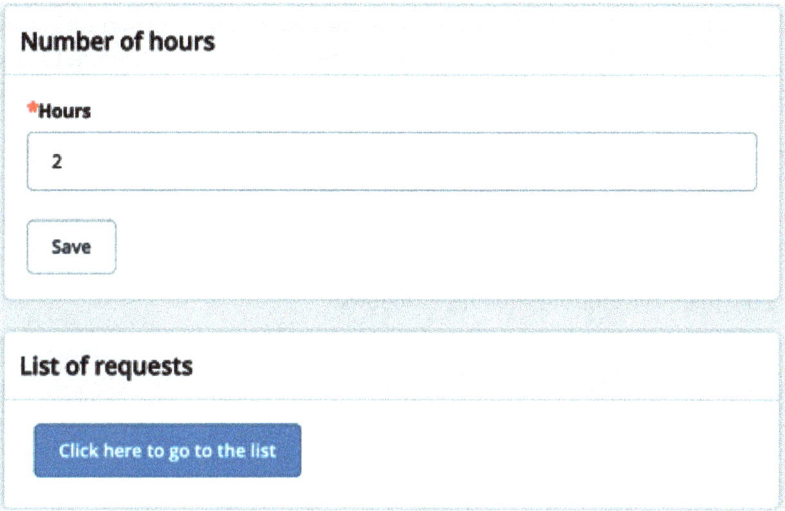

Figure 9.2 – A mockup of the configuration page for our module

Now that we know what we are working toward, we will follow the previously provided checklist for our module creation:

- **Display name**: Customer callback
- **Technical name**: whcallback
- **Tab**: front_office_features
- **need_instance value**: 0
- **Description text**: This is a customer callback module for your front office.
- **Uninstall confirmation text**: Do you still want to uninstall this module?
- **Hooks to register**: displayFooterBefore, actionFrontControllerSetMedia, and registerGDPRConsent (for any GDPR agreement managed by the psgdpr module)
- **Configuration page needed**: Yes

We should have enough elements now to start coding our module. Let's create its structure.

Creating the module's initial structure

Now that you have mastered the folder structure and the main class creation for a module, you can create the /modules/whcallback/ folder containing logo.png, whcallback.php, and index.php.

As a reminder, feel free to go to the GitHub repository of this book at any time if you want to get the code for this module directly, via this URL: https://github.com/PacktPublishing/Practical-Module-Development-for-Prestashop-8/tree/main/Chapter%209/whcallback.

Let's now create the main class for our module, as follows:

```php
<?php

if (!defined('_PS_VERSION_')) {
    exit;
}

class WHCallback extends Module
{
    public function __construct()
    {
    //Required attributes
            $this->name = 'whcallback';
    $this->tab = 'front_office_features';
    $this->version = '1.0.0';
    $this->author = 'Web Helpers';

    //Optional non-localized attributes
    $this->need_instance = 0;
    $this->ps_versions_compliancy = [
      'min' => '1.7.0',
      'max' => '8.99.99',
    ];
    $this->bootstrap = true;
    parent::__construct();

    //Optional localizable attributes
    $this->confirmUninstall = $this->l('Do still you
      want to uninstall this module?');
    $this->description = $this->l('This is a customer
      callback module for your front office.');
    $this->displayName = $this->l('Customer callback');
    }
}
```

Then, we can add the `install()` and `uninstall()` functions, registering to the following hooks:

- `displayFooterBefore` for the FO page's footer display
- `actionFrontControllerSetMedia` for the CSS asset registration
- `registerGDPRConsent` for GDPR agreement management

The `install()` and `uninstall()` functions can be coded as follows:

```
public function install()
{
  if (parent::install() &&
    $this->registerHook('displayFooterBefore') &&
    $this->registerHook('registerGDPRConsent') &&
    $this->registerHook('actionFrontControllerSetMedia'))
    {
    return true;
      }else{
    $this->_errors[] = $this->l('There was an error during
      the installation.');
    return false;
  }
}

public function uninstall()
{
  return parent::uninstall() &&
    $this->unregisterHook('displayFooterBefore') &&
    $this->unregisterHook('registerGDPRConsent') &&
    $this->unregisterHook('actionFrontControllerSetMedia');
}
```

As seen in the previous chapter, we can create an empty `/modules/whcallback/views/css/whcallback.css` file to store our CSS styles. Let's now register this CSS stylesheet and add it to the FO pages via the `hookActionFrontControllerSetMedia()` method:

```
public function hookActionFrontControllerSetMedia($params)
{
  $this->context->controller->registerStylesheet(
    'whcallback-style',
    $this->_path.'views/css/whcallback.css',
    [
            'media' => 'all',
            'priority' => 999,
    ]);
}
```

We won't focus on the CSS part, because that is not one of the main targets of this book. Please find the recommended content for the `whcallback.css` file in the GitHub repository of this book.

Let's now focus on the GDPR agreement required whenever we want customers to provide any personal data. PrestaShop provides the `psgdpr` module, which handles the `registerGDPRConsent` hook, enabling it to manage GDPR compliance for our module. If we register to this hook, our module will be listed as a GDPR-sensitive module, and we will be able to manage the checkbox agreement message for use of personal data. This message and the GDPR agreement checkbox will be automatically provided by the `psgdpr` module to us in any Smarty template by executing `{hook h='displayGDPRConsent' mod='psgdpr' id_module=$id_module}`, with the `$id_module` variable containing the ID of our module in the PrestaShop database. If you need more information about this topic, feel free to read the documentation page: `https://build.prestashop-project.org/howtos/module/how-to-make-your-module-compliant-with-prestashop-official-gdpr-compliance-module/`.

To comply with the fact that all registered hooks need a `hookNameOfTheHook($params)` method corresponding definition, and even if we don't want to add anything special there, let's declare the empty `hookRegisterGDPRContent($params)` method inside our module class, as follows:

```
public function hookRegisterGDPRConsent($params)
{
}
```

Now is the moment for us to create our front HTML form in a Smarty template file to be displayed in the footer of our FO page. It should contain five elements: the `firstname`, `lastname`, and `phone` inputs, the GDPR agreement checkbox, and the `submit` button. We can also provide a div block to contain the success and warning feedback messages. As this book is not about HTML code, let's just create the `/modules/whcallback/views/templates/hook/whcallback.tpl` file and fill it with this HTML and Smarty code:

```
<div id="whcallback_container">
  <span>{l s="Any question? We can call you
    back!"  mod="whcallback"}</span>
  {if isset($alert_message) || isset($success_message)}
    <p class="alert {if isset($alert_message)}
     alert-warning{else}alert-success{/if}">
      {if isset($alert_message)}
        {$alert_message}
      {else}
        {if isset($success_message)}
          {$success_message}
        {/if}
      {/if}
    </p>
  {else}
```

```
<p>{l s="Please leave us your details and we call you
  back" mod="whcallback"} {if $hours>0}{l s="in less
  than" mod="whcallback"} {$hours}{l s="hour(s) "
  mod="whcallback"}{else}{l s="as soon as possible!"
  mod="whcallback"}{/if}</p>
{/if}
<form action="" method="POST">
  <label for="whcbfirstname">{l s="Firstname"
    mod="whcallback"}
    <input type="text" name="whcbfirstname"
      id="whcbfirstname"/>
  </label>
  <label for="whcblastname">{l s="Lastname"
    mod="whcallback"}
    <input type="text" name="whcblastname"
      id="whcblastname"/>
  </label>
  <label for="whcbphone">{l s="Phone number"
    mod="whcallback"}
    <input type="text" name="whcbphone" id="whcbphone"/>
  </label>
  <div>
  {hook h='displayGDPRConsent' mod='psgdpr'
    id_module=$id_module}
  </div>
  <div class="break"></div>
  <input type="submit" name="whcbsubmit" value="{l
    s='Send' mod='whcallback'}" class="btn btn-primary"/>
</form>
</div>
```

There's nothing very special to point out in this code, just {hook h='displayGDPRConsent' mod='psgdpr' id_module=$id_module} for the GDPR part, and you may have noticed the call to the $hours variable that has to be assigned. This variable is the promised maximum number of hours between the request and the phone callback.

Now, let's code the hookDisplayFooterBefore($params) method definition in order to display the previously coded HTML form in the footer of all the FO pages, as follows:

```
private function processFooterForm()
{
  if(Tools::isSubmit('whcbsubmit')){
    if(Tools::getIsset('whcbphone') &&
    Validate::isPhoneNumber(Tools::getValue('whcbphone'))){
      $phone = Tools::getValue('whcbphone');
      $firstname = Tools::getValue('whcbfirstname');
```

```
        $lastname = Tools::getValue('whcblastname');

        //ToDo: Handle the request save and email
        //notification to the customer service
       }else{
       $this->context->smarty->assign([
         'alert_message' => $this->l('Please make sure that
         the phone field is correctly filled!')
       ]);
      }
    }
  }

public function hookDisplayFooterBefore($params)
{
  $this->processFooterForm();
  $this->context->smarty->assign([
    'id_module' => $this->id,
    'hours' => Configuration::get('WHCALLBACK_HOURS'),
  ]);

  return $this->display(__FILE__, 'whcallback.tpl');
}
```

In this code, we create a `processFooterForm()` method, which is responsible for handling the form submission with the input checks and the request persistence in the database. Initially, we'll just do the checks; we'll leave the database business for the next section. We will update this method once that's been explained!

- `Tools::isSubmit('submitName')` detects whether the `submitName` submit button has been clicked

- `Tools::getIsset('inputFieldName')` detects whether the `inputFieldName` input has been sent and set

- `Tools::getValue('inputFieldName')` enables us to retrieve the value of the `inputFieldName` input

If data is missing, we assign the `$alert_message` variable with the appropriate message.

After the form submission process, we assign `$id_module` with the `$id` attribute of the module class to send it to the hook `displayGDPRConsent` payload. We also assign the `$hours` variables to the content of the `WHCALLBACK_HOURS` configuration variable stored in the `prefix_configuration` table.

Finally, we call the `display` method to fetch the `/modules/whcallback/views/templates/hook/whcallback.tpl` Smarty template and return the generated code.

As we need to handle inserting callback requests into the database and the email notifications, let's now discover how to manage the database interface the modern way. We could have created an `ObjectModel` child object and used it to deal with the database, but that's not what we want anymore! Let's do it with the help of **Doctrine** and **Symfony**.

Managing the model the modern way

As we saw in previous chapters, the model interactions in the legacy controllers were handled by the `ObjectModel` child classes. In versions of PrestaShop above v1.7.6, modules can use the Doctrine ORM linked to Symfony. In the Doctrine language, we designate the model object as an **entity**.

Creating the callback request entity

To sum up how the Doctrine way of creating a model works, we have to follow these steps:

1. Create the `src/` folder at the root of your module folder. This is the folder that will contain all the Symfony classes that we will create and use.

2. Create a `composer.json` file at the root of your module folder to handle autoloading classes in our module with a defined namespace following the PSR-4 standard, using the `src/` folder as the root of our namespace.

3. Create a table manually via the `install()` function. *We can't use the Doctrine command-line tools to manage table creation as we are used to doing with a normal Symfony system* because it would use things such as foreign keys, and PrestaShop is still in the migration process and can't handle this yet. It should come later! Then, don't forget to drop the corresponding table, if needed, in the `uninstall()` function.

4. Create a class defining our entity by following the Doctrine annotation mapping (explained at this URL: `https://symfony.com/doc/4.4/doctrine.html#add-mapping-information`).

   The entity classes must be stored in the `src/Entity/` folder of your module.

   But don't worry about it; the more examples you see, the closer you will get to mastering it!

5. Create a corresponding repository class in the `src/Repository/` folder of your module.

6. Create the `config/` folder containing the `config/services.yml` YAML file, within which are the service definitions for Symfony-managed instantiations and injections. We can create the `config/front/services.yml` file containing the service definitions for the FO's use of the **light Symfony container,** available inside the hook calls and the front controllers (enabling us to only use Doctrine-linked services now). Then, we can create the `config/admin/services.yml` file for the BO uses of the **full Symfony container**.

7. Run `composer dumpautoload` in your command line at the root of your module to generate the `vendor/` folder automatically and handle the autoloading of the classes.

Once all of this is done, you can use your new entity!

This may seem a little bit abstract and difficult, but don't go yet! Let's apply these steps to our module now:

1. Create the `/modules/whcallback/src/` folder.

2. Create the `/modules/whcallback/composer.json` file containing this code (by following the Composer syntax):

```json
{
    "name": "webhelpers/whcallback",
    "description": "Customer callback module for your
      front office",
    "authors": [
        {
            "name": "Louis AUTHIE",
            "email": "contact@domain.ext"
        }
    ],
    "require": {
        "php": ">=5.6.0"
    },
    "autoload": {
        "psr-4": {
            "WebHelpers\\WHCallback\\": "src/"
        },
        "classmap": [
            "whcallback.php"
        ],
        "exclude-from-classmap": []
    },
    "config": {
        "preferred-install": "dist",
        "prepend-autoloader": false
    },
    "type": "prestashop-module"
}
```

For this file, we always use the same pattern, and we customize the `name`, `description`, `authors`, and `autoload` fields. The first fields are easy to understand. Let's focus on the `autoload/psr-4` field, which has to be filled with the escaped string of your namespace and the corresponding root folder for this namespace as the value. Then, don't forget to replace the `autoload/classmap` first element with the root class of your module.

3. Let's replace the `install()` method of our main module class with this one:

```
public function install()
{
    if (parent::install() &&
    $this->createTable() &&
    $this->registerHook('displayFooterBefore') &&
    $this->registerHook('registerGDPRConsent') &&
    $this->>
        registerHook('actionFrontControllerSetMedia')
    ){
      Configuration::updateValue('CALLBACK_HOURS', 1);
        return true;
    }else{
    $this->_errors[] = $this->l('There was an error
      during the installation.');
    return false;
    }
}
```

The only added elements are the execution of the `createTable()` method, which will contain the creation of the table for our entity, and the `Configuration::updateValue('CALLBACK_HOURS', 1);` code, which initializes the configuration variable named CALLBACK_HOURS to a value of 1.

The `createTable()` method for the creation of our new entity table can be added as follows:

```
private function createTable()
{
    return Db::getInstance()->execute('
    CREATE TABLE IF NOT EXISTS `' . _DB_PREFIX_ .
      'whcallback_request` (
        `id_request` int(6) NOT NULL AUTO_INCREMENT,
        `phone` varchar(255) NOT NULL,
        `firstname` varchar(255) NOT NULL,
        `lastname` varchar(255) NOT NULL,
        `request_date_add` DATETIME NULL,
        PRIMARY KEY(`id_request`)
    ) ENGINE=' . _MYSQL_ENGINE_ . ' default
      CHARSET=utf8');
}
```

We use the Db singleton to execute the SQL request creating the `prefix_whcallback_request` table containing the `id_request`, `phone`, `firstname`, `lastname`, and `request_date_add` fields defining the structure of our callback request entity. It may seem old-fashioned to use the Db class to create a table for a Doctrine entity, but this will change as soon as all of PrestaShop Core is migrated to Symfony. Please be patient!

As we don't need our callback requests to stay in the database upon uninstalling our module, we can modify the uninstall method of our module's main class as follows:

```
public function uninstall()
{
  $this->dropTable();
      Configuration::deleteByName('CALLBACK_HOURS');
  return parent::uninstall() &&
    $this->unregisterHook('displayFooterBefore') &&
    $this->unregisterHook('registerGDPRConsent') &&
    $this->
      unregisterHook('actionFrontControllerSetMedia');
}
```

We simply added the deletion of our configuration variable with `Configuration::deleteByName('CALLBACK_HOURS');`, and we will now call the `dropTable()` method, which can be created as follows:

```
private function dropTable()
{
    Db::getInstance()->execute('DROP TABLE IF
      EXISTS ' . _DB_PREFIX_ . 'whcallback_request');
}
```

This `dropTable()` function drops the `prefix_whcallback_request` table.

4.   Our table has been created. Let's create the corresponding Doctrine entity following the annotation mapping to link the model class to the MySQL table. We can create the `/modules/whcallback/src/Entity/WHCallbackRequest.php` file, containing the `WHCallbackRequest` entity class, as follows:

```
<?php
namespace WebHelpers\WHCallback\Entity;
use DateTime;
use Doctrine\ORM\Mapping as ORM;
/**
 * @ORM\Table(name="ps_whcallback_request")
 * @ORM\Entity(repositoryClass="WebHelpers\WHCallback\
Repository\WHCallbackRequestRepository")
 */
class WHCallbackRequest
{
}
```

We can add the attributes to link to the columns of our previously created table:

```
/**
 * @var int
 *
 * @ORM\Id
 * @ORM\Column(name="id_request", type="integer")
 * @ORM\GeneratedValue(strategy="AUTO")
 */
private $id;

/**
 * @var string
 *
 * @ORM\Column(name="phone", type="string", length=255)
 */
private $phone;

/**
 * @var string
 *
 * @ORM\Column(name="firstname", type="string", length=255)
 */
private $firstname;

/**
 * @var string
 *
 * @ORM\Column(name="lastname", type="string",
length=255)
 */
private $lastname;

/**
 * @var datetime
 *
 * @ORM\Column(name="request_date_add", type="datetime")
 */
private $requestDateAdd;
```

If you want an explanation of the annotations, feel free to read the official Doctrine documentation.

Then, please add the getters and setters for all the attributes to be able to modify and get the object attributes safely. You can find all of them in the GitHub repository of this book. We will just present one example for `$id`, `$phone`, and `$requestDateAdd` to cover each type:

```php
/**
 * @return int
 */
public function getId()
{
    return $this->id;
}

/**
 * @return string
 */
public function getPhone()
{
    return $this->phone;
}

/**
 * @param string $phone
 *
 * @return WHCallbackRequest
 */
public function setPhone($phone)
{
    $this->phone = $phone;
    return $this;
}

/**
 * @return datetime
 */
public function getRequestDateAdd()
{
    return $this->requestDateAdd;
}
```

Don't be surprised if you don't find the setter for `$requestDateAdd`; it is not there, and we won't create it. As this field just stores the request insertion datetime, we will set it automatically in the constructor of the entity class as follows:

```php
public function __construct()
{
    $this->requestDateAdd = new DateTime();
}
```

5. We can now create the corresponding repository class by creating the /modules/whcallback/ src/Repository/WHCallbackRequestRepository.php file, containing this code:

```php
<?php
namespace WebHelpers\WHCallback\Repository;
use Doctrine\ORM\EntityRepository;
use Doctrine\ORM\QueryBuilder;

class WHCallbackRequestRepository extends EntityRepository
{
}
```

6. Let's create the /modules/whcallback/config/services.yml, /modules/ whcallback/config/admin/services.yml, and /modules/whcallback/ config/front/services.yml files with the following initial content:

```yaml
services:
  _defaults:
    public: true
```

Initially, we will leave it that way. We don't need a repository service for saving, so no service needs to be created yet.

7. Run composer dumpautoload in your command line from the /modules/ whcallback/ folder.

Our WHCallbackRequest entity has now been created and can be used in our module. Let's now add a callback request to save the database inside the processFooterForm() method of our module's main class.

Handling inserting a callback request into the database

To handle saving a customer callback request, you can finally replace the provisional //ToDo: Handle the request save and email notification line with the following code in the processFooterForm() of the main module class:

```php
$entityManager = $this->get('doctrine.orm.entity_manager');
try{
  $callbackRequest = new WHCallbackRequest();
  $callbackRequest
    ->setPhone($phone)
    ->setFirstname($firstname)
    ->setLastname($lastname);
  $entityManager->persist($callbackRequest);
  $entityManager->flush();

  //ToDo: Send a notification email
```

```
$this->context->smarty->assign([
  'success_message' => $this->l('Thank you for your
  interest, we will call you back very soon!'),
]);
}
catch(\Exception $e){
  $this->context->smarty->assign([
    'alert_message' => $e->getMessage()
  ]);
}
```

Let's understand what's going on there.

`$entityManager = $this->get('doctrine.orm.entity_manager');` instantiates the `doctrine.orm.entity_manager` inside the `$entityManager` variable.

If you don't know it, the **Doctrine entity manager** is responsible for implementing the interface between the database and the entities:

```
$callbackRequest = new WHCallbackRequest();
$callbackRequest
  ->setPhone($phone)
  ->setFirstname($firstname)
  ->setLastname($lastname);
```

This creates an instance of the `WHCallbackRequest` entity and sets all the attributes with the submitted form values.

- `$entityManager->persist($callbackRequest);` adds the insertion of `$callbackRequest` into the `$entityManager` queue. The database is not saved at this stage.

- `$entityManager->flush();` executes all the requests in the `$entityManager` queue.

Now we know how to persist our data inside a database with the help of Doctrine and Symfony the modern way! We will be able to use this process whenever we need inside the BO and FO.

In the implementation of the form submission process, we're just missing the ability to send emails to customer services to inform them of a form submission.

Sending a notification email

In `processFooterForm()`, we didn't send the notification email. To do so, you can replace the `//ToDo: Send a notification email` comment with the following code:

```
Mail::Send(
    (int)(Configuration::get('PS_LANG_DEFAULT')),
        //Language id
    'contact', // email template file to be use
    'New Callback Request', // email subject
    array(
        '{email}' => Configuration::get('PS_SHOP_EMAIL'),
            // sender email address
        '{message}' => 'You have a new pending
            customer callback request from '.$firstname.'
            '.$lastname.' -phone: '.$phone
            // email content),
    Configuration::get('PS_SHOP_EMAIL'),
        // receiver email address
    NULL, //receiver name
    NULL, //from email address
    NULL  //from name
);
```

If you want to get deeper into the use of the `Send` function, you can either consult the `/classes/ Mail.php ObjectModel` definition or go to the PrestaShop devdocs article: `https://devdocs. prestashop-project.org/8/development/mail/#using-the-mailsend-method`.

At this stage, our module is able to display the callback request form in the footer of every FO page. It is able to handle a form submission and save its content, also sending a notification to customer services. We're still missing a BO controller page containing a listing of all the registered callback requests for customer services.

Creating a modern BO controller containing a grid to list all the requests

As customer service members may need to review the saved callback requests, we need a new page in the BO of our PrestaShop. Let's use Symfony to create a brand-new BO controller the modern way.

Creating a modern admin controller

Let's create a BO admin controller in our module. The standard process for this starts with the creation of a class extending the `FrameworkBundleAdminController` class in the `src/Controller` folder of your module.

To apply this process to our module, let's create the `/modules/whcallback/src/Controller/AdminWHCallbackRequestController` file. While there is no specification for the naming of a controller, it is important to use a comprehensive one anyway. A good practice could be to prefix it with `Admin` because of its BO destination and to suffix it with `Controller` because it is a BO controller.

The newly created controller will contain the following code for the initial class creation:

```php
<?php
namespace WebHelpers\WHCallback\Controller;

//use... Please find the use instructions in the GitHub repo

class AdminWHCallbackRequestController extends
FrameworkBundleAdminController
{
  private $cache;
  private $commandBus;

  public function __construct(CacheProvider $cache,
    TacticianCommandBusAdapter $commandBus)
  {
        $this->cache = $cache;
        $this->commandBus = $commandBus;
  }
}
```

We initially create two attributes: `$cache`, containing the **Doctrine cache provider**, and `$commandBus`, containing the **Tactician command bus**.

As this controller is a bit empty and simply does nothing yet, let's add a new method responsible for showing the list of registered callback requests. We can call it `listAction()`. The initial definition of it could be as follows:

```php
public function listAction()
{
}
```

As we want to use the dependency injection provided by Symfony for this admin controller, we need to define a new service for this class in /modules/whcallback/config/admin/services. yml by adding the following code to the services list:

```
#CONTROLLERS
WebHelpers\WHCallback\Controller\AdminWHCallbackRequestController:
  class: WebHelpers\WHCallback\Controller\
  AdminWHCallbackRequestController
  arguments:
    - '@doctrine.cache.provider'
    - '@prestashop.core.command_bus'
```

The first line defines the name for the service, which is the same as the controller's namespace, then the class is defined by the namespace, and the arguments are filled with the IDs of the services to inject.

> **How can we list all the services available in the container?**
>
> As in any Symfony system, you can use the following command in the command line from the root of your PrestaShop: php bin/console debug:container.
>
> It will show a two-column table, the first one containing the service ID and the second one the class name. It can be useful if you want to locate the appropriate service for what you need.

Our aim is to be able to access this controller via the BO. To make it accessible in the BO, we need to use the Symfony router and add a new route to it.

Creating a route in the Symfony router

You can add a route to the Symfony router for your module by adding the routes.yml file to the config/ folder of your module. Let's apply it to ours by creating the /modules/whcallback/config/routes.yml file.

We will define the route with this code:

```
admin_whcallbackrequest_list:
  path: whcallback/list
  methods: [GET]
  defaults:
    _controller: 'WebHelpers\WHCallback\Controller\
    AdminWHCallbackRequestController::listAction'
```

The first line is the route name, which must be unique, but you can set it as you want.

`path` being set to `whcall/list` means that your controller will be accessible via the following URL structure depending on your BO folder name and the generated token: `https://www.urlofthewebsite.extension/adminXXX/index.php/modules/whcallback/list?_token=abcdef`.

The `methods` field must be an array. In our case, it contains just the `GET` string, which means that the route will be triggered only for GET HTTP(s) requests.

The `_controller` field contains the namespace of the controller followed by the name of the method to be called, both linked with the `::` symbols.

As our route has now been created, let's get back to the `listAction()` method, as we want to create a list of all the registered callback requests. Even if we could do a simple query to the database via the entity repository and create our table manually, we prefer to use a useful tool available for PrestaShop, the `Grid` component, which is responsible for generating beautiful, rich filtered tables with row actions.

Using the Grid component to generate our callback requests listing view

First, let's have a look at what we're working toward. The grid we want to generate will look like this:

Callback requests (3)

ID ˅	First Name	Last Name	Phone number	Requested at	Actions
Search ID	Search first name	Search last name			🔍 Search
3	D'Esquiria	Natif	0123456789	2022/18/12 21:11:43	🗑
2	AUTHIE	Guiness	0123456789	2022/18/12 21:11:14	🗑
1	AUTHIE	Louis	0123456789	2022/18/12 21:10:42	🗑

Figure 9.3 – The grid we aim to generate

If you remember, we already presented how to use a grid component in *Chapter 4, The Back Office*. As PrestaShop provides a factory class to help create it, we will use it. Our Grid factory will be an instance of the `GridFactory` class. If you look at `/src/Core/Grid/GridFactory.php`, it requires four arguments in its constructor, and the first two of them are the following:

- An object implementing `GridDefinitionFactoryInterface`. Practically, we will create a child class of the `AbstractGridDefinitionFactory` class to provide the column structure, the actions, and all the structural information of the grid.

- An object implementing `GridDataFactoryInterface`. Concretely, we will create a service instantiating the `DoctrineGridDataFactory` class. We will feed it with an `AbstractDoctrineQueryBuilder` child object that we will create. All of this will provide the data to display in the grid.

Let's do this step by step: we will create the services responsible for creating the definition factory and the data factory. Then, we will have enough elements to feed to our grid factory service. We will use the grid factory to generate our grid.

Creating the Grid definition factory

Let's create the /modules/whcallback/src/Grid/Definition/Factory/WHCall-backRequestDefinitionFactory.php file containing a WHCallbackRequestDefinitionFactory class extending AbstractGridDefinitionFactory. The class will initially look like this:

```php
<?php
namespace WebHelpers\WHCallback\Grid\Definition\Factory;
//… use… (see the github repo for details)
final class WHCallbackRequestDefinitionFactory extends
AbstractGridDefinitionFactory
{
  const GRID_ID = 'whcallbackrequest';

  protected function getId()
  {
    return self::GRID_ID;
  }

  protected function getName()
  {
    return $this->trans('Callback requests', [], 'Modules.WHCallback.
    Admin');
  }

  protected function getColumns()
  {
    return (new ColumnCollection());
  }

  protected function getFilters()
  {
    return (new FilterCollection());
    }
}
```

The getId() method returns the unique ID given to this grid. Why not give it the name of the main entity displayed by this list, whcallbackrequest?

The getName() method sets the header presented above the grid table. We put the localized "Callback requests" text there. Let's now generate the columns composing our grid.

Generating the column structure of the grid

We now need to focus on the columns and implement the getColumns() method override. We want six columns in the grid table:

- ID
- First name
- Last name
- Phone number
- Requested at
- An action column to display a delete link to delete a callback request

We will add the columns to the ColumnCollection instance returned by the getColumns() method:

```php
protected function getColumns()
{
  return (new ColumnCollection())
    ->add(
      (new DataColumn('id_request'))
      ->setName($this->trans('ID', [],
        'Modules.WHCallback.Admin'))
      ->setOptions([
        'field' => 'id_request',
        ])
      )
      ->add(
      (new DataColumn('firstname'))
      ->setName($this->trans('First Name', [],
        'Modules.WHCallback.Admin'))
      ->setOptions([
        'field' => 'firstname',
        ])
      )
      ->add(
      (new DataColumn('lastname'))
      ->setName($this->trans('Last Name', [],
        'Modules.WHCallback.Admin'))
      ->setOptions([
          'field' => 'lastname',
        ])
      )
      ->add(
      (new DataColumn('phone'))
```

```
        ->setName($this->trans('Phone number', [],
          'Modules.WHCallback.Admin'))
        ->setOptions([
          'field' => 'phone',
          ])
      )
      ->add(
      (new DateTimeColumn('request_date_add'))
      ->setName($this->trans('Requested at', [],
        'Modules.WHCallback.Admin'))
      ->setOptions([
        'field' => 'request_date_add',
        'format' => 'Y/d/m H:i:s'
        ])
      )
      ->add(
        (new ActionColumn('actions'))
          ->setName('Actions')
          ->setOptions([
            'actions' => (new RowActionCollection())
              ->add((new LinkRowAction('delete'))
                    ->setIcon('delete')
                    ->setOptions(
                    [
                    'route' =>
                    'admin_whcallbackrequest_delete',
                      'route_param_name' =>
                        'idRequest',
                      'route_param_field' =>
                        'id_request',
                      'confirm_message' => $this->
                        trans('Delete this request?',
                        [], 'Modules.
                        WHCallback.Admin'),
                    ])
                  ),
          ])
        );
  }
```

To add a new column, we use the add() method of the ColumnCollection class and give it a DataColumn, DateTimeColumn, or ActionColumn instance as an argument.

Every column must be an instance of a child object of the AbstractColumn class.

We can set the column's localized header name with the `setName()` method, and provide options with an associative array composed of the mandatory `'field'`, enabling the grid to match the content to display with the field name set in the database query.

The `action` column is there to provide a list of possible actions for each row. The actions are made possible by creating a `RowActionCollection` instance and adding to it as many `LinkRowAction` instances as you wish. In our module, we will add only one, to enable customer services to delete any row. As you can see, we will have to define a new route taking the `idRequest` argument and named `admin_whcallbackrequest_delete`. We will do this later in this chapter.

You can find good documentation of the available column types and their available options here: `https://devdocs.prestashop-project.org/8/development/components/grid/columns-reference/`.

Don't forget to put the corresponding namespace `use` instructions before the class definition. We won't list them here because of code length constraints for the book. You can find all of them in the GitHub repository for this book, in the `Chapter 9` folder.

To generate a rich grid, we also need to implement the `getFilters()` method to provide available filtering instructions to our grid.

Generating the filter structure of the grid

We will enable filters on `ID`, `firstname`, and `lastname` only. We will also add a **Search** button and a filter reset link in the last column. The following code should provide all these filters to our grid:

```
protected function getFilters()
{
  return (new FilterCollection())
    ->add((new Filter('id_request', TextType::class))
    ->setTypeOptions([
      'required' => false,
      'attr' => [
        'placeholder' => $this->trans('Search ID', [],
          'Modules.WHCallback.Admin'),
      ],
    ])
    ->setAssociatedColumn('id_request')
    )
  ->add((new Filter('firstname', TextType::class))
  ->setTypeOptions([
    'required' => false,
    'attr' => [
      'placeholder' => $this->trans('Search first name',
        [], 'Modules.WHCallback.Admin'),
    ],
```

```
    ])
        ->setAssociatedColumn('firstname')
    )
    ->add((new Filter('lastname', TextType::class))
      ->setTypeOptions([
        'required' => false,
        'attr' => [
          'placeholder' => $this->trans('Search last name',
            [], 'Modules.WHCallback.Admin'),
          ],
            ])
      ->setAssociatedColumn('lastname')
    )
    ->add(
      (new Filter('actions', SearchAndResetType::class))
        ->setAssociatedColumn('actions')
        ->setTypeOptions([
          'reset_route' =>
            'admin_common_reset_search_by_filter_id',
          'reset_route_params' => [
            'filterId' => self::GRID_ID,
          ],
          'redirect_route' =>
            'admin_whcallbackrequest_list',
        ])
      );
  }
```

To add new filters to the `FilterCollection` instance returned by the `getFilters()` method, we must use the `add()` method and give it an instance of the `Filter` class as an argument. The `Filter` instance requires a name string as the first argument and a `Filter` type as the second argument. The available types provided by PrestaShop are listed here: `https://devdocs.prestashop-project.org/8/development/components/grid/filter-types-reference/`. We need to match each `Filter` with its associated column in the grid column definition via the `setAssociatedColumn($columnName)` method and the options via the `setTypeOptions($optionArray)` method. You will find all the option properties in the developer documentation link provided before.

Here, we just use standard `TextType` and `SearchAndResetType` filters. `TextType` is used for the ID, `firstname`, and `lastname` columns, whereas `SearchAndResetType` is used to manage the **Search** button and the reset link.

We now have a great grid definition factory class. Let's define a service using this class to make it available in the Symfony service container. We need to add the following lines to the services in the `/modules/whcallback/config/admin/services.yml` file to make it available in the BO service container:

```
webhelpers.whcallback.grid.definition.factory.whcallbackrequest_grid_
definition_factory:
  class: 'WebHelpers\WHCallback\Grid\Definition\Factory\
WHCallbackRequestDefinitionFactory'
  parent: 'prestashop.core.grid.definition.factory.abstract_grid_
definition'
  public: true
```

The `webhelpers.whcallback.grid.definition.factory.whcallbackrequest_grid_definition_factory` service name is completely arbitrary and follows a kind of namespace logic.

That's it for the grid definition factory. We should have what we need for the structure. Now, we need to create a data factory to provide data to display to our grid.

Creating the Grid data factory

In order to create a grid data factory, we will use the `DoctrineGridDataFactory` class. Its constructor requires a child class of the `AbstractDoctrineQueryBuilder` class. Let's do it by creating a `/modules/whcallback/src/Grid/Query/WHCallbackRequestQueryBuilder.php` file containing the `WHCallbackRequestQueryBuilder` class.

We can create the class with this code:

```php
<?php
namespace WebHelpers\WHCallback\Grid\Query;
//use... See the list of use instructions in the GitHub

final class WHCallbackRequestQueryBuilder extends
AbstractDoctrineQueryBuilder
{
  private $searchCriteriaApplicator;
  private $filterApplicator;

  public function __construct(Connection $connection,
    $dbPrefix, DoctrineSearchCriteriaApplicatorInterface
    $searchCriteriaApplicator,
    DoctrineFilterApplicatorInterface $filterApplicator)
  {
    parent::__construct($connection, $dbPrefix);
    $this->searchCriteriaApplicator =
      $searchCriteriaApplicator;
```

```php
    $this->filterApplicator = $filterApplicator;
  }
  public function
    getSearchQueryBuilder(SearchCriteriaInterface
    $searchCriteria)
  {
    $qb = $this->getBaseQuery($searchCriteria->
      getFilters());
    $this->searchCriteriaApplicator
    ->applyPagination($searchCriteria, $qb)
    ->applySorting($searchCriteria, $qb);
    return $qb;
  }

  public function getCountQueryBuilder
    (SearchCriteriaInterface $searchCriteria)
  {
    $qb = $this->getBaseQuery($searchCriteria->
      getFilters());
    $qb->select('COUNT(*)');
    return $qb;
  }

    private function getBaseQuery(array $filterValues)
  {
  }
}
```

The only thing required to comply with the `DoctrineQueryBuilderInterface` interface is to implement the `getSearchQueryBuilder()` and `getCountQueryBuilder()` methods. `getSearchQueryBuilder()` is responsible for returning a query builder with `SELECT` containing the fields listed in the data columns of the grid definition. In the same way, `getCountQueryBuilder()` is responsible for returning the query builder with the number of rows returned to the grid corresponding to the filters applied. To make it easier to understand and factorize everything, we will create a common `getBaseQuery()` method to generate the common query.

The query builder creation corresponding to our grid is defined as follows in the `getBaseQuery()` definition:

```php
private function getBaseQuery(array $filterValues)
{
  $query = $this->connection
    ->createQueryBuilder()
    ->select('*')
    ->from($this->dbPrefix.'whcallback_request', 'whcbr');
```

```
    foreach ($filterValues as $filterName => $filter) {
      if($filterName == 'id_request'){
        $query->andWhere('whcbr.`'.$filterName.'` = :'
          .$filterName);
        $query->setParameter($filterName, $filter);
      }else{
        $query->andWhere('whcbr.`'.$filterName.'` LIKE :'
          .$filterName);
        $query->setParameter($filterName, "%".$filter."%");
      }
    }
    return $query;
}
```

We won't cover the use of the **Doctrine query builder** here as it is beyond the scope of this topic. Feel free to use this link to find all the necessary documentation: `https://www.doctrine-project.org/projects/doctrine-orm/en/2.13/reference/query-builder.html`.

As our query builder class is done, let's create its service for the admin service container to make it available to the Grid factory. To do so, please go to the `/modules/whcallback/config/admin/services.yml` file and add it to the service definition:

```
webhelpers.whcallback.grid.query.whcallbackrequest_query_builder:
    class: 'WebHelpers\WHCallback\Grid\Query\
WHCallbackRequestQueryBuilder'
    parent: 'prestashop.core.grid.abstract_query_builder'
    public: true
    arguments:
      - '@prestashop.core.query.doctrine_search_criteria_applicator'
      - '@prestashop.core.grid.query.filter.doctrine_filter_applicator'
```

This service definition creates the query builder service from our class. Then, we can use its alias name to inject it into the data factory service definition, as follows:

```
webhelpers.whcallback.grid.data.factory.whcallbackrequest_data_
factory:
    class:
'PrestaShop\PrestaShop\Core\Grid\Data\Factory\DoctrineGridDataFactory'
    arguments:
      - '@webhelpers.whcallback.grid.query.whcallbackrequest_query_
builder'
      - '@prestashop.core.hook.dispatcher'
      - '@prestashop.core.grid.query.doctrine_query_parser'
      - 'whcallbackrequest'
    public: true
```

Now we have what we need to create our Grid factory!

Creating the Grid factory service and using it in the controller

Indeed, we have enough elements, with the definition and the data factories, to inject into a new service using the Grid factory this way in the services definition in the `/modules/whcallback/config/admin/services.yml` file. Please create the new service definition as follows:

```
webhelpers.whcallback.grid.whcallbackrequest_grid_factory:
  class: 'PrestaShop\PrestaShop\Core\Grid\GridFactory'
  arguments:
    - '@webhelpers.whcallback.grid.definition.factory.
      whcallbackrequest_grid_definition_factory'
    - '@webhelpers.whcallback.grid.data.factory
      .whcallbackrequest_data_factory'
    - '@prestashop.core.grid.filter.form_factory'
    - '@prestashop.core.hook.dispatcher'
```

As you can see, we use our newly created services in the `GridFactory` one.

Let's now go back to `AdminWHCallbackRequestController` and add the grid to the `listAction()` method:

```
public function listAction(WHCallbackRequestFilter $filters)
{
  $callbackRequestGridFactory = $this->get('webhelpers.whcallback.
  grid.whcallbackrequest_grid_factory');
  $callbackRequestGrid = $callbackRequestGridFactory
  ->getGrid($filters);

  return $this->render('@Modules/whcallback/views/templates/admin/
  list.html.twig', [
    'callbackRequestGrid' => $this->presentGrid($callbackRequestGrid)
    ]);
}
```

First, we instantiate `GridFactory` and then retrieve the generated grid with the help of its `getGrid()` method.

This method can take a filter argument, an instance of a child of the `Filters` class. It will generate a grid with some options for default pagination. To have our own parameters, we will create the `/modules/whcallback/src/Filter/WHCallbackRequestFilter.php` file containing the following code:

```
<?php
namespace WebHelpers\WHCallback\Filter;
use PrestaShop\PrestaShop\Core\Search\Filters;
use WebHelpers\WHCallback\Grid\Definition\Factory\
WHCallbackRequestDefinitionFactory;
```

```
final class WHCallbackRequestFilter extends Filters
{
    protected $filterId =
      WHCallbackRequestDefinitionFactory::GRID_ID;

    public static function getDefaults()
    {
        return [
            'limit' => 10,
            'offset' => 0,
            'orderBy' => 'id_request',
            'sortOrder' => 'desc',
            'filters' => [],
        ];
    }
}
```

To be brief, the getDefault() method has to be defined and must return the array containing the pagination options. You should easily be able to interpret the returned array.

Finally, getting back to our listAction() method, we assign to the Twig template via the array given in the second argument of the render() method. Let's see how this template is created.

Creating the Twig template to display the generated grid

As chosen in the listAction() method, the template responsible for displaying the generated grid has to be created. Let's add the /modules/whcallback/views/templates/admin/list.html.twig file with this content:

```
{% extends '@PrestaShop/Admin/layout.html.twig' %}
{% trans_default_domain "Admin.Design.Feature" %}

{% block content %}
  <div class="row">
    <div class="col-sm-12">
    {% include '@PrestaShop/Admin/Common/Grid
      /grid_panel.html.twig' with {'grid':
      callbackRequestGrid} %}
    </div>
  </div>
{% endblock %}

{% block javascripts %}
  {{ parent() }}
  <script src="{{ asset('../modules/whcallback
    /views/public/WHCallbackRequest.bundle.js')
```

```
    }}"></script>
  <script src="{{ asset('themes/default/js
    /bundle/pagination.js') }}"></script>
{% endblock %}
```

The grid is displayed by using `{% include '@PrestaShop/Admin/Common/Grid/grid_panel.html.twig' with {'grid': callbackRequestGrid} %}`. It uses an existing template provided by PrestaShop; we just have to provide the generated grid in the grid value. For us, it is named `callbackRequestGrid`, as assigned in the controller.

In the `javascripts` block, we import two more scripts, one to handle the pagination and another one that we must generate. In fact, the admin common JavaScript files can't handle pagination and a grid search reset. Let's generate ours.

Generating the JavaScript to handle the grid search field and reset

As we will cover this topic in *Chapter 16, Assets Compiling with WebPack*, we won't explain the bundling process of the `/modules/whcallback/views/public/WHCallbackRequest.bundle.js` file. Just remember that you have to create the `/modules/whcallback/views/js/WHCallbackRequest/index.js` Node.js source file, containing just this code:

```
import Grid from '@components/grid/grid';
import FiltersResetExtension from '@components/grid/extension/filters-
reset-extension';
import SortingExtension from '@components/grid/extension/sorting-
extension';

const $ = window.$;

$(() => {
  const callbackGrid = new Grid('whcallbackrequest');

  callbackGrid.addExtension(new FiltersResetExtension());
  callbackGrid.addExtension(new SortingExtension());
});
```

This code imports the `Grid`, `Sorting`, and `FiltersReset` extensions from the BO JavaScript libraries and uses them in our grid defined with the `whcallbackrequest` ID.

The webpack bundler can be used by Node.js with the help of npm to generate the `/modules/whcallback/views/public/WHCallbackRequest.bundle.js` from the `index.js` created file. The recipe provided to webpack is located in the `/modules/whcallback/views/webpack.config.js` file.

To run a compilation, you have to execute `npm install` and `npm run build` in your command-line tool from the `/modules/whcallback/views/` folder. The `webpack.config.js` syntax will be explained in the dedicated chapter.

We now have a nice grid. Let's handle the search requests if a search is carried out in any of the grid columns.

Handling the grid search requests

To handle the filter searches in the generated grid, we need to add the admin_whcallbackrequest_ search route to the /modules/whcallback/config/routes.yml routing configuration file:

```
admin_whcallbackrequest_search:
  path: whcallback/list
  methods: [POST]
  defaults:
    _controller: 'WebHelpers\WHCallback\Controller
    \AdminWHCallbackRequestController::searchAction'
```

Then, we need to create the searchAction() method in the admin controller to handle the search requests. The method to add to AdminWHCallbackRequestController is the following:

```
public function searchAction(Request $request)
{
    $responseBuilder = $this->get('prestashop.bundle.grid
    .response_builder');
    return $responseBuilder->buildSearchResponse(
    $this->get('webhelpers.whcallback.grid.definition.factory
    .whcallbackrequest_grid_definition_factory'),
    $request,
    WHCallbackRequestDefinitionFactory::GRID_ID,
    'admin_whcallbackrequest_list'
    );
}
```

It uses the buildSearchResponse() method of the grid response builder service to generate a grid based on the search requests.

This is enough to generate a grid containing the corresponding results. The only thing we're missing now is how to handle deleting a row from our grid. We'll look at that now.

Handling a callback request delete action from the grid

As we defined it in the grid definition, we need to create a Symfony route to handle the deletion request. Let's add this admin_whcallbackrequest_delete route definition to the /modules/whcallback/config/routes.yml file:

```
admin_whcallbackrequest_delete:
  path: whcallback/delete/{idRequest}
  methods: [GET, POST]
```

```
defaults:
  _controller: 'WebHelpers\WHCallback\Controller\
    AdminWHCallbackRequestController::deleteAction'
```

This route calls the `deleteAction()` method from `AdminWHCallbackRequestController` with the provided argument named `idRequest` containing `id_request` of the row to delete in the database. We make it listen to both `GET` and `POST` HTTP calls.

Following the best practices of PrestaShop, it is recommended to use the **CQRS** design pattern and **Domain-Driven Design (DDD)** to code the database interactions. This enables us to modify the actions done in the database without having to update the controller. Even if it can be longer to code initially, it will save us a lot of time during maintenance tasks.

That's why we need to create a `Command` to delete our request row, instead of doing it directly inside the controller method, with the help of the entity manager. Let's first create the `Command` and its `CommandHandler` to enable the deletion from the command bus, then we will code `deleteAction()` in the admin controller.

Creating the deletion command

As we saw in *Chapter 4, The Back Office*, our delete `Command` represents the deletion task and the required elements to make it. We will create the corresponding `CommandHandler` to execute the deletion task.

Following DDD practices, we need to create the `/modules/whcallback/src/Domain/WHCallbackRequest/` folder, which will contain all the business objects linked to our `WHCallbackRequest` entity.

The `DeleteWHCallbackRequestCommand` class will be our deletion command and we will store it in the `/modules/whcallback/src/Domain/WHCallbackRequest/Command/DeleteWHCallbackRequestCommand.php` file. Let's define it by following this simple code:

```php
<?php
namespace WebHelpers\WHCallback\Domain\WHCallbackRequest\Command;

class DeleteWHCallbackRequestCommand
{
    private $idRequest;
    public function __construct(int $idRequest)
    {
        $this->idRequest = $idRequest;
    }
    public function getIdRequest()
    {
```

```
        return $this->idRequest;
    }
}
```

This Command requires the $idRequest integer representing the id_request of the callback request row to delete in the database. We create the corresponding getter to make it available to CommandHandler.

Creating the deletion CommandHandler

The corresponding DeleteWHCallbackRequestHandler class stored in the /modules/whcallback/src/Domain/WHCallbackRequest/CommandHandler/DeleteWHCallbackRequestHandler.php file will implement the handle() responsible for doing the deletion.

We can use the following code for the DeleteWHCallbackRequestHandler definition:

```php
<?php
namespace WebHelpers\WHCallback\Domain\WHCallbackRequest\
CommandHandler;
//use… see all the use instructions in the GitHub
// repository
class DeleteWHCallbackRequestHandler
{
    private $entityManager;
    private $whCallbackRepository;

    public function __construct(EntityManagerInterface
      $entityManager, $whCallbackRepository)
    {
        $this->entityManager = $entityManager;
        $this->whCallbackRepository =
          $whCallbackRepository;
    }

    public function handle(DeleteWHCallbackRequestCommand
      $deleteWHCallbackRequestCommand)
    {
        try{
            $callbackRequest = $this->whCallbackRepository
              ->findOneById($deleteWHCallbackRequestCommand
              ->getIdRequest());
            $this->entityManager->remove($callbackRequest);
            $this->entityManager->flush();
        }catch(\Exception $e){
            throw new CannotDeleteRequestException(
                sprintf('Failed to delete the request with
```

```
              id "%s".', $deleteWHCallbackRequestCommand
              ->getIdRequest())
        );
    }
  }
}
```

As this `CommandHandler` needs the Doctrine entity manager to remove a row and the `WHCallbackRequest` entity repository to retrieve a record, we initiate that in the constructor, then we code the deletion inside the `handle()` method, which takes the previously created `DeleteWHCallbackRequestCommand` as an argument to get the `id_request`.

You can also see that we throw a `CannotDeleteRequestException` child class of the `DomainException` class, which is provided by PrestaShop and is available in the GitHub repository in the `/modules/whcallback/src/Domain/WHCallbackRequest/Exception/CannotDeleteRequestException.php` file.

To make this `CommandHandler` available in the Symfony service container from the controller, we need to create the service definition in the `/modules/whcallback/config/admin/services.yml` file. Also, as this command needs `WHCallBackRequestRepository` as an injected service, let's add the repository service definition too:

```
webhelpers.whcallback.repository.whcallbackrequest_repository:
  class: WebHelpers\WHCallback\Repository\WHCallbackRequestRepository
  factory: ['@doctrine.orm.default_entity_manager', getRepository]
  arguments:
    - WebHelpers\WHCallback\Entity\WHCallbackRequest

webhelpers.whcallback.domain.whcallbackrequest.command_handler.delete_
request:
  class: 'WebHelpers\WHCallback\Domain\WHCallbackRequest\
CommandHandler\DeleteWHCallbackRequestHandler'
  arguments:
    - '@doctrine.orm.default_entity_manager'
    - '@webhelpers.whcallback.repository.whcallbackrequest_repository'
  tags:
    - { name: tactician.handler, command: WebHelpers\WHCallback\
Domain\WHCallbackRequest\Command\DeleteWHCallbackRequestCommand }
```

Nothing very special here; you just have to make sure that the `Command` namespace corresponding to your handler is the right one.

We can now use this `Command` to code our `deleteAction()` method in the admin controller.

Creating the deleteAction() method

We can now implement our `deleteAction($idRequest)` method in `AdminWHCallback-RequestController` like this:

```
public function deleteAction(int $idRequest)
{
    $this->commandBus->handle(new
      DeleteWHCallbackRequestCommand($idRequest));
    return $this->redirectToRoute('admin_whcallbackrequest_list');
}
```

This function uses `CommandBus` to handle `DeleteWHCallbackRequestCommand`. Then, it redirects to the request list. It is very simple. To make our example simple, we won't add any feedback messages at the moment.

As our modern BO admin controller is done now, we can leave it like this. We now need to make it accessible from the BO menu to make it easier for customer services to get the request list.

Adding the BO controller to the BO menu

We can add simply an item to the BO menu by adding the `$tabs` class public array variable to our main module class by following a pattern. In our example, we can add the `$tabs` variable to the `/modules/whcallback/whcallback.php` file, inside the class definition, like this:

```
public $tabs = [
        [
            'name' => [
                'en' => 'Callback Requests',
                'fr' => 'Demandes de rappel'
            ],
            'class_name' => 'AdminWHCallbackRequest',
            'route_name' => 'admin_whcallbackrequest_list',
            'parent_class_name' => 'AdminParentCustomer',
            'wording' => 'Callback Requests',
              // Ignored in PS < 1.7.8
            'wording_domain' => 'Modules.WHCallback.Admin',
              // Ignored in PS < 1.7.8
        ]
    ];
```

This `$tab` variable is an array of associative arrays. Each associative array represents a menu tab to create. Let's explain each key of these associative arrays:

- The `name` value is the localized array containing the displayed name of the menu item that will appear in the BO menu.

- `class_name` is the name of the admin controller class without the `Controller` suffix.

- `route_name` is the name of the route to redirect to by clicking on the menu link.

- `parent_class_name` is the class name of the parent item in the menu. For us, it is the customer item. You can quickly get all the possible parent class names at this URL: `https://devdocs.prestashop-project.org/8/modules/concepts/controllers/admin-controllers/tabs/#which-parent-to-choose`.

- `wording` is the translation key to localize the item label.

- `wording_domain` is the translation domain.

The tab will be added during the module installation process automatically. We will now have a callback request link inside the customer BO submenu. The only remaining feature we're missing now is the configuration page to set the `WHCALLBACK_HOURS` configuration variable.

Creating a configuration page for our module and adding a Symfony form

If you want your module line on the **Improve | Modules | Module manager** BO page to contain a **Configure** button in the drop-down list on the right-hand side of the line, you must add the `getContent()` method to your main module class. This method should return the content of the configuration page.

If you go back to *Figure 9.2* in the first section of this chapter, you will see what we want. First, we want to create a Symfony form that allows the user to set the maximum number of hours before being called back by customer services. As we are not providing a full lesson on how to create a form with Symfony, just remember that PrestaShop provides a **Form Builder** service. It requires two arguments to work and generate your Symfony form: a **data provider**, which will retrieve and provide all the data to fill the inputs, and a **form type**, to define the form structure with the list of inputs.

First, let's focus on the form type to define the structure of our form.

Defining our form type

Our form is very simple. It will be composed of only one text field containing an integer.

All the form-related classes will have to be stored in the `src/Form/` folder in your module folder. Let's create our form type definition by creating the `/modules/whcallback/src/Form/Type/SettingType.php` file. Let's define the `SettingType` class as follows:

```php
<?php
namespace WebHelpers\WHCallback\Form\Type;
//use... to get the use instructions refer to the GitHub
//repo.
class SettingType extends AbstractType
{
    public function buildForm(FormBuilderInterface
      $builder, array $options): void
    {
        $builder
            ->add('hours', TextType::class)
            ->add('save', SubmitType::class)
        ;
    }
}
```

If you already know how to create a form type with Symfony, you should recognize that the `buildForm()` method is where we define our form structure by applying updates to our Form Builder object with the help of the `add($name, $inputType)` method.

In our case, we add a `TextType` item and a `SubmitType` button.

If you need more information about Symfony forms, you will find what you need here: `https://symfony.com/doc/4.4/forms.html`.

Now, we just need a form data provider to be able to generate our form with our PrestaShop Form Builder.

Defining our form data provider

Let's create our data provider for our setting form in a new `/modules/whcallback/src/Form/Setting/DataProvider/SettingFormDataProvider.php` file. All the data related to our setting form will be stored in `/modules/whcallback/src/Form/Setting/`, which will make it easy to understand.

This data provider will use a **query bus** following the **CQRS pattern** to retrieve the data to display. We know how to use the **command bus**. The **query bus** works in exactly the same way, but it returns data through **Data Transfer Objects** (**DTOs**) to make the results easy to use and transfer between classes.

Our SettingFormDataProvider class should look like this:

```php
<?php
namespace WebHelpers\WHCallback\Form\Setting\DataProvider;
//use… please find the use instructions in the GitHub repo.
final class SettingFormDataProvider implements
FormDataProviderInterface
{
    private $queryBus;
    private $setting;

    public function __construct(CommandBusInterface
      $queryBus)
    {
        $this->queryBus = $queryBus;
        $this->setting = $this->queryBus->handle(new
          GetSettingForEditing());
    }

    public function getData($id=0)
    {
        return [
            'hours' => $this->setting->getHours(),
        ];
    }

    public function getDefaultData()
    {
        return [
            'hours' => $this->setting->getHours(),
        ];
    }
}
```

This class is simple. It implements FormDataProviderInterface, which consists of defining getData($id) and getDefaultData(), returning an array with one key per form input name. In the edition mode, the getData($id) method will be called; if not, it will call the getDefaultData() method instead.

We created a $hours variable to store our data to provide to the hours form input. We hydrate it with the help of our GetSettingForEditing query, which is executed in the constructor via the query bus.

Exactly like the deletion Command we created before, you will find the GetSettingForEditing query defined in the /modules/whcallback/src/Domain/Setting/Query/GetSettingForEditing.php file and GetSettingForEditingHandler defined in the /modules/whcallback/src/Domain/Setting/QueryHandler/GetSettingForEditingHandler.php file responsible for retrieving the data and packaging it into the Setting DTO defined in the /modules/whcallback/src/Domain/Setting/DTO/Setting.php file.

> **Exercise**
>
> As an exercise, try to guess their content and find their real content in the GitHub repository of this book.

The GetSettingForEditing query needs to be added to the Symfony service container to be used easily. It is defined by adding the following code to the /modules/whcallback/config/admin/services.yml file:

```
webhelpers.whcallback.domain.setting.query_handler.get_setting_for_
editing_handler:
  class: 'WebHelpers\WHCallback\Domain\Setting\QueryHandler\
  GetSettingForEditingHandler'
  arguments:
    - '@prestashop.adapter.legacy.configuration'
    - '%default_conf_key%'
  tags:
    - { name: tactician.handler, command: WebHelpers\WHCallback\
      Domain\Setting\Query\GetSettingForEditing }
```

In the service arguments, the first one is the Configuration class, which is used to easily retrieve the configuration variable. The second argument is the configuration variable key name to store the max number of hours before a callback. As we want this key name to be easily editable in the service definition, we also need to put this code at the beginning of the file:

```
parameters:
  default_conf_key: 'WHCALLBACK_HOURS'
```

It defines the default_conf_key variable for us to be able to use it in the service definition.

Generating the form and displaying it

As we now have our form type and our form data provider, we can define our Form Builder service in the same services.yml file with this code:

```
#FORM SERVICES
#--> DATA PROVIDER - Responsible for providing data
webhelpers.whcallback.form.identifiable_object.data_provider.setting_
```

```
form_data_provider:
  class: 'WebHelpers\WHCallback\Form\Setting\DataProvider\
  SettingFormDataProvider'
  arguments:
    - '@prestashop.core.query_bus'
#--> FORM BUILDER - Responsible for generating the form
webhelpers.whcallback.form.identifiable_object.builder.setting_form_
builder:
  class: 'PrestaShop\PrestaShop\Core\Form\Setting\Builder\FormBuilder'
  factory: 'prestashop.core.form.builder.form_builder_factory:create'
  arguments:
    - 'WebHelpers\WHCallback\Form\Type\SettingType'
    - '@webhelpers.whcallback.form.identifiable_object.data_provider
      .setting_form_data_provider'
```

First, we defined our data provider service, then we used it in our form builder arguments.

We can now display our form and create our module configuration page by adding the getContent() method to our main WHCallback module class:

```
public function getContent()
{
  $settingFormBuilder = $this->get('webhelpers.whcallback.form.
  identifiable_object.builder.setting_form_builder');
  $settingForm = $settingFormBuilder->getForm();

  //ToDo: Handling the form submission and update the hours
  //configuration variable

  $link = Context::getContext()->link;
  $symfonyUrl = $link->getAdminLink(null, true, array('route'
  => 'admin_whcallbackrequest_list'));
  return $this->get('twig')->render('@Modules/whcallback/views
  /templates/admin/configure.html.twig', [
    "settingForm"=>$settingForm->createView(),
    "linkGrid"=>$symfonyUrl,
  ]);
}
```

First, we instantiate our Form Builder service named webhelpers.whcallback.form. identifiable_object.builder.setting_form_builder, and we store the build Form object in a $settingForm variable.

We will assign the result of its createView() method to Twig, which will enable us to generate all the HTML for the form with {{ form(form) }}. We also assign the link to the request list grid to create a button redirecting to it.

Our Twig template responsible for generating the configuration view has to be created in the `/modules/whcallback/views/templates/admin/configure.html.twig` file containing this:

```
<div class="panel">
  <div class="panel-heading">{{ 'Number of hours'|trans({},
    'Modules.WHCallback.Admin') }} </div>
  {{ form(settingForm) }}
</div>

<div class="panel">
  <div class="panel-heading">{{ 'List of requests'
    |trans({}, 'Modules.WHCallback.Admin') }}</div>
  <a href="{{ linkGrid }}" class="btn btn-info">{
    { 'Click here to go to the list'|trans({},
    'Modules.WHCallback.Admin') }}</a>
</div>
```

We have two panels, one for the form display and the second one for the link to the request list. The last thing we need to complete our configuration page is the form submission process. For that, we will use the Symfony form handler.

Handling form submission with a form handler

The best tool to manage our form submission is to create a **form handler**, which will tell our module how to process the form submissions for creation or edition.

The form handler requires the creation of a form data handler. Please create the `/modules/whcallback/src/Form/Setting/DataHandler/SettingFormDataHandler.php` file and define the `SettingFormDataHandler` class as follows:

```php
<?php
namespace WebHelpers\WHCallback\Form\Setting\DataHandler;
//use… please find the use instructions in the GitHub repo.
final class SettingFormDataHandler implements FormDataHandlerInterface
{
    private $commandBus;

    public function __construct(CommandBusInterface $commandBus)
    {
        $this->commandBus = $commandBus;
    }
    public function create(array $data)
    {
        $this->update(0, $data);
    }
```

```
    public function update($id, array $data)
    {
        $editSettingCommand = new
          EditSettingCommand($data['hours']);
        $this->commandBus->handle($editSettingCommand);
    }
}
```

As required by `FormDataHandlerInterface`, we have to define `create($data)` for the creation mode of the form and `update($id, $data)` for the edition mode. For us, it will always be in edition mode, but as we don't really need to edit an entity, we can't really use the form edition mode. That's why we simulate it by providing `id=0` to the system.

We use the CQRS pattern with `EditSettingCommand`, which is created to handle updating our configuration variable. As we have already covered an example of the use and creation of a `Command`, please feel free to create one yourself as an exercise and see the solution by going to the GitHub repository for this book.

Now that we have our form data handler, we can add a new service to `/modules/whcallback/config/admin/services.yml` and use it to create a form handler service. Please add this code to the services list:

```
#--> FORM DATA HANDLER
webhelpers.whcallback.form.identifiable_object.data_handler.setting_
form_data_handler:
  class: 'WebHelpers\WHCallback\Form\Setting\DataHandler\
SettingFormDataHandler'
  arguments:
    - '@prestashop.core.command_bus'
#--> FORM HANDLER - Responsible for handling a form request
webhelpers.whcallback.form.identifiable_object.handler.setting_form_
handler:
  class: 'PrestaShop\PrestaShop\Core\Form\Setting\Handler\FormHandler'
  factory: 'prestashop.core.form.identifiable_object.handler.form_
handler_factory:create'
  arguments:
    - '@webhelpers.whcallback.form.identifiable_object.data_handler.
setting_form_data_handler'
```

Finally, use your brand-new form handler service in your configuration page by replacing the `//ToDo: Handling the form submission and update the hours configuration variable` comment in the `WHCallback` class with the following code:

```
$request = Request::createFromGlobals();
$settingForm->handleRequest($request);
$settingFormHandler = $this->get(
```

```
'webhelpers.whcallback.form.identifiable_object
.handler.setting_form_handler');
$result = $settingFormHandler->handle($settingForm);
```

First, we instantiate a `Request` object to get all the data sent by the form. By the way, don't forget to add the use `Symfony\Component\HttpFoundation\Request;` instruction to the use declarations to use this object. Then, we instantiate the form handler in the `$settingFormHandler` variable via `webhelpers.whcallback.form.identifiable_object.handler.setting_form_handler` and apply its handle method to the form. That's it for the configuration page.

Now, our module is finished. Feel free to install it from the Modules manager BO page and test it from the BO and the FO!

Summary

This chapter showed us how to create a front form and process its data from the hooks definition using modern Doctrine entities. We also saw how to send emails from the module class, and we created a complete Symfony controller presenting a grid. We mastered the creation of a simple grid, from the structure definition to the templating, as well as bundling JavaScript assets with a configured webpack. We also explored the creation commands and queries from the ground up, as well as examples of their use, by following the CQRS design pattern. We added a new tab to the BO menu and created a configuration page for our module by generating and handling a form with the Symfony Form component.

Even if this chapter was full of many new ideas, you were able to concretely visualize how things are articulated and organized. Feel free to apply this new knowledge to one of your personal projects!

In the next chapter, we will create a lighter module by extending the BO category form. We will learn how to add fields to an already existing form and how to process it.

10

Category Extension Module

With the customer callback module, we learned about many important features of module creation, from the Symfony-based BO controllers and using the CQRS design pattern to entity creation, grid component creation, and form creation/handling. This was sometimes tough, but it was necessary to see all the possibilities offered by Symfony in PrestaShop.

In this chapter, we will create a new module, adding two localized fields and a file upload input to the category creation and edition modes of the Symfony form by using hooks, after which we will display their saved content. We will reuse some knowledge from previous modules and will look at new features in more detail.

We will cover the following topics to achieve our goal:

- Presenting the most useful hooks to extend a form and handle it
- Defining our module design
- Creating the module's initial structure
- Creating the entities
- Extending the Category form in creation mode
- Improving the Category form in edition mode
- Handling the extended form submission
- Handling a Category deletion
- Displaying saved content on the FO Category page
- Testing our module

By the end of this chapter, we will know how to extend a migrated Symfony-based form and handle its submission without overriding any core class.

Technical requirements

You will need the following elements to create this category form extension module:

- Any PHP editor to code your module

- An (s)FTP client to browse your module files and folders (only if you work on a remote server; this is not necessary if you work on a local server)

- A web browser to install and test your module

- A working PrestaShop installation (v1.7.x minimum)

- A downloaded version of our module, which is available in this book's GitHub repository at `https://github.com/PacktPublishing/Practical-Module-Development-for-Prestashop-8/tree/main/Chapter%2010`

Before getting into the module creation process, please keep in mind that all the chapters of this book about module creation have been provided with the corresponding module folders in the GitHub repository. For efficiency reasons, even if we try to cover all the module aspects, we have to avoid too much repetition; refer to the previous chapters if needed at your discretion. The further you go into this book, the more new notions we will cover.

Presenting the most useful hooks to extend a form and handle it

Before we get into module design and creation, since finding the best hook for our needs can sometimes be tricky, let's perform reverse engineering on the form building and form handling aspects to identify the hooks we want to register our module to. We will then explore the Category `ObjectModel` class to find the right hook to clean our created content on Category deletion.

We will divide our hook exploration into three parts while following our targets:

- Extending the Category Symfony-based form on the BO Category controller by adding three fields to it

- Handling new input from the extended form for both creation and edition modes

- Cleaning our extended fields database stored content on Category deletions

Let's get into the first target and learn how to find the best hook for our Category form extension.

Extending the Category Symfony-based form on the BO Category controller

Let's explore the code of the Category BO controller, which is located in the `/src/PrestaShopBundle/Controller/Admin/Sell/Catalog/CategoryController.php` file. If you read the definition of the `createAction()` method, you will see that the form builder service is named `prestashop.core.form.identifiable_object.builder.category_form_builder`.

If you search the `/src/PrestaShopBundle/Resources/config/services/core/form/form_builder.yml` file while defining this service, you will find that it instantiates the `FormBuilder` object by using a form factory with the corresponding Category form definition and data provider. This is similar to how we created our form in the customer callback module!

So, let's get to the `FormBuilder` object definition located in the `/src/Core/Form/IdentifiableObject/Builder/FormBuilder.php` file and look at its `buildForm()` method. There, just after its creation in the factory, the form builder is stored in the `$formBuilder` variable. Then, the `'action' . $this->camelize($formBuilder->getName()) . 'FormBuilderModifier'` hooks are executed.

For us, the executed hook will be the `actionCategoryFormBuilderModifier` hook. The corresponding code snippet for these executions is this one:

```
$this->hookDispatcher->dispatchWithParameters('action' . $this->camelize($formBuilder->getName()) . 'FormBuilderModifier', [
        'form_builder' => $formBuilder,
        'data' => &$data,
        'options' => &$options,
        'id' => $id,
    ]);
```

This will enable us to use the `form_builder` parameter that's sent with the hook call in our module class. By using the `add()` method of `formBuilder`, we can do what we need.

That's it for the form definition extension. Now, we can try to find a hook to retrieve the data that's sent by our added inputs from our category form.

Handling new input from the extended form

In the customer callback request module from the previous chapter, we saw that after creating a form and handling its result, we needed to implement a form handler to get the submitted data and handle it. If we go back to the Symfony Category BO controller class in the `createAction()` or `editAction()` method for generating the creation or update forms and handling them, we will see that the form handler responsible for these form submissions is called `prestashop.core.form.identifiable_object.handler.category_form_handler`.

In the corresponding service definition located in the `/src/PrestaShopBundle/Resources/config/services/core/form/form_handler.yml` file, we can see that the FormHandler object was instantiated and located in the `/src/Core/Form/IdentifiableObject/Handler/FormHandler.php` file.

Usually, handling form submissions is done with the help of the `handle()` method of the `FormHandler` instance. By exploring it, we discover that it directly calls the `handleForm()` method. Depending on the creation or edition mode of the Category entity, it will call `handleFormCreate()` for the creation mode or `handleFormUpdate()` for the edition. Here, we find one hook execution per mode. In the creation mode, the `'actionAfterCreate'` . `Container::camelize($form->getName())` . `'FormHandler'` hook executions will be the best for us. These are defined like this:

```
$this->hookDispatcher->dispatchWithParameters('actionAfterCreate' .
Container::camelize($form->getName()) . 'FormHandler', [
        'id' => $id,
        'form_data' => &$data,
    ]);
```

In our specific case, the executed hook will be `actionAfterCreateCategoryFormHandler` for the Category form.

In the same way, in the edition mode, the `'actionAfterUpdate'` . `Container::camelize($form->getName())` . `'FormHandler'` hook executions will enable us to perform our edition business from our module. The corresponding definition is this one:

```
$this->hookDispatcher->dispatchWithParameters('actionAfterUpdate' .
Container::camelize($form->getName()) . 'FormHandler', [
        'id' => $id,
        'form_data' => &$data,
    ]);
```

In our case, it will be the `actionAfterUpdateCategoryFormHandler` hook that will help us to update/create our data in the database from the module.

Finally, we need to cover the last possible scenario for our entity: deletion.

Cleaning our saved content on Category deletions

The first way to find a hook for a deletion operation would be to go back to the Category BO controller and read its `deleteAction()` method, which is called for any deletion action. As there are no hook calls there, we need to go to the deletion command handler of the `DeleteCategoryCommand` command. As it deals with non-migrated old Category ObjectModels, it is defined in the adapter part in the `/src/Adapter/Category/CommandHandler/DeleteCategoryHandler.php` file. The command handler instantiates the Category object defined in the `/classes/Category.php` file and calls the `delete()` method. Let's look at this method definition and see whether we can find a hook execution somewhere to help us.

Here is our solution – on deletion, the `actionCategoryDelete` hook is executed in this way:

```
Hook::exec('actionCategoryDelete', ['category' => $this, 'deleted_
children' => $deletedChildren]);
```

There, our corresponding data will be deleted whenever this hook is called. With that, we have finished our hook exploration, and so we have a complete definition of our module design. Let's go for it!

Defining our module design

As usual, we need to describe our target module to do the job efficiently.

We want to create a module by adding two localizable fields to the Category creation/edition form in the BO:

- The first field will be named `Short text field extension` and will be a simple localized text input

- The second field will be named `Long text field extension` and will be a localized textarea input

- We will add a non-localized file upload field to add a JPG or PNG image named `Image file extension`

The following screenshot shows the layout we aim to get at the end of our module creation for the Category form:

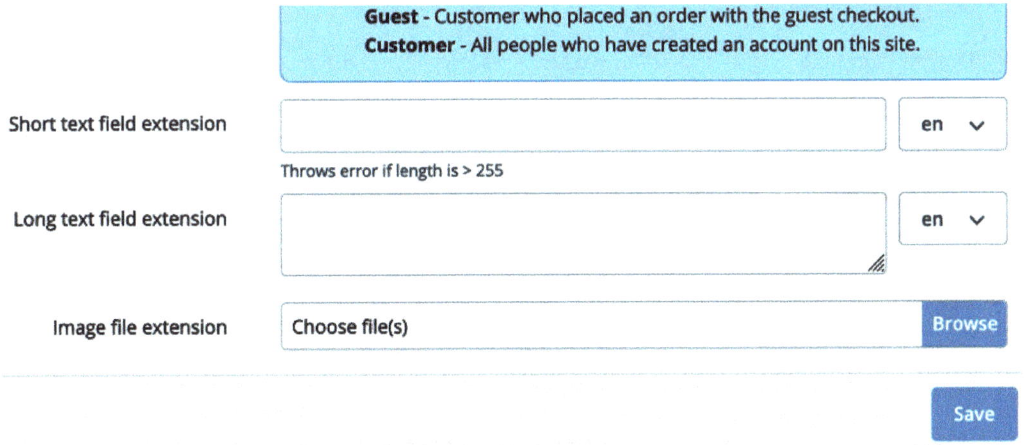

Figure 10.1 – A preview of the three fields to create

Once we have added our fields, we will simply display the corresponding content of those fields without any styles on the Category FO template, like this:

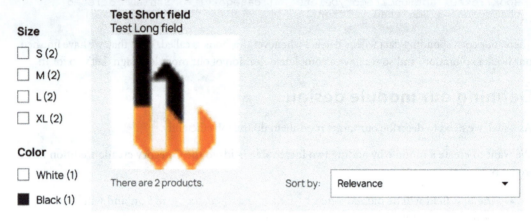

Figure 10.2 – A preview of the FO template

Now that we know our target, we will follow our usual checklist that's necessary for module creation:

- **Display name**: Category field extension
- **Technical name**: `whcategoryfields`
- **Tab**: `front_office_features`
- **need_instance value**: 0
- **Description text**: `This is a module adding fields to the categories.`
- **Uninstall confirmation text**: `Do you still you want to uninstall this module?`
- **Hooks to register**: `displayHeaderCategory` (to display the content on the FO), `actionCategoryFormBuilderModifier`, `actionAfterCreateCategoryFormHandler`, `actionAfterUpdateCategoryFormHandler`, and `actionCategoryDelete`
- **Configuration page needed**: No

We now have enough information to start creating our module efficiently.

Creating the module's initial structure

Since this is our fourth module, you should now know how to create a complete module structure by creating a /modules/whcategoryfields/ and its mandatory files called whcategoryfields.php, index.php, and logo.png.

We can continue by creating our /modules/whcategoryfields/views/ folder and a /modules/whcategoryfields/views/templates/ subfolder.

Initially, we can create the main module class in the whcategoryfields.php file, thereby focusing on the install() and uninstall() functions since the rest is standard:

```php
// … Beginning of the file in the GitHub repo…

class WHCategoryFields extends Module
{
  private $commandBus;
  public function __construct()
  {
    $this->name = 'whcategoryfields';
    //…Please find the rest in the GitHub repo
  }

  public function install()
  {
    if (parent::install() &&
      $this->createTable() &&
      $this->createLangTable() &&
      $this->registerHook('displayHeaderCategory') &&
      $this->registerHook(
        'actionCategoryFormBuilderModifier') &&
      $this->registerHook(
        'actionAfterCreateCategoryFormHandler') &&
      $this->registerHook(
        'actionAfterUpdateCategoryFormHandler') &&
      $this->registerHook('actionCategoryDelete'))
    {
      return true;
    }else{
      $this->_errors[] = $this->l('There was an error
        during the installation.');
      return false;
    }
  }
  public function uninstall()
  {
    $this->dropTables();
    return parent::uninstall() &&
      $this->unregisterHook('displayHeaderCategory') &&
      $this->unregisterHook(
        'actionCategoryFormBuilderModifier') &&
      $this->unregisterHook(
```

```
        'actionAfterCreateCategoryFormHandler') &&
    $this->unregisterHook(
        'actionAfterUpdateCategoryFormHandler') &&
    $this->unregisterHook('actionCategoryDelete');
  }
}
```

In the `install()` and `uninstall()` functions, we call the `createTable()`, `createLang-Table()`, and `dropTables()` functions. We need to create them.

As we want to extend our Category `ObjectModel` entity, we could try to extend it or override it. However, this is not recommended anymore because we don't want to change the database's core structure to avoid problems during possible PrestaShop updates. Therefore, we will create a new Doctrine entity linked to the core Category entity by using a **one-to-one** relationship.

Let's create the database tables for our new data in `createTable()` and `createLangTable()`, one for the non-localized fields and another for the localized fields linked to the `Lang` entity:

```
private function createTable()
{
  return Db::getInstance()->execute('
  CREATE TABLE IF NOT EXISTS `' . _DB_PREFIX_ .
  'whcategoryfields_extension` (
    `id_extension` int(6) NOT NULL AUTO_INCREMENT,
    `id_category` int(6) NOT NULL,
    `filename` varchar(255) NOT NULL,
    `extension_date_add` DATETIME NULL,
    `extension_date_update` DATETIME NULL,
    PRIMARY KEY (`id_extension`)
  ) ENGINE=' . _MYSQL_ENGINE_ . ' default CHARSET=utf8');
}

private function createLangTable()
{
  return Db::getInstance()->execute('
  CREATE TABLE IF NOT EXISTS `' . _DB_PREFIX_ .
  'whcategoryfields_extension_lang` (
    `id_extension` int(6) NOT NULL,
    `id_lang` int(6) NOT NULL,
    `short_text` varchar(255) NOT NULL,
    `long_text` text NOT NULL,
    PRIMARY KEY (`id_extension`, `id_lang`)
  ) ENGINE=' . _MYSQL_ENGINE_ . ' default CHARSET=utf8');
}
```

In the `prefix_whcategoryfields_extension` table, we will store the following information:

- The relationship with the Category entity
- The name of the uploaded file
- The add and update datetimes

In the `prefix_whcategoriyfields_extension_lang` table, we will store the following information:

- The relationship with the `Lang` entity
- The `short_text` field
- The `long_text` field

We also need to create the `dropTables()` function to drop the created tables to clean the data on uninstall. We can create it as follows:

```
private function dropTables()
{
  Db::getInstance()->execute('DROP TABLE IF EXISTS ' . _DB_PREFIX_ .
'whcategoryfields_extension');
  Db::getInstance()->execute('DROP TABLE IF EXISTS ' . _DB_PREFIX_ .
'whcategoryfields_extension_lang');
}
```

Nothing is unusual there! Now, we only need to create all the hook callback functions – that is, `hookDisplayHeaderCategory($params)`, `hookActionCategoryFormBuilder-Modifier($params)`, `hookActionAfterCreateCategoryFormHandler($params)`, `hookActionAfterUpdateCategoryFormHandler($params)`, and `hookActionCat-egoryDelete($params)`. Let's leave them empty for now. We will code them separately in the next few sections.

Before coding the form extension, let's create the corresponding **Doctrine** entities.

Creating the entities

As we want to store localized and non-localized fields in the database, we need to create two **Doctrine** entities. Before we get into the code, we need to create the `/modules/whcategoryfields/composer.json` file to manage how these classes are autoloaded from the module `src/` folder that we will create.

Please have a look at the corresponding file provided in this book's GitHub repository. You will notice that we just mapped the `WebHelpers\WHCategoryFields` namespace to the `src/` folder. Don't forget to execute the `composer dumpautoload` command from the `/modules/whcategoryfields/` folder.

> **Exercise**
>
> As you already know how to create a simple non-localized entity from the previous chapter, you can try and create a `WHCategoryFieldsExtension` class by defining the first entity representing `prefix_whcategoryfields_extension`, which contains the `id` integer primary key field, the `filename` string field, and the `extension_date_add` and `extension_date_update` datetime fields, along with their getters and setters. We will add features to it after.

As a correction, let's create the `/modules/whcategoryfields/src/Entity/WHCategoryFieldsExtension.php` file to create the entity:

```
/**
 * @ORM\Table(name="ps_whcategoryfields_extension")
 *
@ORM\Entity(repositoryClass="WebHelpers\WHCategoryFields\Repository\
WHCategoryFieldsExtensionRepository")
 * @ORM\HasLifecycleCallbacks
 */
class WHCategoryFieldsExtension
{
}
```

Now, let's add the attribute variables to it, as follows:

```
/**
 * @var int
 *
 * @ORM\Id
 * @ORM\Column(name="id_extension", type="integer")
 * @ORM\GeneratedValue(strategy="AUTO")
 */
private $id;

/**
 * @var int
 *
 * @ORM\Column(name="id_category", type="integer")
 */
private $idCategory;

/**
 * @var string
 *
 * @ORM\Column(name="filename", type="string", length=255)
 */
```

```
private $filename;

/**
 * @var datetime
 *
 * @ORM\Column(name="extension_date_add", type="datetime")
 */
private $extensionDateAdd;

/**
 * @var datetime
 *
 * @ORM\Column(name="extension_date_update", type="datetime")
 */
private $extensionDateUpdate;
```

Then, we can create the getters/setters for all those fields. Please check their definitions in this book's GitHub repository.

Please note that we can add an `updatedTimestamps()` method with the following annotation to trigger it on `persist()` or `update()` execution of this entity:

```
/**
 * @ORM\PrePersist
 * @ORM\PreUpdate
 */
public function updatedTimestamps(): void
{
    $this->setExtensionDateUpdate();
    if ($this->getExtensionDateAdd() == null) {
        $this->setExtensionDateAdd();
    }
}
```

That's it for the moment regarding this new entity object. We will come back to it to create the relationship with the corresponding localized table very soon!

Now, let's create the second entity, named `WHCategoryFieldsExtensionLang`, in the `/modules/whcategoryfields/src/Entity/WHCategoryFieldsExtensionLang.php` file. It will contain the localized fields from our inputs and can be initially created with the following code:

```
/**
 * @ORM\Table(name="ps_whcategoryfields_extension_lang")
 * @ORM\Entity()
 */
class WHCategoryFieldsExtensionLang
```

```
{
    /**
     * @var WHCategoryFieldsExtension
     * @ORM\Id
     * @ORM\ManyToOne(targetEntity="WebHelpers\WHCategoryFields\
Entity\WHCategoryFieldsExtension", inversedBy="extensionLangs")
     * @ORM\JoinColumn(name="id_extension", referencedColumnName="id_
extension", nullable=false)
     */
    private $extension;

    /**
     * @var Lang
     * @ORM\Id
     *
@ORM\ManyToOne(targetEntity="PrestaShopBundle\Entity\Lang")
     * @ORM\JoinColumn(name="id_lang", referencedColumnName="id_lang",
nullable=false, onDelete="CASCADE")
     */
    private $lang;

    /**
     * @var string
     *
     * @ORM\Column(name="short_text", type="string", length=255)
     */
    private $shortText;

    /**
     * @var string
     *
     * @ORM\Column(name="long_text", type="text")
     */
    private $longText;
}
```

As you can see, the $extension variable has specific annotations. Their meanings are very well explained in the online Doctrine documentation. To summarize, Doctrine will consider that there is a **many-to-one** relationship with our WHCategoryFieldsExtension entity, and even if this entity is represented by this variable there, the inverse will be the $extensionLang variable in the WHCategoryFieldsExtension entity. We will add it to the corresponding class shortly.

In the same way, we define the $lang variable, which represents the Lang object in a **many-to-one** relationship. If any lang is deleted from the prefix_lang table, Doctrine will delete all the rows representing this lang in our table in a cascading fashion.

As all the getters/setters of this `WHCategoryFieldsExtensionLang` class are easy to create and understand, we won't dive into this any further. You will find them in this book's GitHub repository if needed.

Let's get back to our `WHCategoryFieldsExtension` class definition and add the `$extensionLang` variable and some cool methods to benefit from its **one-to-many** relationship with `WHCategoryFieldsExtensionLang` by adding the following code to its definition:

```
/**
 * @ORM\OneToMany(targetEntity="WebHelpers\WHCategoryFields\Entity\
WHCategoryFieldsExtensionLang", cascade={"persist", "remove"},
mappedBy="extension")
 */
private $extensionLangs;
```

The following getters/setters and other functions will make our life easier in the next few steps of module creation:

```
public function getExtensionLangs(): ArrayCollection
{
  return $this->extensionLangs;
}


public function getExtensionLangByLangId(int $langId):
?WHCategoryFieldsExtensionLang
{
  foreach ($this->extensionLangs as $extensionLang) {
    if ($langId === $extensionLang->getLang()->getId()) {
      return $extensionLang;
    }
  }
  return null;
}


public function getShortTextLangs(): array
{
  $shortTextLangs = [];
  foreach($this->extensionLangs as $extensionLang)
  {
    $shortTextLangs[$extensionLang->getLang()
      ->getId()]=$extensionLang->getShortText();
  }
  return $shortTextLangs;
}


public function getLongTextLangs(): array
```

```
{
  $longTextLangs = [];
  foreach($this->extensionLangs as $extensionLang)
  {
    $longTextLangs[$extensionLang->getLang()
      ->getId()]=$extensionLang->getShortText();
  }
  return $longTextLangs;
}

public function addExtensionLang(WHCategoryFieldsExtensionLang
$extensionLang): self
{
  $extensionLang->setExtension($this);
  $this->extensionLangs->add($extensionLang);

  return $this;
}
```

Nothing is very difficult in those functions' definitions:

- `getExtensionLangByLangId(int $langId)` enables the `WHCategoryFieldsExtensionLang` item corresponding to the provided lang ID.

- We can add a new linked `WHCategoryFieldsExtensionLang` instance by using the `addExtensionLang($extensionLang)` function.

- We can get an associative array of all the `$shortText` values from the `WHCategoryFieldsExtensionLang` linked instances with the lang IDs as keys by using the `getShortTextLangs()` function. The same is possible for `$longText` with the `getLongTextLangs()` function.

We have to create `WHCategoryFieldsExtensionRepository` to be able to retrieve our content easily in the `/modules/whcategoryfields/src/Repository/WHCategoryFieldsExtensionRepository.php` file. We won't explain its creation here as it is an empty class that only extends the `EntityRepository` class.

Don't forget to create the `webhelpers.whcategoryfields.repository.whcategoryfieldsextension_repository` service in the `/modules/whcategoryfields/config/services.yml` file.

That's the first time we have implemented two entities linked by a **one-to-many** relationship. This relationship is very useful to manage the localized fields of a Doctrine entity. We will have the opportunity to use these entities in the next few sections. Now, let's get back to our module class and extend the Category form builder definition to add our fields.

Extending the Category form in creation mode

In the *Presenting the most useful hooks to extend a form and handle it* section, we saw that we can use the `actionCategoryFormBuilderModifier` hook to enable our module to add the three fields to our form. The corresponding `hookActionCategoryFormBuilderModifier($params)` function can initially be defined as follows:

```
public function hookActionCategoryFormBuilderModifier($params)
{
    $formBuilder = $params['form_builder'];
    $formBuilder->add('short_text', TranslatableType::class, [
        'type' => TextType::class,
        'label' => $this->trans('Short text field extension', [],
        'Modules.WHCategoryFields.Admin'),
        'help' => $this->trans('Throws error if length is > 255',
        [],'Modules.WHCategoryFields.Admin'),
        'required' => false,
        'options' => [
            'constraints' => [
                new Length([
                    'max' => 255,
                ]),
            ],
        ],
    ])
    ->add('long_text', TranslatableType::class, [
        'type' => TextareaType::class,
        'label' => $this->trans('Long text field extension', [],
        'Modules.WHCategoryFields.Admin'),
        'required' => false,
    ]);

    //ToDo - Manage edition mode

    $formBuilder->add('image_file_extension', FileType::class, [
        'label' => 'Image file extension',
        'required' => false,
        'constraints' => [
            new File([
                'maxSize' => '8024k',
                'mimeTypes' => [
                    'image/jpeg',
                    'image/png',
                ],
                'mimeTypesMessage' => $this->trans('Please choose only JPG of
                PNG files', [], 'Modules.WHCategoryFields.Admin'),
```

```
        ])
     ]
  ]);

  $formBuilder->setData($params['data']);
}
```

Let's explain how it works.

With `$formBuilder = $params['form_builder']`;, we retrieve the form builder object from the hook call.

Then, we apply the `add` method to the form builder to add fields after its already existing fields. Here, we add two localized fields named `short_text` and `long_text` by using the `TranslatableType::class` input type.

You can find the full specification for this form input type in the official PrestaShop developer documentation: `https://devdocs.prestashop-project.org/8/development/components/form/types-reference/translatable/`.

Let's focus on the type options provided for the `short_text` field:

- `type`: We want some input text, so we set its value to `TextType::class`.
- `label`: The simple string label is set to `'Short text field extension'` and localized in the BO language.
- `help`: The help legend displayed below the field is set to the `'Throws error if length is > 255'` localized text with the BO language.
- `required`: This is set to false as it is not required.
- `options`: The `constraints` key is provided the `Length` object constraint to set the maximum field length to 255 characters. If you want to know more about validation, please go to the Symfony documentation at `https://symfony.com/doc/4.4/validation.html`.

The `long_text` field is created the same way by using `TextareaType::class` as the type option value.

The `image_file_extension` field is using `FileType::class` directly as it isn't localized.

Finally, `$formBuilder->setData($params['data']);` will replace the data to insert into the fields with the content of the `$params['data']` array. It has no real utility in creation mode, but it does in edition mode!

Improving the Category form in edition mode

The same form is used in creation and edition mode, which is why we need to add the ability to pre-fill the newly created fields with the existing saved content to our hook, either for localized or non-localized content.

For the file upload field, it is better to have a picture preview of what's already been uploaded and available. We can also provide a delete button near the preview of the uploaded file to be able to delete the existing file.

The final layout should look like this:

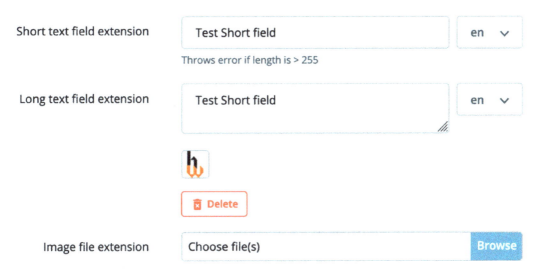

Figure 10.3 – The extended fields in edition mode

Let's manage this edition mode by replacing the `//ToDo - Manage edition mode` comment with the following code:

```
if(isset($params['id']) && $params['id']>0){
  $extensionRepository = $this->get('webhelpers.whcategoryfields.
repository.whcategoryfieldsextension_repository');
  $extension = $extensionRepository->findOneBy(['idCategory'=>$params
['id']]);

  if(!is_null($extension)){
    $params['data']['short_text'] = $extension->getShortTextLangs();
    $params['data']['long_text'] = $extension->getLongTextLangs();

    if(isset($extension) && $extension->getFileName()!=""){
      $link = New Link();
```

```
            $deletionLink = $link->getAdminLink(
            'AdminWHCategoryFields', true, ['route'=>
            'admin_whcategoryfields_file_delete', 'idCategory'
            =>$extension->getIdCategory()], []);
            $formBuilder->add('image_file_icon', CustomContentType::class, [
                'required' => false,
                'template' => '@Modules/whcategoryfields/views/templates
                /admin/upload_image.html.twig',
                'data' => [
                    'pathDeletion' => $deletionLink,
                    'filenameUrl' => $link->getBaseLink()."/modules/"
                    .$this->name."/views/img/uploads/"
                    .$extension->getFileName(),
                ],
            ]);
        }
    }
}
```

In this code snippet, the `if (isset($params['id']) && $params['id']>0)` condition checks whether we are in edition mode.

If `true`, we retrieve the repository service in the `$extensionRepository` variable. We look for the instances of the `WHCategoryFieldsExtension` class with the same category as the one we are editing. If the result is not null, then we pre-fill the two localized fields with their values via the `$params['data']['short_text'] = $extension->getShortTextLangs();` and `$params['data']['long_text'] = $extension->getLongTextLangs();` instructions, storing the data in the `$params['data']` array that will populate the form fields.

If our `WHCategoryFieldsExtension` retrieved object contains a non-empty `filename`, which means that a file has already been uploaded with this name (we will decide to store the uploaded files in the `/modules/whcategoryfields/views/img/uploads/` folder), we must add a `CustomContentType` form field before the upload field. This will enable us, via the `template` and `data` option keys of the field addition, to create a custom file preview and add a delete button to it in a Twig template. To do so, we need to create a custom template in the `/modules/whcategoryfields/views/templates/admin/upload_image.html.twig` file. Its content is as follows. The variables assigned to the Twig template are only the target path for the deletion link (`pathDeletion`) and the path where the uploaded file is stored (`filenameUrl`):

```
<div class="form-group row mt-3">
  <div class="col-sm">
    <figure class="figure">
      <img src="{{ filenameUrl }}" class="figure-img img-fluid
      img-thumbnail">
      <figcaption class="figure-caption">
```

```
                <button class="btn btn-outline-danger btn-sm
                 js-form-submit-btn" data-form-submit-url
                ="{{ pathDeletion }}"data-form-csrf-token
                ="{{ csrf_token('delete-icon-image') }}"type="button">
                  <i class="material-icons">delete_forever</i>
                  {{ 'Delete'|trans({}, 'Admin.Actions') }}
                </button>
            </figcaption>
          </figure>
      </div>
  </div>
```

Please note that we need to create a Symfony-based BO controller called `AdminWHCategory-FieldsController` to handle the uploaded file's deletion because we use `$deletionLink = $link->getAdminLink('AdminWHCategoryFields', true, ['route'=>'ad-min_whcategoryfields_file_delete', 'idCategory'=>$extension->get-IdCategory()], [])`; as the link URL. This controller will be stored in the `/modules/whcategoryfields/src/Controller/AdminWHCategoryFieldsController.php` file. As you already know how to create a BO controller, we will not provide many details about it – feel free to read the full file in this book's GitHub repository.

We just need to create a new route in the `/modules/whcategoryfields/config/routes.yml` file named `admin_whcategoryfields_file_delete` that calls a `deleteFileAction()` function. This `deleteFileAction()` function can call a Command named `DeleteExtensionFileCommand` to delete the uploaded file like so:

```
public function deleteFileAction(Request $request, $idCategory)
{
  $this->commandBus->handle(new
  DeleteExtensionFileCommand($idCategory));
  return $this->redirectToRoute('admin_categories_edit', [
                'categoryId' => $idCategory,
  ]);
}
```

We won't present `DeleteExtensionFileCommand` here; it aims to set the `filename` field of our current Doctrine entity to an empty string, and it deletes the uploaded file from the `/modules/whcategoryfields/views/img/uploads/` folder via the `unlink` PHP function. The full command and command handler files are available in the `/modules/whcategoryfields/src/Domain/WHCategoryFieldsExtension/Command/` and `/modules/whcategoryfields/src/Domain/WHCategoryFieldsExtension/CommandHandler/` folders in this book's GitHub repository. Don't forget to create the corresponding services for the commands in the `services.yml` file!

With that, we now have an extended form for our Category entities. Like all the forms, only half of the job is done, because, without handling, a form itself does nothing! In the following section, we will learn how to do it.

Handling the extended form submission

In the *Presenting the most useful hooks to extend a form and handle it* section, we decided to handle the form submission via two hooks that are called depending on the mode used (creation or edition) for the form: `actionAfterCreateCategoryFormHandler` and `actionAfterUpdateCategoryFormHandler`.

In our module class, we can create the two following functions to implement the hook calls:

```
public function hookActionAfterCreateCategoryFormHandler($params)
{
   $this->updateWHFieldsExtension($params);
}

public function hookActionAfterUpdateCategoryFormHandler($params)
{
   $this->updateWHFieldsExtension($params);
}
```

We will use the same behavior by calling a common `updateWHFieldsExtension($params)` function for both because their `$params` arrays have the same structure with two elements:

- `id` of the Category sent
- The `form_data` array containing the data sent by the form

Let's create this `updateWHFieldsExtension($params)` function:

```
private function updateWHFieldsExtension(array $params)
{
   $this->commandBus = $this->get('prestashop.core.command_bus');
   $entityManager = $this->get('doctrine.orm.entity_manager');
   $extensionRepository = $this->get('webhelpers.whcategoryfields
   .repository.whcategoryfieldsextension_repository');

   $categoryId = $params['id'];
   $categoryFormData = $params['form_data'];
   $shortText = $categoryFormData['short_text'];
   $longText = $categoryFormData['long_text'];

   $extension = $extensionRepository->findOneBy(['idCategory'=>(int)
   $categoryId]);
```

```php
    $fileToUpload = $categoryFormData['image_file_extension'];
    $filename = "";
    if(!is_null($fileToUpload)){
      $originalFilename = pathinfo($fileToUpload
      ->getClientOriginalName(), PATHINFO_FILENAME);
      $filename = uniqid().'.'.$fileToUpload->guessExtension();
      try {
        $fileToUpload->move(
          _PS_MODULE_DIR_."whcategoryfields/views/img/
          uploads/",$filename);
      }catch (FileException $e) {
      }
      $this->commandBus->handle(new DeleteExtensionFileCommand(
      $categoryId));
    }else{
      $filename=$extension->getFilename();
    }
    if(is_null($extension)){
      $this->commandBus->handle(new AddExtensionCommand(
      $categoryId,$shortText,$longText,$filename));
    }else{
      $this->commandBus->handle(new EditExtensionCommand(
      $extension->getId(),$categoryId,$shortText,$longText,$filename));
    }
  }
}
```

Let's explain this code quickly:

1. `$this->commandBus = $this->get('prestashop.core.command_bus');` and `$entityManager = $this->get('doctrine.orm.entity_manager');` allow us to retrieve the command bus and the Doctrine entity manager by instantiating the corresponding services.

2. Then, we instantiate our entity repository by using `$extensionRepository = $this->get('webhelpers.whcategoryfields.repository.whcategoryfieldsextension_repository');` with the corresponding service.

   We retrieve the necessary data to be able to update or create our recording process into the database via doctrine with the following code.

   ```php
       $categoryId = $params['id'];
       $categoryFormData = $params['form_data'];
       $shortText = $categoryFormData['short_text'];
       $longText = $categoryFormData['long_text'];
   ```

3. We use our `$extensionRepository` repository instance to select the current category extension record if it exists with `$extension = $extensionRepository->findO neBy(['idCategory'=>(int)$categoryId])`; based on the current category ID.

4. In `$fileToUpload`, we store the value of `$categoryFormData['image_file_ extension']`; to retrieve the data of the file sent in the `'image_file_extension'` file upload field.

5. If the file upload field is not null, we manage the file upload just like any uploading process in PHP. Please note that we decided to rename our uploaded file with the `uniqid()` function to make sure that we won't have the same filenames in our destination upload folder. Then, we take care of deleting the existing uploaded file (if it exists) by using `DeleteExtensionFileCommand` with `$this->commandBus->handle(new DeleteExtensionFileCommand($categoryId))`;

    If the file upload field is not filled and null, we don't delete the existing uploaded file from previous submissions if it exists. We just make sure we store the existing filename in the `$filename` variable with `$filename=$extension->getFilename()`;.

6. Once the upload business has been completed, we can test whether we are in creation mode or edition mode for our category by testing `if (is_null($extension))`:

    -   If `true`, we are in creation mode and we use `$this->commandBus->handle(new AddExtensionCommand($categoryId,$shortText,$longText,$file- name))`; to invoke `AddExtensionCommand`. This command persists our fields.

    -   If `false`, we are in edition mode and we use `$this->commandBus->handle(new EditExtensionCommand($extension->getId(),$categoryId,$short- Text,$longText,$filename))`; to invoke `EditExtensionCommand`. This command updates our fields.

> **Exercise**
> Please try and create the `AddExtensionCommand` and `EditExtensionCommand` commands and their corresponding handlers. Don't forget to create the corresponding services in the `/modules/whcategoryfields/config/services.yml` file. Please look at the correction files in this book's GitHub repository.

Once the commands and command handlers have been created, our module can handle the form submission. Now, let's implement the deletion of our `WHCategoryFieldsExtension` entity rows on a Category deletion to clean the table.

Handling Category deletion

When a Category is deleted, we saw that the `actionCategoryDelete` hook was called. Let's implement its `hookActionCategoryDelete($params)` function in the main module class to handle our cleaning:

```
public function hookActionCategoryDelete($params)
{
  $this->commandBus = $this->get('prestashop.core.command_bus');
  $category = $params['category'];
  if(!is_null($category)){
    $this->commandBus->handle(new DeleteExtensionFileCommand(
    $category->id));
    $this->commandBus->handle(new DeleteExtensionCommand(
    $category->id));
  }
}
```

The previous code is short and easy to understand:

1. We instantiate the command bus service.
2. We retrieve the deleted `Category` instance object to get its `id`.
3. Then, if `$category` is not null, we call `DeleteExtensionFileCommand` to clean the uploaded file and `DeleteExtensionCommand` to clean any row linked to the deleted `$category->id`.

You can go to this book's GitHub repository to see how `DeleteExtensionCommand` is designed. It simply retrieves the extension with the category ID corresponding to the one provided as an argument and removes it via Doctrine.

Now that we've covered data handling, let's learn how to retrieve the extension fields that have been registered and display them in the FO category template.

Displaying saved content on the FO Category page

The `displayHeaderCategory` hook will be used in this example. We won't create a super cool layout for this data presentation because that is not the challenge in this module. It is more focused on the form component extension.

Before going further, please create the `/modules/whcategoryfields/config/front/`
`services.yml` file and add the following repository service definition to make it possible to use
`WHCategoryFieldsExtensionRepository` from the legacy context:

```
webhelpers.whcategoryfields.repository.whcategoryfieldsextension_
repository:
  class: WebHelpers\WHCategoryFields\Repository\
  WHCategoryFieldsExtensionRepository
  factory: ['@doctrine.orm.default_entity_manager', getRepository]
  arguments:
    - WebHelpers\WHCategoryFields\Entity\WHCategoryFieldsExtension
```

As we already saw in previous modules, if we declare a service in the `config/services.yml`
file, it doesn't have the same availability and possibilities as if we declare it in the `config/admin/`
`services.yml` file or `config/front/services.yml` file. Let's look at this in more detail:

- All the services declared in the `config/services.yml` file of your module are only
  available in the Symfony service container. You will be able to use all the Symfony services and
  the `PrestaShopBundle` services from there.

- All the services declared in the `config/front/services.yml` file are only available
  in the Symfony services container and the front legacy container. You will only be able to use
  Doctrine and a few services declared in the YAML files of the `/config/services/front/`
  folder of your PrestaShop system from there.

- All the services declared in the `config/admin/services.yml` file are only available
  in the Symfony services container and the admin legacy container. You will only be able to
  use Doctrine and a few services declared in the YAML files of the `/config/services/`
  `admin/` folder of your PrestaShop system from there.

If you go to `https://devdocs.prestashop-project.org/8/modules/concepts/`
`services/#environments`, you will find more details about the services that are available in
the different environments.

Now, we can use our repository in the front legacy container. Let's implement the definition of the
`hookDisplayHeaderCategory($params)` function:

```
public function hookDisplayHeaderCategory($params)
{
  $categoryId = Tools::getValue('id_category');
  $extensionRepository = $this->get('webhelpers.whcategoryfields
  .repository.whcategoryfieldsextension_repository');
  $extension = $extensionRepository->findOneBy(['idCategory'
  =>(int)$categoryId]);
  $idLang = $this->context->language->getId();
  if(!is_null($extension)){
```

```
    $this->context->smarty->assign([
        'short_text' => $extension->getExtensionLangByLangId($idLang)
        ->getShortText(),
        'long_text' => $extension->getExtensionLangByLangId($idLang)
        ->getLongText(),
    ]);
    if($extension->getFilename()!=""){
        $this->context->smarty->assign('filename_path',
        _MODULE_DIR_."whcategoryfields/views/img/uploads/"
        .$extension->getFilename());
    }
    return $this->display(__FILE__, 'whcategoryfields.tpl');
}else{
    return "";
}
}
```

At this point, you should understand everything about this function:

1. It simply retrieves the category ID and uses the repository to find the fields extension entity stored in the database corresponding to this category.

2. Then, it assigns the necessary data to display the fields, depending on the active lang and whether the uploaded file is not empty.

The only missing file to create is the Smarty template file. For this, create the /modules/ whcategoryfields/views/templates/hook/whcategoryfields.tpl file and fill it with the following simple code:

```
<div id="whcategoryfields">
    <strong>{$short_text}</strong>
    <div>
        {$long_text}
    </div>
    {if isset($filename_path)}
    <img src="{$filename_path}" width="300"/>
    {/if}
</div>
```

Now, we know how to display freshly created field values in the category FO controller. We can now test our module and see how it works.

Testing our module

Our module is now ready for testing. It can be downloaded from this book's GitHub repository at `https://github.com/PacktPublishing/Practical-Module-Development-for-Prestashop-8/tree/main/Chapter%2010/whcategoryfields`. Let's get started:

1. Let's install the module by browsing the **Modules | Module Manager** page of the PrestaShop BO.

2. Search for your `Category fields extension` module inside the **Design & Navigation** section and click on the **Install** button.

3. After the success toast message appears, go to **Catalog | Categories** and create a new category or edit one.

At the bottom of the form, you should see our new fields! If you add some content to a category and go to the corresponding category FO page, you will find your content in the header of the category before the product list.

Summary

In this chapter, we learned how to extend a Symfony form from a BO controller by adding multiple fields, localized or otherwise. We also learned how to handle a form submission in creation and edition mode. We discovered how to display a custom field that shows an uploaded file in the form. It was also a means to reuse the CQRS pattern in a different context.

Then, we covered the category deletion event by cleaning our database and displaying our stored field data in the front office.

In the next chapter, we will create a new module to add a blog system to the front office of our shop. Here, we will reuse our Doctrine entity creation, grid display, and form creation knowledge. We will also discover how to create a new legacy module FO controller as it still exists!

11
A Simple Blogging Module

With all the previous modules' examples provided by the previous chapters, we know how to create many of the features offered by PrestaShop's new core. In this chapter, we will create a simple blogging module, presenting simple blog posts regrouped and presented by categories. It will be a good means for us to apply all the previous knowledge and discover how to easily create legacy **front office (FO)** controllers.

As you have already seen most of the components we will use there, we will try to put the accent on the general workflow instead of the core programming. As always, you will be able to find all the files of this module in the GitHub public repo provided with this book.

We will go through the following steps to create our module:

- Defining our module design
- Designing the general architecture of this module
- Creating the entities and the relationships, the repositories, and the database tables
- Creating commands, queries, and data transfer objects
- Creating BO controllers and routes
- Adding forms for creation and editions of entities
- Creating Grids
- Handling deletions
- Creating the FO controllers and displaying the data

By the end of this chapter, you will know how to create a full standard module from its **back office (BO)** to its FO side.

Technical requirements

You will need the following elements to create this blogging module:

- Any PHP editor to code your module

- An (s)FTP client to browse your module files and folders (only if you work on a remote server; this is not necessary if you are working on a local server)

- A web browser to install and test your module

- A working PrestaShop installation (**v1.7.x** minimum)

- A downloaded version of our module is available on the GitHub repository of this book available at `https://github.com/PacktPublishing/Practical-Module-Development-for-Prestashop-8/tree/main/Chapter%2011`

Defining our module design

Let's follow our usual design process: we want to create a light blogging module for our PrestaShop website.

This blog is made of posts composed of a localized title and content. Each post can contain uploaded images in JPEG or PNG, and every post can be displayed in an FO controller to look like the following:

Home / Category name / Post title

Post title

Lorem ipsum dolor sit amet, consectetur adipiscing elit, sed do eiusmod tempor incididunt ut labore et dolore magna aliqua. Ut enim ad minim veniam, quis nostrud exercitation ullamco laboris nisi ut aliquip ex ea commodo consequat. Duis aute irure dolor in reprehenderit in voluptate velit esse cillum dolore eu fugiat nulla pariatur. Excepteur sint occaecat cupidatat non proident, sunt in culpa qui officia deserunt mollit anim id est laborum.

Categorie(s)
Category name

Figure 11.1 – The post FO controller appearance

Each post can be linked to one or many post categories. A post category is made of a title localized field. Every category displays the list of posts linked to it as follows:

Category name

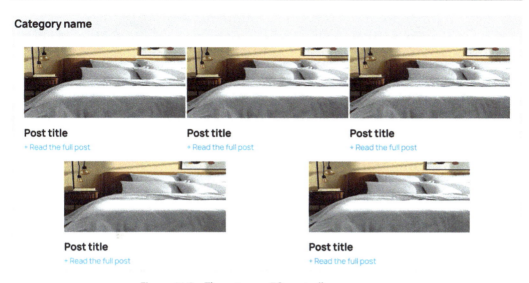

Figure 11.2 – The category FO controller appearance

A home blog FO controller will display the three latest published posts like this:

Figure 11.3 – The home blog FO controller appearance

In the BO, the module comprises a creation/edition form for posts. The following screenshot shows how edition forms can be displayed:

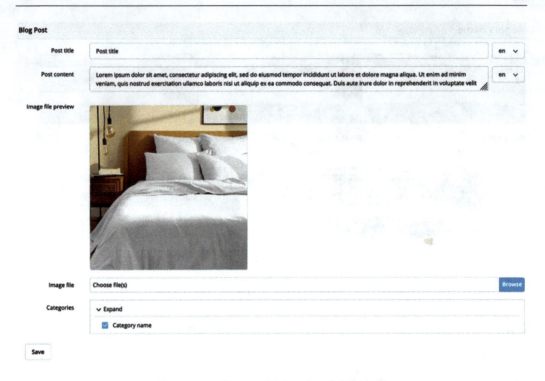

Figure 11.4 – The post-BO form in edition mode

Still in the BO, the module provides a creation/edition form for categories. The following screenshot shows what it should look like:

Figure 11.5 – The category BO form in editing mode

It also shows the list of categories in a grid listing view and lists of posts in grid listing views per linked categories or for all posts. Here, you can see the wanted list of categories in a grid:

Figure 11.6 – The categories Grid layout in the BO controller

The grid for posts will be as shown in the following screenshot:

Figure 11.7 – The post Grid layout in the BO controller

As you may have noticed in the previous grid listings, we need to add buttons for navigation at the top of the views. In the categories listing, we need to have a **Add a new category** button, and everywhere in the blog BO controller, we need the **Add a new Post** and **View all posts** buttons.

Every row of a grid can be edited and deleted with an action button. And for the categories, we need to show all the linked posts for the corresponding row.

Now that we know our plan, we will follow our usual checklist necessary for our module creation:

- **Display name**: Blog
- **Technical name**: `whblog`
- **Tab**: `front_office_features`
- **need_instance value**: 0
- **Description text**: `This is a simple blog module.`
- **Uninstall confirmation text**: `Do you still want to uninstall this module?`
- **Hooks to register**: None
- **Configuration page needed**: No

We now have enough information to start creating our module.

Designing the general architecture of this module

This module will be bigger than the previous ones, which is why it is better to think about the technical design before getting deep into the code. First, let's define the data structure.

Defining the data structure

As a blog category is defined by a localized title, we will use a Doctrine Entity for the blog category containing a date add field and a date update field. We will also have to create another Doctrine lang category entity containing the title localized field as a string, linked to the `Lang` entity with a **many-to-one** relationship, and linked to the previous blog category with a **many-to-one** relationship too.

We will have to create a table named `prefix_whblog_category` in the database with the following structure:

Column name	Column type
`id_category`	int (primary autoincrement)
`category_date_add`	datetime
`category_date_update`	datetime

Table 11.1 – The prefix_whblog_category table structure

Then, we will have to create another table named `prefix_whblog_category_lang` with the following structure:

Column name	Column type
id_category	int
id_lang	int
title	varchar(255)

Table 11.2 – The prefix_whblog_category_lang table structure

For the blog posts part, it will be defined by a Doctrine blog post entity containing the filename field to store the name of the uploaded image file linked to each post, and we will also store the add and update datetimes in dedicated fields. This entity will be linked to the blog category entity with a **many-to-many** relationship. Also, we will have to store the localized title and content information in another Doctrine post lang entity with two dedicated fields. As it deals with localization, it will be linked to the Lang entity in a **many-to-one** relationship and with the blog post entity in a **many-to-one** relationship too.

The resulting structure for the `prefix_whblog_post` table will be the following:

Column name	Column type
id_post	int (primary autoincrement)
filename	varchar(255)
post_date_add	datetime
post_date_update	datetime

Table 11.3 – The prefix_whblog_post table structure

And the structure for the `prefix_whblog_post_lang` table will be as follows:

Column name	Column type
id_post	int
Id_lang	int
title	varchar(255)
content	text

Table 11.4 – The prefix_whblog_post_lang table structure

As implementing a **many-to-many** relationship between two entities is like implementing two **one-to-many** relationships between each entity and a matching one, we can create a table named `prefix_whblog_category_post` responsible for storing the matching for it as follows:

Column name	Column type
id_category_post	Int (primary autoincrement)
id_post	int
id_category	int

Table 11.5 – The prefix_whblog_category_post table structure

We now have a full data structure edible for our target. Now we can design the BO controllers' structure and behavior to manage those entities.

Designing the BO controllers

As seen in our module definition in the previous section, we want a BO controller that contains the list of blog categories in a `Grid`, enabling us to create and edit categories in a form and delete a category.

First, we need to create a BO controller named `AdminWHBlogCategoryController` that will contain one method for all these needs:

- `listAction()`: This will display a Grid component to list all the categories. It will instantiate a `Grid` defined in a definition factory named `WHBlogCategoryDefinitionFactory` for the structure definition, with a query builder named `WHBlogCategoryQueryBuilder` for the data retrieval.

- `createAction()`: This will display a form defined by the `WHBlogCategoryType` class for the list of fields definition, handled by the `WHBlogCategoryFormDataHandler` class to create a category. The data handler will use the `CreateCategoryCommand` in the `CommandBus` to manage the creation business.

- `editAction()`: This will display the same form defined by the `WHBlogCategoryType` class for the list of fields definition, handled by the `WHBlogCategoryFormDataHandler` class to update the edited category. The data handler will use `EditCategoryCommand` in the `CommandBus` to manage the update business. The form data will be retrieved by the `WHBlogCategoryFormDataProvider` class using the `GetCategoryForEditing` command.

- `deleteAction()`: This will delete a category from the database using the `DeleteCategoryCommand` in the `CommandBus`.

Then, we want to have a BO controller containing the list of blog posts in a `Grid`, filtered or not by category, enabling us to create and edit posts on a form and delete a post.

For that, we need to create a BO controller named `AdminWHBlogPostController` that will contain one method for all these needs:

- `listAction()`: This will display a `Grid` component to list all the posts. It will instantiate a `Grid` defined in a definition factory named `WHBlogPostDefinitionFactory` for the structure definition, with a query builder named `WHBlogPostQueryBuilder` for the data retrieval.

- `listFromCategoryAction()`: This will display the same Grid, filtered by category. With this, we can show all the posts linked to a category.

- `createAction()`: This will display a form defined by the `WHBlogPostType` class for the list of fields definition, handled by the `WHBlogPostFormDataHandler` class to create a category. The data handler will use `CreatePostCommand` in `CommandBus` to manage the creation business.

- `editAction()`: This will display the same form defined by the `WHBlogPostType` class for the list of fields definition, handled by the `WHBlogPostFormDataHandler` class to update the edited category. The data handler will use `EditPostCommand` in the `CommandBus` to manage the update business. The form data will be retrieved by the `WHBlogPostFormDataProvider` class using the `GetPostForEditing` command.

- `deleteAction()`: This will delete a category from the database by using the `DeletePostCommand` in `CommandBus`.

We will see in the next section how to create all those files. As we have finished the BO design, let's think about the FO part.

Designing the FO controllers

In the previews available for this module FO part, we can see that we will need three front controllers to generate the FO pages. As the FO is not yet migrated to Symfony, we need to create legacy FO controllers.

We haven't used them yet. If you look at the `/classes/controller/ModuleFrontController.php` file, you will find that we can extend the `ModuleFrontController` class to add a new FO controller from our module.

We will also need to comply with some naming conventions to create module FO controllers: Each child class of `ModuleFrontController` must be named in three parts:

- It must start with the **module's main class name**

- Then it must be followed by the **Capitalized name of the FO controller**

- It must end with the `ModuleFrontController` suffix

That's why we will create the following classes:

- The `WHBlogHomeModuleFrontController` class for the three last published posts of our blog, from all the blog categories

- The `WHBlogCategoryModuleFrontController` class for the list of the posts of a same blog category

- The `WHBlogPostModuleFrontController` class for a post detailed view

As we can use Doctrine services in our legacy FO controllers, we will use the repositories linked to our entities to retrieve the necessary data.

Now that we have a complete high-level view of our module architecture, we can safely start programming our classes. It is also an opportunity for us to train ourselves on some coding challenges!

Creating entities and relationships, repositories, and database tables

As you now know how to create the skeleton of a module, we will suppose for brevity that you know how to create the `/modules/whblog/` folder and the main module class named `WHBlog`. Please have a look at the GitHub repository if you need it.

> **Reminder**
>
> It would be too long to present all the code for the commands, queries, and **data transfer objects (DTOs)** in this book, which is why all the code for those classes is provided in the GitHub repository of this book and we recommend you have it open while reading this book.

As we can't yet use the Symfony console command to automatically generate the migrations necessary to build our tables, let's do it manually via the `install()` function by following the data structure defined in the previous section.

As the table creation is a bit longer than before, we will divide it into two parts:

- The localized tables (suffixed by `_lang`)
- The non-localized ones

For the non-localized tables, let's create the `createTables()` method:

```
{
  Db::getInstance()->execute('
  CREATE TABLE IF NOT EXISTS `' . _DB_PREFIX_ . 'whblog_post` (
    `id_post` int(6) NOT NULL AUTO_INCREMENT,
    `filename` varchar(255) NOT NULL,
    `post_date_add` DATETIME NULL,
    `post_date_update` DATETIME NULL,
    PRIMARY KEY(`id_post`)
  ) ENGINE=' . _MYSQL_ENGINE_ . ' default CHARSET=utf8');

  Db::getInstance()->execute('
  CREATE TABLE IF NOT EXISTS `' . _DB_PREFIX_ . 'whblog_category` (
    `id_category` int(6) NOT NULL AUTO_INCREMENT,
    `category_date_add` DATETIME NULL,
    `category_date_update` DATETIME NULL,
    PRIMARY KEY(`id_category`)
  ) ENGINE=' . _MYSQL_ENGINE_ . ' default CHARSET=utf8');

  Db::getInstance()->execute('
  CREATE TABLE IF NOT EXISTS `' . _DB_PREFIX_ . 'whblog_category_post`
(
    `id_category_post` int(6) NOT NULL AUTO_INCREMENT,
    `id_category` int(6) NOT NULL,
    `id_post` int(6) NOT NULL,
    PRIMARY KEY(`id_category_post`)
  ) ENGINE=' . _MYSQL_ENGINE_ . ' default CHARSET=utf8');
  return true;
}
```

And for the localized tables, let's create the `createLangTables()` method:

```
private function createLangTables()
{
  Db::getInstance()->execute('
  CREATE TABLE IF NOT EXISTS `' . _DB_PREFIX_ . 'whblog_post_lang` (
    `id_post` int(6) NOT NULL,
    `id_lang` int(6) NOT NULL,
    `title` varchar(255) NOT NULL,
    `content` text NOT NULL,
    PRIMARY KEY(`id_post`, `id_lang`)
  ) ENGINE=' . _MYSQL_ENGINE_ . ' default CHARSET=utf8');
```

```
    Db::getInstance()->execute('
    CREATE TABLE IF NOT EXISTS `' . _DB_PREFIX_ . 'whblog_category_lang`
(
      `id_category` int(6) NOT NULL,
      `id_lang` int(6) NOT NULL,
      `title` varchar(255) NOT NULL,
      PRIMARY KEY(`id_category`, `id_lang`)
    ) ENGINE=' . _MYSQL_ENGINE_ . ' default CHARSET=utf8');
    return true;
}
```

The `install()` function using the preceding functions will look like the following:

```
public function install()
{
  if (parent::install() && $this->createTables() && $this
  ->createLangTables())
  {
    return true;
  }
  else{
    $this->_errors[] = $this->l('There was an error during the
    installation.');
    return false;
  }
}
```

Regarding the `uninstall()` function, we will also create two sub-functions, `dropTables()` and `dropLangTables()`, performing a sequence of table drops. Please review GitHub if you want to see their full implementation.

Having the table's full structure, we can now implement the corresponding entities named `WHBlogCategory`, `WHBlogCategoryLang`, `WHBlogPost`, and `WHBlogPostLang` located in the `/modules/whblog/src/Entity/` folder.

> **Entities challenge!**
>
> A good challenge to practice entity creation is to implement all these classes without coding the **many-to-many** relationships between `WHBlogCategory` and `WHBlogPost` yet. Go on and correct yourself by looking at the corresponding classes in the GitHub repository folder. Please don't consider the `$categoryPostRelationship` attributes yet. We will see them in the coming paragraphs.

The new aspect in this module, as you have already mastered entity creation, is the **many-to-many** relationship between the `WHBlogPost` and `WHBlogCategory` entities. Therefore, we need to create two **one-to-many** relationships between each of those classes and a new matching entity called `WHBlogCategoryPost`. This new class will contain one `$id` attribute to identify each instance and one attribute per side of the relationship. It can be coded like this:

```php
//... namespace and use can be found in the GitHub repository
/**
 * @ORM\Table(name="ps_whblog_category_post")
 * @ORM\Entity(repositoryClass="WebHelpers\WHBlog\Repository\
   WHBlogCategoryPostRepository")
 * @ORM\HasLifecycleCallbacks
 */
class WHBlogCategoryPost
{
  /**
   * @var int
   *
   * @ORM\Id
   * @ORM\Column(name="id_category_post", type="integer")
   * @ORM\GeneratedValue(strategy="AUTO")
   */
  private $id;

  /**
   * @var WHBlogCategory
   * @ORM\ManyToOne(targetEntity="WebHelpers\WHBlog\Entity\
     WHBlogCategory", inversedBy="categoryPostRelationship")
   * @ORM\JoinColumn(name="id_category", referencedColumnName
     ="id_category", nullable=false)
   */
  private $category;

  /**
   * @var WHBlogPost
   * @ORM\ManyToOne(targetEntity="WebHelpers\WHBlog\Entity\
     WHBlogPost", inversedBy="categoryPostRelationship")
   * @ORM\JoinColumn(name="id_post", referencedColumnName
     ="id_post", nullable=false)
   */
  private $post;
}
```

If you want to read more detail about Doctrine annotations, feel free to go to the official documentation here: `https://www.doctrine-project.org/projects/doctrine-orm/en/2.14/reference/association-mapping.html`.

Don't forget to create the getters and setters for the entity attributes as usual.

The $post and $category attributes require that we create their inverse attribute named $categoryPostRelationship in the WHBlogPost and WHBlogCategory entities with this code:

```
/**
*
@ORM\OneToMany(targetEntity="WebHelpers\WHBlog\Entity\
WHBlogCategoryPost", cascade={"persist", "remove"}, mappedBy="post")
*/
protected $categoryPostRelationship;
```

To end with the entity creation, we also need to create the following three repositories: WHBlogCategoryPostRepository, WHBlogCategoryRepository, and WHBlogPostRepository, in the /modules/whblog/src/Repository/ folder.

Remember that we need to create the corresponding services in the /modules/whblog/config/ services.yml file to make the repositories accessible by the Symfony service container.

Useful trick

When your config/services.yml is too big and hard to understand, it means that you must divide it into parts. You can use the import function for this:

```
imports:
  - {resource: 'entities.yml'}
  - {resource: 'forms.yml'}
```

It enables you to create sub-YAML files named entities.yml and forms.yml containing your YAML code. If you look at the whblog module in the GitHub repository, you will see an example using this function and the YAML subdivision.

Once the repository services definitions are created in the YAML file, we can jump into the **commands, queries, and DTO** that we will have to use in our controllers, forms, and Grids.

Creating commands, queries, and data transfer objects

In the previous sections of this chapter, we have seen that our controller will need the following commands, queries, and DTOs to be able to manage the blog categories and posts. We can divide them by the entities they enable to manage. That's why we can create the following folders: /modules/ whblog/src/Domain/WHBlogCategory/ and /modules/whblog/src/Domain/ WHBlogPost/. We can then create all the files in both folders, as listed here:

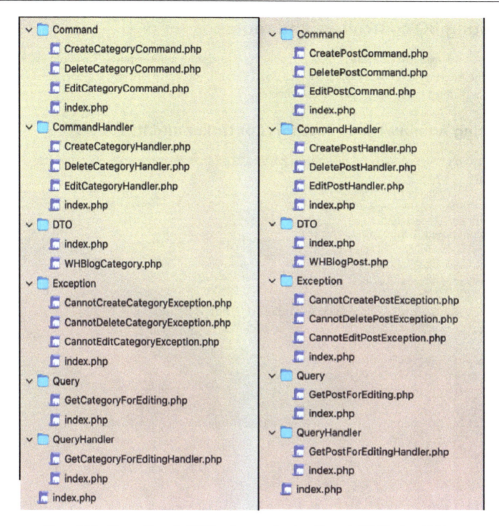

Figure 11.8 – The src/Domain/WHBlogCategory/ and src/Domain/WHBlogPost/ folders

Challenge

The creation of commands, queries, and DTOs was covered in previous chapters. Please create all the previously listed commands, command handlers, queries, queries handlers, and DTOs.

Don't forget to create the services definition in /modules/whblog/config/services. yml or in a sub YAML file named commands.yml or queries.yml.

As usual, you can check this in the GitHub repository of this book!

When our commands, queries, and DTOs are created, we can jump to the BO controller creation and use those newly created classes.

Creating BO controllers and routes

In the BO, we need two controllers to manage the blog categories and the posts. Therefore, we will create the `AdminWHBlogCategoryController` and `AdminWHBlogPostController` classes as planned in the design part of this chapter.

Creating AdminWHBlogCategoryController and its routes

Let's focus on `AdminWHBlogCategoryController` first. We can create the controller class as follows:

```
//namespace and uses are available in the GitHub repository
class AdminWHBlogCategoryController extends
FrameworkBundleAdminController
{
  private $cache;
  private $commandBus;

  public function __construct(CacheProvider $cache,
  TacticianCommandBusAdapter $commandBus)
  {
    $this->cache = $cache;
    $this->commandBus = $commandBus;
  }

  public function listAction(WHBlogCategoryFilter $filters)
  {
    return "";
  }

  public function deleteAction(int $idCategory)
  {
    //ToDo
  }

  public function createAction(Request $request)
  {
    //ToDo
  }

  public function editAction($idCategory, Request $request)
  {
    //ToDo
  }
}
```

Now, we need to create the service definition in `config/services.yml` or in a sub YAML file named `controllers.yml` via an import:

```
WebHelpers\WHBlog\Controller\AdminWHBlogCategoryController:
   class: WebHelpers\WHBlog\Controller\AdminWHBlogCategoryController
   arguments:
      - '@doctrine.cache.provider'
      - '@prestashop.core.command_bus'
```

There is nothing special there; we just tell the service container to inject the cache provider and the command bus services for the instantiation.

Each function must be implemented now. Let's start by creating `listAction()` like this:

```
public function listAction(WHBlogCategoryFilter $filters)
{
   $categoryGridFactory = $this->
   get('webhelpers.whblog.grid.category_grid_factory');
   $categoryGrid = $categoryGridFactory->getGrid($filters);

   return $this->
   render('@Modules/whblog/views/templates/admin
   /list.html.twig',[
      'grid' => $this->presentGrid($categoryGrid),
      'layoutHeaderToolbarBtn' => $this->
      getGridToolbarButtons(),
   ]);
   return "";
}
```

First, we store an instance of the `webhelpers.whblog.grid.category_grid_factory` Grid factory service in `$categoryGridFactory`. We will create it in the *Creating Grids* section of this chapter.

Then we generate a grid with the help of the `$categoryGridFactory` grid factory and we assign it to the Twig template.

You may have noticed that we send the presented Grid in the `grid` variable to the Twig template, and we send a `layoutHeaderToolbarBtn` variable too. This last variable is an array containing a list of buttons to put in the header toolbar of the BO page as the Twig extends the `@PrestaShop/Admin/layout.html.twig` processing this variable.

In our example we create a `getGridToolbarButtons()` method to generate this toolbar array as follows:

```
private function getGridToolbarButtons()
{
  $toolbarButtons['add'] = [
    'href' => $this->
    generateUrl('admin_whblog_category_create'),
    'desc' => $this->trans('Add a new category',
    'Admin.WHBlog.Text'),
    'icon' => 'add_circle_outline',
  ];
  $toolbarButtons['post'] = [
    'href' => $this->
    generateUrl('admin_whblog_post_create'),
    'desc' => $this->trans('Add a new post',
    'Admin.WHBlog.Text'),
    'icon' => 'add_circle_outline',
  ];
  $toolbarButtons['view_all'] = [
    'href' => $this->generateUrl('admin_whblog_post_list'),
    'desc' => $this->trans('View all posts',
    'Admin.Whblog.Text'),
    'icon' => 'visibility',
  ];
  return $toolbarButtons;
}
```

Focusing on the creation of this array, we see that a button is an associative array composed of three keys:

- `href`: This contains the target path of the link to generate
- `desc`: This contains the localized text of the link
- `icon`: This contains the CSS class for the **Material** icon displayed

Feel free to check out the Twig code and the `WHBlogCategoryFilter` class in the GitHub repository. They are standard, that's why we will jump directly to the `deleteAction()` method of our BO Controller. We can create it easily as follows:

```
public function deleteAction(int $idCategory)
{
  $this->commandBus->handle(new
  DeleteCategoryCommand($idCategory));
  $this->addFlash('success', $this->trans('Successful
  deletion.', 'Admin.Notifications.Success'));
```

```
    return $this->
    redirectToRoute('admin_whblog_category_list');
}
```

This simple function calls the `DeleteCategoryCommand` via the `CommandBus` responsible for a category row deletion from the database.

Then, we call the `addFlash()` method, which is a Symfony method: it adds the provided message in the session, and once read by a template, it will be deleted from the session automatically. The BO PrestaShop theme will display this success message at the top of the page to give feedback to the user.

After that, we redirect the user to the categories list with the `redirectToRoute()` Symfony method.

The last part of our BO controller is the implementation of the creating and editing methods displaying and handling the category forms.

Please find a possible implementation for `createAction()` as follows:

```
public function createAction(Request $request)
{
    $categoryFormBuilder = $this->
    get('webhelpers.whblog.form.identifiable_object.builder
    .category_form_builder');
    $categoryForm = $categoryFormBuilder->getForm();
    $categoryForm->handleRequest($request);
    $categoryFormHandler = $this->
    get('webhelpers.whblog.form.identifiable_object.handler
    .category_form_handler');
    $categoryFormHandler->handle($categoryForm);
    if ($categoryForm->isSubmitted() && $categoryForm->
    isValid())
    {
        $this->addFlash('success', $this->trans('Successful
        creation.', 'Admin.Notifications.Success'));
        return $this->
        redirectToRoute('admin_whblog_category_list');
    }
    return $this->
    render('@Modules/whblog/views/templates/admin
    /formCategory.html.twig', [
        "categoryForm"=>$categoryForm->createView()
    ]);
}
```

Nothing is special in the previous code. We use the `webhelpers.whblog.form.identifiable_object.builder.category_form_builder` form builder to create the category form.

Then we handle the form submission with the help of the `webhelpers.whblog.form.identifiable_object.handler.category_form_handler` form handler. Finally, we display the form view in a Twig template.

You will find the form builder definition, the data handler, and the data provider in the *Adding forms for the creation and editions of the entities* section of this chapter.

The `editAction()` method will be almost the same as the `createAction()` one. It can be coded as follows:

```php
public function editAction($idCategory, Request $request)
{
  $categoryFormBuilder = $this->
  get('webhelpers.whblog.form.identifiable_object.builder
  .category_form_builder');
  $categoryForm = $categoryFormBuilder->
  getFormFor((int)$idCategory);
  $categoryForm->handleRequest($request);
  $categoryFormHandler = $this->
  get('webhelpers.whblog.form.identifiable_object.handler
  .category_form_handler');
  $categoryFormHandler->handleFor($idCategory,
  $categoryForm);
  if ($categoryForm->isSubmitted() &&
  $categoryForm->isValid())
  {
    $this->addFlash('success', $this->trans('Successful
    update.', 'Admin.Notifications.Success'));
    return $this->
    redirectToRoute('admin_whblog_category_list');
  }
  return $this->
  render('@Modules/whblog/views/templates/admin
  /formCategory.html.twig', [
    "categoryForm"=>$categoryForm->createView()
  ]);
}
```

The only differences are the following:

- The use of `getFormFor($idCategory)` instead of `getForm()`, because we need to prefill the form fields with the existing stored data for our blog category

- The use of `handleFor($idCategory, $categoryForm)` instead of `handle($categoryForm)` to handle the updates in the database

That's all for this BO controller. The only missing point is the routes definition in the /modules/ whblog/config/routes.yml file. We can define the routes with the following code:

```
admin_whblog_category_list:
  path: whblog/category/list
  methods: [GET]
  defaults:
    _controller: 'WebHelpers\WHBlog\Controller\
    AdminWHBlogCategoryController::listAction'
admin_whblog_category_create:
  path: whblog/category/create
  methods: [GET, POST]
  defaults:
    _controller: 'WebHelpers\WHBlog\Controller\
    AdminWHBlogCategoryController::createAction'
admin_whblog_category_delete:
  path: whblog/category/delete/{idCategory<\d+>?0}
  methods: [GET, POST]
  defaults:
    _controller: 'WebHelpers\WHBlog\Controller\
    AdminWHBlogCategoryController::deleteAction'
  requirements:
    idCategory: \d+
admin_whblog_category_edit:
  path: whblog/category/edit/{idCategory<\d+>?0}
  methods: [GET, POST]
  defaults:
    _controller: 'WebHelpers\WHBlog\Controller\
    AdminWHBlogCategoryController::editAction'
  requirements:
    idCategory: \d+
```

As nothing is special about these route definitions, we won't provide more explanation about them.

Once we have created all the category routes, we can create the AdminWHBlogPostController BO controller for the blog posts.

Creating AdminWHBlogPostController and its routes

First, like the category controller, we can create the skeleton of AdminWHBlogPostController as follows:

```
class AdminWHBlogPostController extends FrameworkBundleAdminController
{
  private $cache;
  private $commandBus;
```

```
  public function __construct(CacheProvider $cache,
  TacticianCommandBusAdapter $commandBus)
  {
    $this->cache = $cache;
    $this->commandBus = $commandBus;
  }
  //--- ToDo: Implement the following functions ----
  public function listAction(WHBlogPostFilter $filters){}
  public function listFromCategoryAction(int $idCategory){}
  public function deleteAction(int $idPost){}
  public function createAction(Request $request){}
  public function editAction($idPost, Request $request){}
}
```

The only new thing there is the implementation of a `listFromCategoryAction(int $idCategory)` method. It will display a list of posts linked to the category with `id_category` equal to `$idCategory`.

As all the methods follow the same pattern as those previously created in `AdminWHBlogCategoryController`, we will just focus on the new `listFromCategoryAction(int $idCategory)` method. It will be coded this way (with a reminder of the `listAction()` method):

```
public function listAction(WHBlogPostFilter $filters)
{
  $postGridFactory = $this->
  get('webhelpers.whblog.grid.post_grid_factory');
  $postGrid = $postGridFactory->getGrid($filters);

  return $this->
  render('@Modules/whblog/views/templates/admin
  /list.html.twig', [
    'grid' => $this->presentGrid($postGrid),
    'layoutHeaderToolbarBtn' => $this->
    getGridToolbarButtons(),
  ]);
  return "";
}

public function listFromCategoryAction(int $idCategory)
{
  $filters = new WHBlogPostFilter();
  $filters->replace([
    'limit' => 10,
    'offset' => 0,
    'orderBy' => 'id_post',
```

```
      'sortOrder' => 'asc',
      'filters' => [
        'id_category'=>$idCategory
      ],
    ]);
    return $this->listAction($filters);
}
```

In this filtered `listFromCategoryAction($idCategory)` method, we instantiate `WHBlog-PostFilter()`, and we use its `replace()` method to add `'id_category'=>$idCategory` to its filters key. With this, we will be able to retrieve `$idCategory` in the query builder of the post grid. Then we reinject the amended filters into the `listAction()` method designed to display the blog posts grid.

As the blog post routes are standard, feel free to read about them in the `/modules/whblog/config/routes.yml` file.

With our BO controllers now created, we can now focus on the components used in these controllers, starting with the forms for creation and edition.

Adding forms for creating and editing entities

In our BO controllers, we use two forms: one for the category and one for the posts. As the **category form** is really simple, we will focus on the **blog post creation/edition form**. It follows the same concept as in the previous chapter form builder extension, but it's a nice way to rediscover it in another context.

As a reminder, a form is defined by a structure definition type for our form and the data provider for inputs to prefill before display.

First, let's create the `/modules/whblog/src/Form/Type/WHBlogPostType.php` file to implement the field structure for our form as follows:

```
class WHBlogPostType extends TranslatorAwareType
{
  private $categoryRepository;
  private $categoriesChoiceTree;

  public function __construct($translator, $locales,
  $categoryRepository)
  {
    parent::__construct($translator, $locales);
    $this->categoryRepository = $categoryRepository;
  }

  public function buildForm(FormBuilderInterface $builder,
  array $options): void
```

```
      {
      }
  }
```

You should notice that we want to retrieve the category repository as a service instance to be able to get all the available blog categories to link our posts to one or many of them.

To continue, we can code the buildForm() method as follows to define the form structure:

```
public function buildForm(FormBuilderInterface $builder, array
$options): void
{
  $this->buildChoiceTree($this->locales[0]["id_lang"]);
  $builder
    ->add('title', TranslatableType::class, [
      'type' => TextType::class,
      'label' => $this->trans('Post title',
      'Modules.Whblog.Admin'),
      'required' => false,
      'options' => [
        'constraints' => [
          new Length([
            'max' => 255,
          ]),
        ],
      ],
    ])
    ->add('content', TranslatableType::class, [
      'type' => TextareaType::class,
      'label' => $this->trans('Post content',
      'Modules.Whblog.Admin'),
      'required' => false
    ]);
  if(isset($options['data']['image_file_preview']['
  filenameUrl']) && $options['data']['
  image_file_preview']['filenameUrl']!="")
  {
    $builder->add('image_file_preview',
    CustomContentType::class, [
      'required' => false,
      'template' => '@Modules/whblog/views/templates
      /admin/upload_image.html.twig',
      'data' => $options['data']['image_file_preview'],
    ]);
  }
  $builder->add('image_file', FileType::class, [
```

```
                'label' => $this->trans('Image file',
                'Modules.Whblog.Admin'),
                'required' => false,
                'constraints' => [
                  new File([
                     'maxSize' => '8024k',
                     'mimeTypes' => [
                       'image/jpeg',
                       'image/png',
                     ],
                     'mimeTypesMessage' => $this->trans('Please choose
                     only JPG of PNG files',
                     'Modules.WHCategoryFields.Admin'),
                  ])
                ]
            ])
            ->add('categories', CategoryChoiceTreeType::class, [
                'label'=> $this->trans('Categories',
                'Modules.Whblog.Admin'),
                'multiple' => true,
                'choices_tree' => $this->categoriesChoiceTree,
            ])
            ->add('save', SubmitType::class);
    }
```

All the fields should ring a bell to you, as we used them or comparable fields in the previous chapter. The only type of field you don't know yet is CategoryChoiceTreeType. It enables us to display a list of checkboxes or radio buttons in a choice tree. It is usually used in the list of product categories, but we can use it in another context. You can find its official documentation here: https://devdocs. prestashop-project.org/8/development/components/form/types-reference/ category-choice-tree/.

We set the multiple option to true and we put the blog categories list into the choices_tree one via the use of our categoriesChoiceTree class variable. This variable content is previously built via the $this->buildChoiceTree($this->locales[0]["id_lang"]); instruction at the beginning of the function definition.

The buildChoiceTree() definition is as follows:

```
    private function buildChoiceTree($id_lang)
    {
      $this->categoriesChoiceTree = [];
      $categories = $this->categoryRepository->findAll();
      foreach($categories as $category)
      {
        $name = $category->getCategoryLangByLangId($id_lang)->
```

```
    getTitle();
    if($name=="")
    {
      $name = "No title - ID: ".$category->getId();
    }
    $this->categoriesChoiceTree[] = ['id_category'
    =>(string)$category->getId(), 'name'=>$name];
  }
}
```

In this function, we use the blog categories repository to retrieve all the categories information (ID and title), and we add a new subarray to the `categoriesChoiceTree` array for each blog category containing the following:

- An `id_category` key containing the category ID
- A `name` key containing the title of the category or a substitution string if empty.

The rest should be easy for you. If not, please go back to the previous chapter, where you should find many common points.

As we are done with the form type definition, we need to implement a data provider to use the form factory to build it. Therefore, let's create the `/modules/whblog/src/Form/WHBlogPost/DataProvider/WHBlogPostFormDataProvider.php` file with the following content:

```
//namespace and uses available in the GitHub repository
final class WHBlogPostFormDataProvider implements
FormDataProviderInterface
{
  private $queryBus;

  public function __construct(CommandBusInterface
  $queryBus)
  {
    $this->queryBus = $queryBus;
  }

  public function getData($id)
  {
    $postForEditing = $this->queryBus->handle(new
    GetPostForEditing($id));
    $filename = "";
    if($postForEditing->getFilename() != "")
    {
      $filename = "/modules/whblog/
      views/img/uploads/".$postForEditing->getFilename();
```

```
    }
    return [
      'title' => $postForEditing->getTitle(),
      'content' => $postForEditing->getContent(),
      'image_file_preview' => ['filenameUrl' => $filename],
      'categories' => $postForEditing->getCategories(),
    ];
  }

  public function getDefaultData()
  {
    return ['title' => [], 'content' => [], 'filename'
    => "", 'categories' => []];
  }
}
```

As we implement FormDataProviderInterface there, we need to define the getDefaultData() method to return an array with empty values for each field. We also need to implement the getData($id) method to pass data to the form to prefill the form fields. The general idea here is to use a GetPostForEditing query, which returns a DTO to provide the fetched data.

These two Type and Data Provider classes enable us to create the services definition to create our form factory used in the controller createAction() and editAction() methods. We can add the form factory services definition as follows in the config/services.yml file or in a sub YAML imported file, like in the GitHub repository example:

```
webhelpers.whblog.form.identifiable_object.data_provider.post_form_
data_provider:
  class: 'WebHelpers\WHBlog\Form\WHBlogPost\DataProvider\
  WHBlogPostFormDataProvider'
  arguments:
    - '@prestashop.core.query_bus'

webhelpers.whblog.form.type.post_type:
  class: 'WebHelpers\WHBlog\Form\Type\WHBlogPostType'
  parent: 'form.type.translatable.aware'
  public: true
  tags:
    - { name: form.type }
  arguments:
    - '@webhelpers.whblog.repository.whblogcategory_repository'

webhelpers.whblog.form.identifiable_object.builder.post_form_builder:
  class: 'PrestaShop\PrestaShop\Core\Form\Setting\Builder\FormBuilder'
  factory: 'prestashop.core.form.builder.form_builder_factory:create'
  arguments:
```

```
    - 'WebHelpers\WHBlog\Form\Type\WHBlogPostType'
    - '@webhelpers.whblog.form.identifiable_object.data_provider
      .post_form_data_provider'
```

The new thing here is the definition of the `webhelpers.whblog.form.type.post_type` service definition. It enables us to inject the blog categories repository service into our form type class constructor. If no dependencies are required in the form Type class, there is no need to define this kind of service.

Even if we have a great form to display, we need to implement the corresponding form data handler to process a form submission via a form handler service. Let's create a `/modules/whblog/src/Form/WHBlogPost/DataHandler/WHBlogPostFormDataHandler.php` file with the following content:

```
//namespace and uses available in the GitHub repository
final class WHBlogPostFormDataHandler implements
FormDataHandlerInterface
{
  private $commandBus;

  public function __construct(CommandBusInterface
  $commandBus)
  {
    $this->commandBus = $commandBus;
  }

  public function create(array $data)
  {
    $createPostCommand = new CreatePostCommand(
    $data['title'],$data['content'],$data['image_file'],
    $data['categories']);
    $this->commandBus->handle($createPostCommand);
  }

  public function update($id, array $data)
  {
    $editPostCommand = new EditPostCommand($id,
    $data['title'],$data['content'],$data['image_file'],
    $data['categories']);
    $this->commandBus->handle($editPostCommand);
  }
}
```

This class implements `FormDataHandlerInterface`; that's why we need to implement the `create($data)` and the `update($id, $data)` methods to handle the form submission. Those two methods use simple commands with the **Command Query Responsibility Segregation (CQRS)** design pattern. All the data sent by the form is available in the `$data` argument array.

Finally, we need to create the corresponding services to define the form data handler and the form handler in the `config/services.yml` file or in an imported sub YAML file:

```
webhelpers.whblog.form.identifiable_object.data_handler.post_form_
data_handler:
  class: 'WebHelpers\WHBlog\Form\WHBlogPost\DataHandler\
WHBlogPostFormDataHandler'
  arguments:
    - '@prestashop.core.command_bus'
webhelpers.whblog.form.identifiable_object.handler.post_form_handler:
  class: 'PrestaShop\PrestaShop\Core\Form\Setting\Handler\FormHandler'
  factory: 'prestashop.core.form.identifiable_object.handler.form_
handler_factory:create'
  arguments:
    - '@webhelpers.whblog.form.identifiable_object.data_handler.post_
form_data_handler'
```

This way, we can handle a post form submission for a creation in the controller via this code:

```
$postForm->handleRequest($request);
$postFormHandler = $this->
  get('webhelpers.whblog.form.identifiable_object
  .handler.post_form_handler');
$postFormHandler->handle($postForm);
if ($postForm->isSubmitted() && $postForm->isValid())
{
  //… redirection to the list
}
```

We now have what we need to create and handle more complex forms using the CQRS pattern. We can now go into more detail on the Grids used in listing the methods of our controllers.

Creating Grids

We use Grids in our BO controller implementations in the methods to display the lists of blog categories and blog posts.

Here, we will only focus on the blog post Grids enabling us to display a full list and a filtered list of blog posts linked to a category. Remember that anytime you can have a look at the GitHub repository of this book containing the module files to get the blog categories Grid.

As seen in previous chapters, a Grid is generated by a Grid Factory, which uses the following objects:

- A definition factory for the structure of the column

- A data factory that retrieves the data to display

In the case of the blog posts, let's define the structure of the column for our Grid in the `/modules/whblog/src/Grid/Definition/Factory/WHBlogPostDefinitionFactory.php` file with the following content:

```
//namespace and uses available in the GitHub repository
final class WHBlogPostDefinitionFactory extends
AbstractGridDefinitionFactory
{
  protected function getId()
  {
    return "whblogpost";
  }

  protected function getName()
  {
    return $this->trans('Blog posts', [],
    'Modules.WHBlog.Admin');
  }

  protected function getColumns()
  {
    //Todo column definition
  }
}
```

Everything is pretty standard in this factory. If you need more information, go back to the previous module chapters, as everything is well explained. We will focus on the `getColumns()` implementation to define the structure of the column for this Grid:

```
protected function getColumns()
{
  return (new ColumnCollection())
  ->add(
    (new DataColumn('id_post'))
    ->setName($this->trans('ID', [],
    'Modules.WHBlog.Admin'))
    ->setOptions([
      'field' => 'id_post',
    ])
  )
  ->add(
```

```php
            (new DataColumn('title'))
            ->setName($this->trans('Post title', [],
            'Modules.WHBlog.Admin'))
            ->setOptions([
              'field' => 'title',
            ])
        )
        ->add(
          (new ActionColumn('actions'))
          ->setName('Actions')
          ->setOptions([
            'actions' => (new RowActionCollection())
            ->add(
              (new LinkRowAction('edit'))
              ->setIcon('edit')
              ->setOptions([
                'route' => 'admin_whblog_post_edit',
                'route_param_name' => 'idPost',
                'route_param_field' => 'id_post'
              ])
            )
            ->add(
              (new LinkRowAction('delete'))
              ->setIcon('delete')
              ->setOptions([
                'route' => 'admin_whblog_post_delete',
                'route_param_name' => 'idPost',
                'route_param_field' => 'id_post'
              ])
            ),
          ])
        );
}
```

As you can see, we add two columns to display the post ID and the title. A third column is added to display an action button to edit or delete each post.

Let's take some more time to define the query builder responsible for getting the data to display in the Grid. We can now create the `/modules/whblog/src/Grid/Query/WHBlogPostQueryBuilder.php` file containing all the data retrieval business:

```php
//namespace and uses available in the GitHub repository
final class WHBlogPostQueryBuilder extends
AbstractDoctrineQueryBuilder
{
    private $searchCriteriaApplicator;
```

```
    private $filterApplicator;
    private $contextIdLang;

    public function __construct(Connection $connection,
    $dbPrefix, DoctrineSearchCriteriaApplicatorInterface
    $searchCriteriaApplicator,
    DoctrineFilterApplicatorInterface $filterApplicator,
    int $contextIdLang)
    {
      parent::__construct($connection, $dbPrefix);
      $this->searchCriteriaApplicator =
      $searchCriteriaApplicator;
      $this->filterApplicator = $filterApplicator;
      $this->contextIdLang = $contextIdLang;
    }

    public function getSearchQueryBuilder(
    SearchCriteriaInterface $searchCriteria) {
      $qb = $this->getBaseQuery($searchCriteria->
      getFilters());

      $this->searchCriteriaApplicator
        ->applyPagination($searchCriteria, $qb)
        ->applySorting($searchCriteria, $qb)
      ;

      return $qb;
    }

    public function getCountQueryBuilder(
    SearchCriteriaInterface $searchCriteria)
    {
      $qb = $this->getBaseQuery($searchCriteria->
      getFilters());
      $qb->select('COUNT(*)');
      return $qb;
    }

    // Base query can be used for both Search and Count
    // query builders
    private function getBaseQuery(array $filterValues)
    {
      //ToDo
    }
}
```

Like in every query builder class for Grids, we need to implement the getSearchQueryBuilder()
and getCountQueryBuilder() methods. We usually create a common getBaseQuery()
method responsible for creating the common base query for factory needs.

The getBaseQuery() method can be implemented as follows:

```
private function getBaseQuery(array $filterValues)
{
  $query = $this->connection
    ->createQueryBuilder()
    ->select('whp.id_post, whpl.title')
    ->from($this->dbPrefix.'whblog_post', 'whp')
    ->leftJoin('whp', $this->dbPrefix . 'whblog_post_lang',
    'whpl', 'whp.`id_post` = whpl.`id_post` AND
    whpl.`id_lang` = :contextIdLang')
    ->setParameter('contextIdLang', $this->
    contextIdLang);
  foreach ($filterValues as $filterName => $filter) {
    if($filterName == 'id_category'){
    $query->innerJoin('whp', $this->dbPrefix .
    'whblog_category_post', 'whcp', 'whp.`id_post` =
    whcp.`id_post` AND whcp.`id_category` = :idCategory');
    $query->setParameter('idCategory', $filter);
    }
  }
  return $query;
}
```

In our case, we want to get all the posts from the prefix_whblog_post table and the joined
localized title from prefix_blog_post_lang on id_post. In the case of a blog posts list
filtered by blog category, we add an inner join that matches a relationship between the blog post and
the potentially filtered category.

As you can see, all the filters are provided to the query builder by an associative array via the getFil-
ters() method of the injected SearchCriteriaInterface $searchCriteria argument.

Now that we have the classes required to create a grid factory, we can define the corresponding services
definitions in the config/services.yml or in any imported sub YAML file with the following code:

```
webhelpers.whblog.grid.definition.factory.post_grid_definition_
factory:
  class: 'WebHelpers\WHBlog\Grid\Definition\Factory\
WHBlogPostDefinitionFactory'
  parent: 'prestashop.core.grid.definition.factory.abstract_grid_
definition'
  public: true
```

```
webhelpers.whblog.grid.query.post_query_builder:
    class: 'WebHelpers\WHBlog\Grid\Query\WHBlogPostQueryBuilder'
    arguments:
        - '@prestashop.core.query.doctrine_search_criteria_applicator'
        - '@prestashop.core.grid.query.filter.doctrine_filter_applicator'
        - "@=service('prestashop.adapter.legacy.context').getContext().
language.id"
    parent: 'prestashop.core.grid.abstract_query_builder'
    public: true

webhelpers.whblog.grid.data.factory.post_data_factory:
    class: 'PrestaShop\PrestaShop\Core\Grid\Data\Factory\
DoctrineGridDataFactory'
    arguments:
        - '@webhelpers.whblog.grid.query.post_query_builder'
        - '@prestashop.core.hook.dispatcher'
        - '@prestashop.core.grid.query.doctrine_query_parser'
        - 'whblogpost'
    public: true

webhelpers.whblog.grid.post_grid_factory:
    class: 'PrestaShop\PrestaShop\Core\Grid\GridFactory'
    arguments:
        - '@webhelpers.whblog.grid.definition.factory.post_grid_
definition_factory'
        - '@webhelpers.whblog.grid.data.factory.post_data_factory'
        - '@prestashop.core.grid.filter.form_factory'
        - '@prestashop.core.hook.dispatcher'
```

After the Grids definitions and their use in the controllers, we can dive into the remaining BO process, deletions.

Handling deletions

We have seen in the BO controllers that we use commands to delete each entity, the `DeleteCategoryCommand` for the categories and the `DeletePostCommand` for posts.

Each command is linked to its `CommandHandler`. Now that we have mastered the command creation, we will focus on `CommandHandlers`.

Let's create the `/modules/whblog/src/Domain/WHBlogCategory/CommandHandler/DeleteCategoryHandler.php` file to implement `DeleteCategoryHandler` linked to `DeleteCategoryCommand`. Its content can be seen in the following code:

```
//namespace and uses available in the GitHub repository
class DeleteCategoryHandler
```

```
{
  private $entityManager;
  private $categoryRepository;

  public function __construct($entityManager,
  $categoryRepository)
  {
    $this->entityManager = $entityManager;
    $this->categoryRepository = $categoryRepository;
  }

  public function handle(DeleteCategoryCommand
  $deleteCategoryCommand)
  {
    try{
      $blogCategory = $this->categoryRepository->
      findOneBy(['id' => $deleteCategoryCommand->
      getIdCategory()]);
      if(!is_null($blogCategory)){
        $this->entityManager->remove($blogCategory);
        $this->entityManager->flush();
      }
    }catch(\Exception $e){
      throw new CannotDeleteCategoryException(
        sprintf('Failed to delete the blog category')
      );
    }
  }
}
```

In the constructor, we store the entity manager and the category repository instances into member variables. And in the `handle()` method responsible for handling `DeleteCategoryCommand`, we retrieve the ID of the category to delete, and we simply remove it from the database with Doctrine.

Now let's create the `/modules/whblog/src/Domain/WHBlogPost/CommandHandler/ DeletePostHandler.php` file handling the post deletion commands. We can implement it with the following code:

```
//namespace and uses available in the GitHub repository
class DeletePostHandler
{
  private $entityManager;
  private $postRepository;

  public function __construct($entityManager,
  $postRepository)
```

```php
{
    $this->entityManager = $entityManager;
    $this->postRepository = $postRepository;
}


public function handle(DeletePostCommand
$deletePostCommand)
{
    try{
        $blogPost = $this->postRepository->findOneBy(['id' =>
        $deletePostCommand->getIdPost()]);
        if(!is_null($blogPost)){
            if($blogPost->getFilename()!="" &&
            file_exists(_PS_MODULE_DIR_."whblog/views/img
            /uploads/".$blogPost->getFilename())){

                unlink(_PS_MODUzLE_DIR_."whblog/views/img/uploads/"
                .$blogPost->getFilename());
            }
            $this->entityManager->remove($blogPost);
            $this->entityManager->flush();
        }
    }catch(\Exception $e){
        throw new CannotDeletePostException(
            sprintf('Failed to delete the blog post')
        );
    }
}
}
```

Exactly like for categories, we retrieve the entity manager and the post repository instances via the constructor. Then we handle `DeletePostCommand` by retrieving the blog post to delete via the repository. If a file is uploaded and linked to the corresponding post, we delete it physically from its folder, and we follow by removing the corresponding post record from the database.

Don't forget to create the corresponding services definition for these commands in the `config/services.yml` file with this code:

```yaml
webhelpers.whblog.domain.whblogcategory.command_handler.delete_
category:
  class:
'WebHelpers\WHBlog\Domain\WHBlogCategory\CommandHandler\
DeleteCategoryHandler'
  arguments:
    - '@doctrine.orm.default_entity_manager'
    - '@webhelpers.whblog.repository.whblogcategory_repository'
```

```
  tags:
    - { name: tactician.handler, command: WebHelpers\WHBlog\Domain\
WHBlogCategory\Command\DeleteCategoryCommand }

webhelpers.whblog.domain.whblogpost.command_handler.delete_post:
    class: 'WebHelpers\WHBlog\Domain\WHBlogPost\CommandHandler\
DeletePostHandler'
    arguments:
      - '@doctrine.orm.default_entity_manager'
      - '@webhelpers.whblog.repository.whblogpost_repository'
    tags:
      - { name: tactician.handler, command: WebHelpers\WHBlog\Domain\
WHBlogPost\Command\DeletePostCommand
}
```

As we should now understand the YAML routes definition, the previous code should be clear to us and we won't get deeper into it.

We are done with the BO business. We need to create now the FO pages to display the data.

Creating the FO controllers and displaying the data

In the first section of this chapter, we designed the module to display three types of pages in the FO. Before getting into the practical coding, let's present how to create a FO controller to display a front page for our module.

We saw that we needed to extend the ModuleFrontController class to create a new FO controller by following the naming conventions already presented. As ModuleFrontController is a child class of the FrontController class, we can override the existing method of its life cycle.

As a reminder, we have the following methods sequence:

1. init()
2. setMedia()
3. postProcess()
4. initHeader()
5. initContent()
6. initFooter()
7. display()

In our case, as we need to add content to the body of our page layout, we will override the initContent() method in our classes.

Let's start by creating the blog home FO controller displaying the three latest blog posts published. The first thing to do is to create the /modules/whblog/controllers/front/home.php file. There we can create the WHBlogHomeModuleFrontController class and override the initContent() method this way:

```
class WHBlogHomeModuleFrontController extends ModuleFrontController
{
  public function initContent()
  {
    parent::initContent();
    $postRepository = $this->
    get('webhelpers.whblog.repository.whblogpost
    _repository');

    $posts = $postRepository->findBy([],['id'=>"DESC"], 3);

    $this->context->smarty->assign(
    array(
      'title' => $this->trans('My shop blog', [],
      "Modules.Whblog.Shop"),
      'posts' => $posts,
      'module_dir' => _PS_MODULE_DIR_ . $this->module->name
    ));
    $this->setTemplate('module:whblog/
    views/templates/front/category.tpl');
  }
}
```

We retrieve the post repository and get the three last created posts. Then we assign it to Smarty and send the module_dir variable with the path to the module to be able to display the uploaded image files. The Smarty template is in the views/templates/front/category.tpl. For all the FO controllers' views, the best practice is to store them in the views/templates/front/ folder. In our case, we will use the same category.tpl Smarty view, it simply displays a list of posts.

Once the controller is created, we will access it via the URL (https://www.nameofthesite. extension/en/module/whblog/home) as soon as the module is installed following the same pattern after the lang code, with /module/technicalnameofthemodule/controllername.

How can we set up pretty URLs for our module FO controllers?

You can still create custom routes by using the `ModuleRoutes` hook. The `hookModuleRoutes($params)` must return an associative array with one custom route per key/value couple.

Please find an example of an array returned by this hook for a custom route as follows:

```
[
    'module-technicalnameofmodule-controllername' => [
        'controller' => 'controllername', //front controller name
        'rule' => 'customurlstring', //the desired page URL
        'keywords' => [
            'link_rewrite' => [
                'regexp' => '[_a-zA-Z0-9-\pL]*',
                'param' => 'link_rewrite'
            ],
        ],
        'params' => [
            'fc' => 'module',
            'module' => 'technicalnameofmodule', //module technical name
        ]
    ]
];
```

For the FO blog category posts list, we must create the `/modules/whblog/controllers/front/category.php` file containing the `WHBlogCategoryModuleFrontController` class. As it is not really different from the home FO controller, we won't give more information about it. As usual, go to the GitHub repository for this book to see the full file.

Finally, we will have a closer look at the post detail FO controller that has to be implemented in the `/modules/whblog/controllers/front/post.php` file. Here, we can implement the `WHBlogPostModuleFrontController` class overriding the `initContent()` method to display our data this way:

```
public function initContent()
{
    parent::initContent();

    $categoryPostRepository = $this->
    get('webhelpers.whblog.repository.whblogcategorypost
```

```php
_repository');
$relationships = $categoryPostRepository->
findBy(['post'=>Tools::getValue('id_post')]);

$categories = [];
if(!is_null($relationships) && count($relationships)>0)
{
  foreach($relationships as $relation)
  {
    $id_category = $relation->getCategory()->getId();
    $categoryRepository = $this->
    get('webhelpers.whblog.repository.whblogcategory
    _repository');
    $category = $categoryRepository->
    findOneById($id_category);
    $category_data = ["title"=>$category->
    getCategoryLangByLangId($this->context->language->
    id)->getTitle(),"url"=>Context::getContext()->link->
    getModuleLink('whblog', 'category',
    array('id_category' => $id_category))];
    $categories[] = $category_data;
  }
}

$postRepository = $this->
get('webhelpers.whblog.repository.whblogpost
_repository');
$post = $postRepository->
findOneById(Tools::getValue('id_post'));
$this->context->smarty->assign(
array(
  'title' => $post->getTitleLangs(),
  'content' => $post->getContentLangs(),
  'filename' => $post->getFilename(),
  'categories' => $categories,
));
$this->
setTemplate('module:whblog/views/templates/front
/post.tpl');
}
```

This override is made of two parts. First, we extract the parent category data to send it to the Smarty view. The second part is responsible for retrieving the post details via the post repository to also send it to the view. The Smarty template displays the content of the post and the parent category link. We can also add an override of the `getBreadcrumbLinks()` method to control the content of the displayed breadcrumb on the FO page with the following implementation:

```
protected function getBreadcrumbLinks()
{
    $postRepository = $this->
    get('webhelpers.whblog.repository.whblogpost
    _repository');
    $post = $postRepository->
    findOneById(Tools::getValue('id_post'));

    $categoryPostRepository = $this->
    get('webhelpers.whblog.repository.whblogcategorypost
    _repository');
    $relationships = $categoryPostRepository->
    findBy(['post'=>Tools::getValue('id_post')]);

    $breadcrumb = parent::getBreadcrumbLinks();

    if(!is_null($relationships) && count($relationships)>0){
        $id_category_parent = $relationships[0]->
        getCategory()->getId();
        $categoryRepository = $this->
        get('webhelpers.whblog.repository.whblogcategory
        _repository');
        $category = $categoryRepository->
        findOneById($id_category_parent);

        $breadcrumb['links'][] = [
            'title' => $category->getCategoryLangByLangId($this->
            context->language->id)->getTitle(),
            'url' => Context::getContext()->link->
            getModuleLink('whblog', 'category',
            array('id_category' => $id_category_parent))
        ];

        $breadcrumb['links'][] = [
            'title' => $post->getPostLangByLangId($this->context
            ->language->id)->getTitle(),
            'url' => Context::getContext()->link->
            getModuleLink('whblog', 'post', array('id_post' =>
            Tools::getValue('id_post')))
```

```
    ];
  }
  return $breadcrumb;
}
```

We simply retrieve the parent category data if available; then we can set an array with the `links` key containing an array with all the elements of the breadcrumb. Each link of the breadcrumb must be an array with the target URL in the `url` key and the displayed label of the link in the `title` key.

Do it yourself

To apply this new knowledge, why not try to create a FO controller with the list of existing categories, each of the displayed categories linking to the blog category FO controller?

The algorithm will follow these steps:

- Create the `categorylist` module FO controller

- Override the `initContent()` method

- In the `initContent()` method, retrieve all the categories information via the categories repository, then put it into an array and assign it to the Smarty view

- Set the Smarty view responsible for displaying the categories list

- Create the corresponding view template

That's all with our module's FO controllers. Now we know how to create module FO controllers practically, we can install and check our module by going into the modules manager in the BO and browsing the menu to go to the blog management BO controller. We can also get into the FO and browse the FO pages via the URL structure presented previously.

Summary

In this chapter, we have created a large module containing the most used components: BO `Grids`, filtered or not, `Forms` in creation and edition mode, and all the data management processing via the CQRS design pattern.

Finally, we saw how the created data can be displayed with the legacy module FO controller that extends the `FrontController` and `Controller` classes.

The huge amount of information provided for this module obliged us to focus on the new knowledge and the most important information. That's why we sometimes jumped from one component to another. Remember that the GitHub repository contains the full resulting module if you need to get all the complete files, don't hesitate and go through it anytime.

We now know most of what a developer needs to create standard PrestaShop modules. In the next chapter, we will discover the Payment modules that enable us to add new payment solutions to our shop.

12

A Cash Payment Module

In the last chapter, we applied our different knowledge of module components and design patterns to a blogging module. That enables us to modify and add content to the **Front Office** (**FO**) and the **Back Office** (**BO**). Even if it is very important for online sellers to customize their website's content and tools, they also need to have full control over payment options. As modules can provide new custom payment solutions, we will understand how to create a cash payment solution with a simple example.

Creating this module will follow these steps:

- Defining our module design
- Defining a PrestaShop payment module
- Creating our module structure
- Creating the payment validation controller
- Testing our module

By the end of this chapter, you will know how to create a standard payment module. You will master enough notions on payment modules to be able to create a new one for PrestaShop.

Technical requirements

You will need the following elements to create this payment module:

- Any PHP editor to code your module
- An (s)FTP client to browse your module files and folders (only if you work on a remote server, not necessary if you work on a local server)
- A web browser to install and test your module

- A working PrestaShop installation (v1.7.x minimum)
- A downloaded version of our module is available in the GitHub repository of this book at this URL: `https://github.com/PacktPublishing/Practical-Module-Development-for-Prestashop-8/tree/main/Chapter%2012/whcashpayment`.

Defining our module design

As we want to create a Cash Payment module, we need to define it. Let's follow our standard process. This module aims to provide a cash payment option in our checkout process:

- The customer will have to pay the order by cash, picking it up at the physical store or the delivery center.
- When the customer has validated the payment solution, the order will be created, and its state will switch to **Awaiting cash payment**. As this order state does not already exist, our module will automatically create it on installation.

The payment option at the payment step of the checkout process should look as follows:

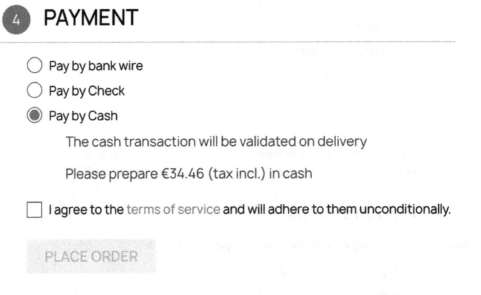

Figure 12.1 – The payment module step in the checkout process

Then, the following order confirmation step should display this feedback message when our module has been chosen:

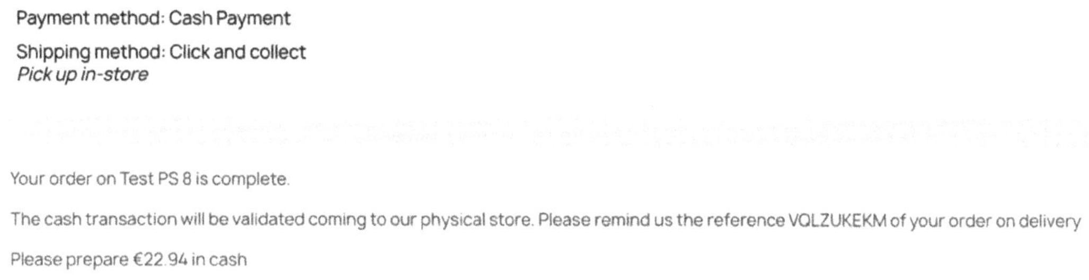

Payment method: Cash Payment

Shipping method: Click and collect
Pick up in-store

Your order on Test PS 8 is complete.

The cash transaction will be validated coming to our physical store. Please remind us the reference VQLZUKEKM of your order on delivery

Please prepare €22.94 in cash

Figure 12.2 – The order confirmation page in the checkout process

Now that we know our targets, we will follow our usual checklist necessary for our module creation:

- **Display name**: Cash Payment
- **Technical name**: whcashpayment
- **Tab**: payment_gateways
- **need_instance value**: 0
- **Description text**: This module displays a cash payment option.
- **Uninstall confirmation text**: Do you still want to uninstall this module?
- **Hooks to register**: paymentOptions and displayPaymentReturn
- **Configuration page needed**: No

The chosen hooks may be unclear as we don't know them. But don't worry; in the next section, defining what a payment method is, we will explain it.

We now have enough information in order to start creating our module. First, we will present the specificities of a Payment module to make sure that we comply with the standards.

Defining a PrestaShop payment module

Even if we know what a module is, we don't know yet what a payment module is and what is needed to create one. If you browse the core files, you should find the classes/PaymentModule.php file, which defines a child class of Module.

Practically, instead of extending the Module class to create our main module class, we will extend this PaymentModule class.

The only way to offer one or many new payment options to our shop is to register our module to the paymentOptions hook and to implement the hookPaymentOptions($params) method, which will have to return an array of PaymentOption instances. We will focus on it while creating our module.

Also, we need to register our module to the `displayPaymentReturn` hook and implement its `hookDisplayPaymentReturn($params)` method, which will return the view to display on the order confirmation page.

Let's have a further look at this `PaymentModule` class to understand how to use it efficiently. Among others, we can point out the following useful methods:

- The `install()` method is overridden and triggers the following:

  - The `addCheckboxCurrencyRestrictionsForModule()` method if `$currencies_mode` is set to `checkbox`. This method simply adds in the `prefix_module_currency` table one row per active currency for each shop. It enables us to activate the current module for 0 to *n* currencies.

  - The `addRadioCurrencyRestrictionsForModule()` method if `$currencies_mode` is set to `radio`. This method adds only one row in the `prefix_module_currency` table for each shop. It enables us to activate the current module for only one currency at a time.

  - The `addCheckboxCountryRestrictionsForModule()` method is responsible for adding checkbox country restrictions for the current module.

  - The `addCheckboxCarrierRestrictionsForModule()` method is responsible for adding checkbox restrictions.

  - The update/creation of multiple configuration keys/values for the current module.

- The `validateOrder()` method enables us to create an order from a cart and multiple parameters. It handles all consecutive actions such as notification emails, stock decreases, and invoice creation.

- The `getCurrency()` method enables us to know which currencies are enabled for the current module.

- The `getInstalledPaymentModules()` method enables us to list all the modules hooked to `paymentOptions`.

Knowing how the `PaymentModule` class is defined, we know how to use it. Let's start creating our module.

Creating our module structure

Theoretically, we know how to create a payment module, so let's apply it to our example module. As seen before, we can create the `/modules/whcashpayment/` folder containing a `logo.png` file, the `index.php` file, and the main module class file named `whcashpayment.php`.

Our /modules/whcashpayment/whcashpayment.php file should initially look like this:

```php
<?php
use PrestaShop\PrestaShop\Core\Payment\PaymentOption;

if (!defined('_PS_VERSION_')) {
  exit;
}

class WHCashPayment extends PaymentModule
{
  const CONFIG_OS_WHCASH = 'WH_OS_CASH_VALIDATION';

  public function __construct()
  {
    $this->name = 'whcashpayment';
    $this->tab = 'payments_gateways';
    $this->version = '1.0.0';
    $this->author = 'Web Helpers';
    $this->need_instance = 0;
    $this->ps_versions_compliancy = [
     'min' => '1.7.0',
     'max' => '8.99.99',
    ];
    $this->bootstrap = true;

    $this->currencies = true;
    $this->currencies_mode = 'checkbox';
    $this->controllers = ['validation'];

    parent::__construct();

    $this->confirmUninstall = $this->l('Do you still you
      want to uninstall this module?');
    $this->description = $this->l('This module displays a
      cash payment option');
    $this->displayName = $this->l('Cash Payment');
  }

  public function install()
  {
    return parent::install()
      && $this->registerHook('paymentOptions')
      && $this->registerHook('displayPaymentReturn')
      && $this->installOrderState()
```

```
    ;
  }

  public function uninstall()
  {
    return parent::uninstall();
  }

  public function hookPaymentOptions($params)
  {
    //ToDo
  }

  public function hookDisplayPaymentReturn($params)
  {
    //ToDo
  }

  public function installOrderState()
  {
    //ToDo
  }
}
```

First, we add use `PrestaShop\PrestaShop\Core\Payment\PaymentOption;` to be able to create the `PaymentOption` instances to return to our `paymentOptions` hook.

Then, we define our `WHCashPayment` class by extending the `PaymentModule` object.

As we want our payment module to set the order to a new order state labeled `Awaiting cash payment` in English, we will have to create a new order state on module installation; then, we will store the new order state ID in a configuration variable named `WH_OS_CASH_VALIDATION`. We will set this configuration variable name in a constant named `CONFIG_OS_WHCASH`.

Then, we can create the standard skeleton of the module class by adding the `__construct()`, `install()`, (optional) `uninstall()`, `hookPaymentOptions($params)`, and `hookDisplayPaymentReturn($params)` methods.

The `install()` method registers the payment mandatory hooks, as seen before; then, we trigger a method named `installOrderState()`, which will be responsible for the order state creation.

Let's focus on provisioning the payment options.

Implementing the hookPaymentOptions($params) method

A nice implementation for the hookPaymentOptions(params) method could be the following:

```
public function hookPaymentOptions($params)
{
  if (!$this->active) {
    return;
  }

  if (!$this->checkCurrency($params['cart'])) {
    return;
  }

  $cart = $this->context->cart;
  $total = $this->context->getCurrentLocale()->formatPrice(
    $cart->getOrderTotal(true, Cart::BOTH),
    (new Currency($cart->id_currency))->iso_code
  );

  $taxLabel = '';
  if ($this->context->country->display_tax_label) {
    $taxLabel = $this->trans('(tax incl.)', [],
      'Modules.Whcashpayment.Admin');
  }

  $this->smarty->assign([
    'totalPrice' => $total,
    'taxLabel' => $taxLabel
  ]);

  $cashOfflineOption = new PaymentOption();
  $cashOfflineOption->setModuleName($this->name)
    ->setCallToActionText($this->trans('Pay by Cash', [],
      'Modules.Whcashpayment.Admin'))
    ->setAction($this->context->link->getModuleLink($this->
      name, 'validation', [], true))
    ->setAdditionalInformation($this->
      fetch('module:whcashpayment/views/templates/hook
      /payment_infos.tpl'));

  return [$cashOfflineOption];
}
```

In this implementation, we first check whether the module is active, and if not, we won't return any payment options. Then, we also need to check whether our module is enabled for the current cart currency. If not, we won't return any payment options. That can be easily done with the help of the following `checkCurrency($cart)` method inserted into our class:

```
private function checkCurrency($cart)
{
  $currency_order = new Currency((int) ($cart->
    id_currency));
  $currencies_module = $this->getCurrency((int) $cart->'
    id_currency);

  if (is_array($currencies_module)) {
    foreach ($currencies_module as $currency_module) {
      if ($currency_order->id ==
        $currency_module['id_currency']) {
        return true;
      }
    }
  }
  return false;
}
```

After these eligibility tests on the currency and the module activation, we assign to Smarty the necessary data such as `totalPrice` for the cart and `taxLabel` to add all the information to our `PaymentOption` instance, which will be returned as an array.

Finally, we store a new `PaymentOption` instance in the `$cashOfflineOption` variable. And we use the following methods to prepare our object:

- `setModuleName()`: This is used to set the name of the module responsible for this payment option.

- `setCallToAction()`: This is used to set the corresponding call-to-action text.

- `setAction()`: This is used to set the URL of the front controller responsible for the order validation handling. For us, it will be the front validation controller of our module.

- `setAdditionnalInformation()`: This is used to set the HTML view to display additional information.

Feel free to read the `/src/Core/Payment/PaymentOption.php` file to find all the possible setters to add additional information to our `PaymentOption`. Moreover, if you want to get all the possible types of payment options, please browse this URL: `https://devdocs.prestashop-project.org/8/modules/payment/#paymentoption-types`.

The Smarty view for the additional display information will be stored in the `/modules/whcashpayment/views/templates/hook/payment_infos.tpl` file filled with this code:

```
<section>
  <p>{l s='The cash transaction will be validated on delivery'
d='Modules.Whcashpayment.Shop'}</p>
  <p>{l s='Please prepare %s %s in cash'
sprintf=[$totalPrice,$taxLabel] d='Modules.Whcashpayment.Shop'}</p>
</section>
```

Finally, the `hookPaymentOptions(params)` method returns an array containing our `$cashOfflineOption` variable.

If you want, you can add all the payment options needed to this array. For us, the preceding code will be enough! Let's implement the `displayPaymentReturn` hook.

Implementing the hookDisplayPaymentReturn($params) method

As a reminder, this hook is responsible for displaying the necessary information to explain to the customer that the order has been confirmed, but it will be invoiced only on cash payment when the order is picked up at the physical store.

A good solution for the `hookDisplayPaymentReturn($params)` implementation could be the following:

```
public function hookDisplayPaymentReturn($params)
{
  if (!$this->active) {
    return;
  }

  $totalAmount = $params['order']->getOrdersTotalPaid();

  $this->smarty->assign([
    'totalAmount' => $this->context->getCurrentLocale()->
      formatPrice(
      $totalAmount,
      (new Currency($params['order']->id_currency))->
        iso_code
    ),
    'shop_name' => $this->context->shop->name,
    'reference' => $params['order']->reference,
  ]);
```

```
    return $this->
      fetch('module:whcashpayment/views/templates/hook/
    payment_return.tpl');
}
```

First, we check whether the module is still active, then compute the total amount, shop name, and order reference. We assign all those variables to Smarty and generate the corresponding HTML using the /modules/whcashpayment/views/templates/hook/payment_return.tpl template file. Its content could be the following code:

```
<p>{l s='Your order on %s is done and complete.' sprintf=[$shop_name]
d='Modules.Whcashpayment.Shop'}</p>
<p>{l s='The cash transaction will be validated coming to our physical
store. Please remind us the reference %s of your order on delivery'
sprintf=[$reference] d='Modules.Whcashpayment.Shop'}</p>
<p>{l s='Please prepare %s in cash' sprintf=[$totalAmount] d='Modules.
Whcashpayment.Shop'}</p>
```

All of this is simple and beneficial for the final customer, who will understand what to do after the confirmation.

Before diving into the creation of the validation module FO controller responsible for converting our cart into an order, we need to create the new order state labeled Awaiting cash payment that will be assigned to it.

Creating a new order status for orders pending cash payment

As seen before, we decided to create the installOrderState() method in order to create our new order state. Its implementation can be done as follows:

```
private function installOrderState()
{
  if (Configuration::getGlobalValue(WHCashPayment::CONFIG_OS_WHCASH))
{
    $orderState = new OrderState((int)
Configuration::getGlobalValue(WHCashPayment::CONFIG_OS_WHCASH));
    if (Validate::isLoadedObject($orderState) && $this->name ===
$orderState->module_name) {
      return true;
    }
  }
  return $this->createOrderState(
    static::CONFIG_OS_WHCASH,
    [
      'en' => 'Awaiting cash payment',
      'fr' => 'En attente de paiement en cash',
    ],
```

```
    '#E5C143'
  );
}
```

There, we check whether we already have an ID stored in the `WHCashPayment::CONFIG_OS_WHCASH` global configuration variable:

- If true: If the order state with the stored ID is valid and is linked to the current module, as the order state exists, we don't have anything to do

- If false: We use the `createOrderState()` method, which creates an order state, by using the localized `Awaiting cash payment` label and the `#E5C143` hexadecimal color in the BO

The `createOrderState()` method is defined like this:

```
private function createOrderState($configurationKey, array
$nameByLangIsoCode, $color, $isLogable = false, $isPaid = false,
$isInvoice = false, $isShipped = false, $isDelivery = false,
$isPdfDelivery = false, $isPdfInvoice = false, $isSendEmail = false,
$template = '', $isHidden = false, $isUnremovable = true, $isDeleted =
false) {
  $tabNameByLangId = [];
  //ToDo: fill the $tabNameByLangId array
  $orderState = new OrderState();
  $orderState->module_name = $this->name;
  $orderState->name = $tabNameByLangId;
  $orderState->color = $color;
  $orderState->logable = $isLogable;
  $orderState->paid = $isPaid;
  $orderState->invoice = $isInvoice;
  $orderState->shipped = $isShipped;
  $orderState->delivery = $isDelivery;
  $orderState->pdf_delivery = $isPdfDelivery;
  $orderState->pdf_invoice = $isPdfInvoice;
  $orderState->send_email = $isSendEmail;
  $orderState->hidden = $isHidden;
  $orderState->unremovable = $isUnremovable;
  $orderState->template = $template;
  $orderState->deleted = $isDeleted;
  $result = (bool) $orderState->add();

  if (false === $result) {
    $this->_errors[] = sprintf('Failed to create OrderState
      %s', $configurationKey);
    return false;
  }
  $result = (bool) Configuration::
```

```
        updateGlobalValue($configurationKey,
        (int) $orderState->id);
    if (false === $result) {
        $this->_errors[] = sprintf('Failed to save OrderState
            %s to Configuration', $configurationKey);
        return false;
    }
    //ToDo: setting the order state icon
    return true;
}
```

In this function, we instantiate an `OrderState` object and hydrate it with the provided arguments. Then we store the ID of the new `OrderState` object in the global configuration variable with the provided name.

We now miss two parts of the code; the first one is the creation of the `$tabNameByLangId` array with the names/labels of the order state to create. We can replace the `//ToDo: fill the $tabNameByLangId array` comment with the following code:

```
foreach ($nameByLangIsoCode as $langIsoCode => $name) {
    foreach (Language::getLanguages(false) as $language) {
        if (Tools::strtolower($language['iso_code']) === $langIsoCode) {
            $tabNameByLangId[(int) $language['id_lang']] = $name;
        } elseif (isset($nameByLangIsoCode['en'])) {
            $tabNameByLangId[(int) $language['id_lang']] =
            $nameByLangIsoCode['en'];
        }
    }
}
```

Then we omit the code copying the icon of the order state to create the corresponding folder. For this, we can replace the `//ToDo: setting the order state icon` comment with the following code:

```
    $orderStateImgPath = $this->getLocalPath() . 'views/img/orderstate/'
    . $configurationKey . '.gif';

    if (false === (bool)Tools::file_exists_cache($orderStateImgPath)) {
        $this->_errors[] = sprintf(
            'Failed to find icon file of OrderState %s',
            $configurationKey
        );
        return false;
    }

    if (false === (bool) Tools::copy($orderStateImgPath, _PS_ORDER_
```

```
STATE_IMG_DIR_ . $orderState->id . '.gif')) {
    $this->_errors[] = sprintf(
      'Failed to copy icon of OrderState %s',
      $configurationKey
    );
    return false;
}
```

In this code, we check whether the icon file exists, and if true, we copy the file to the order states folder of PrestaShop by naming it with the ID of the new order state. As you may have understood, the icon file has to be added to the module via the /modules/whcashpayment/views/img/orderstate/WH_OS_CASH_VALIDATION.gif file.

All this code enables handling the mandatory behaviors of the Payment module. The only thing we need is to create the payment validation FO controller called by our module payment option form if it is selected.

Creating the payment validation controller

The payment validation controller is set as the action target URL of our module payment option by using this code:

```
$cashOfflineOption->setAction($this->context->link-
>getModuleLink($this->name, 'validation', [], true))
```

We can now implement this validation controller responsible for creating a new order from the cart. As we already have seen how to create a module front controller, we can create the /modules/whcashpayment/controllers/front/validation.php file containing the WHCashPaymentValidationModuleFrontController class.

It can be implemented with the following code:

```php
<?php
class WHCashPaymentValidationModuleFrontController extends
ModuleFrontController
{
  public function postProcess()
  {
    if (!($this->module instanceof WHCashPayment)) {
      Tools::redirect('index.php?controller=order&step=1');
      return;
    }
    $cart = $this->context->cart;

    if ($cart->id_customer == 0 || $cart->id_address_delivery == 0 ||
      $cart->id_address_invoice == 0 || !$this->module->active) {
```

```
    Tools::redirect('index.php?controller=order&step=1');
    return;
}

$authorized = false;
foreach (Module::getPaymentModules() as $module) {
  if ($module['name'] == 'whcashpayment') {
    $authorized = true;
    break;
  }
}
if (!$authorized) {
  exit($this->trans('This payment method is not available.', [],
 'Modules.Whcashpayment.Shop'));
}

$customer = new Customer($cart->id_customer);
if (!Validate::isLoadedObject($customer)) {
  Tools::redirect('index.php?controller=order&step=1');
  return;
}

$currency = $this->context->currency;
$total = (float) $cart->getOrderTotal(true, Cart::BOTH);

$mailVars = [];
$order_status_id = (int)
Configuration::getGlobalValue(WHCashPayment::CONFIG_OS_WHCASH);

$this->module->validateOrder((int)$cart->id, $order_status_id,
$total, $this->module->displayName, null, $mailVars,
(int)$currency->id, false, $customer->secure_key);
Tools::redirect('index.php?controller=order-confirmation&id_cart='
. (int) $cart->id . '&id_module=' . (int) $this->module->id
. '&id_order=' . $this->module->currentOrder . '&key='
. $customer->secure_key);
  }
}
```

In this simple FO controller, we make some checks on the module name, the mandatory cart information, and the availability of the current payment module.

If all the conditions are checked, we retrieve the ID for the `Awaiting cash payment` order state and create an order from the current cart with the help of the `validateOrder()` method.

Finally, it redirects to the order confirmation FO controller.

Our controller is now fully complete. We can test it and check whether everything works.

Testing our module

To test our newly created module we can apply these steps:

1. We can now install our module via the BO modules manager controller.

2. Then, we can add products to our cart on the FO of PrestaShop.

3. Then, we can go to the checkout page. There, we can check in the payment options whether our Cash Payment module is available and displays the **Pay by Cash** option.

4. By choosing it, we can check whether the confirmation page displays the appropriate information.

5. Then, we can check whether the order was created with the `Awaiting cash payment` order state.

Summary

In this chapter, we discovered what makes the `PaymentModule` child modules so special with the necessary registration of the `paymentOptions` and `displayPaymentReturn` hooks and their implementation. We also found out how to create a new `OrderState` for our orders. Then, we saw how to create a validation controller to convert our cart into a new order.

Now that we have mastered Payment modules, we will discover another main module type with the creation of a Shipping module.

13
A Drive Delivery Module

Now that we know most of what we need to create standard and payment modules, we must discover how to add a delivery option to PrestaShop programmatically. Here, we will learn how to create a drive delivery module that displays a list of relay points where we can pick up our order, even though anyone can add a carrier with the **Back Office** (**BO**) controller responsible for transport management. It will be a great occasion to demonstrate how to create a carrier, handle the delivery price computation, and save and display the chosen relay delivery point for an order.

In creating this module, we will go through the following steps:

- Defining our module design
- Defining a PrestaShop `Carrier` module
- Creating our module structure
- Creating a `WHRelayCart` entity to save our chosen relay points
- Creating a Carrier programmatically
- Displaying the relay pickup points list during the checkout
- Handling a relay pickup point choice via an Ajax **Front Office** (**FO**) controller
- Displaying the pickup point on the order view BO controller
- Creating a Widget to promote our module anywhere on the FO
- Testing our module

By the end of this chapter, we will know how to create a full custom shipping module by showing a new delivery option during the checkout shipping method step. Moreover, you will know how to add a drive delivery pickup points list and how to create a widget for your FO pages.

Technical requirements

You will need the following elements to create this `Carrier` module:

- Any PHP editor to code your module

- An (s)FTP client to browse your module files and folders (only if you work on a remote server, not necessary if you work on a local server)

- A web browser to install and test your module

- A working PrestaShop installation (v1.7.x minimum)

- A downloaded version of our module is available in the GitHub repository of this book, available at this URL: `https://github.com/PacktPublishing/Practical-Module-Development-for-Prestashop-8/tree/main/Chapter%2013/whrelaycarrier`

Defining our module design

Our drive delivery module will programmatically add a new carrier named `Relay Carrier` available for any order on our website. On the checkout page, the `Carrier` module will be displayed in the shipping options this way:

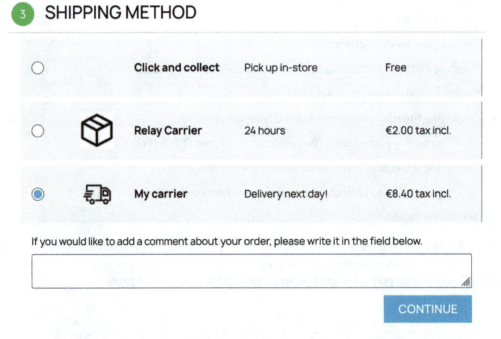

Figure 13.1 – The shipping option

When we select our drive relay delivery option, we should get a list of available relay points from where to pick up our order. You should be able to choose one. If no point is selected, the next steps of the order won't be available (we will hide the validation button to go to the payment step). The modal for choosing our point should look like this:

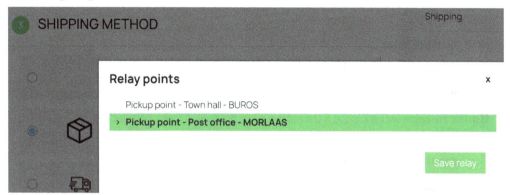

Figure 13.2 – The Relay points modal

The module will add €2 to the computed shipping price if this `Carrier` module is used to complete this order. We should be able to see the chosen pickup relay point in the order details BO view in a new panel like this:

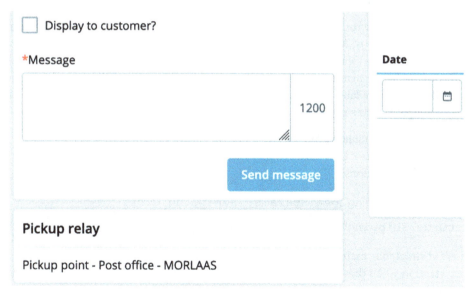

Figure 13.3 – The pickup relay point panel in the BO order view controller

Then, the module needs to display a widget available anywhere on the website to promote the number of relay pickup points.

Now that we know our targets, we will follow our usual checklist necessary for our module creation:

- **Display name**: Drive relay delivery carrier
- **Technical name**: `whrelaycarrier`
- **Tab**: `shipping_logistics`
- **need_instance value**: 0
- **Description text**: `This module displays a new carrier.`
- **Uninstall confirmation text**: `Do you still want to uninstall this module?`
- **Hooks to register**: `actionCarrierUpdate`, `displayAfterCarrier`, `displayAdminOrderSideBottom`, and `actionFrontControllerSetMedia`
- **Configuration page needed**: No

We now have enough information to start creating our module. First, we will present what makes a `Carrier` module so special.

Defining a PrestaShop Carrier module

We will see what a `Carrier` module is in the same way that we previously defined what a `payment` module was. What's the difference between a `Carrier` module and a Carrier?

In fact, `Carrier` is the `ObjectModel` representing a shipping option for your shop. We can have 0 to N available `Carriers`. A `Carrier` will be available depending on the cart weight or price and on the delivery address location. Customer `Group` restrictions can also exist. A Carrier module is a module responsible for managing the availability or price of a corresponding linked `Carrier`; it adds capacity to it. It's available as the upper layer of a `Carrier`. Be aware that a Carrier module can manage multiple `Carriers`.

Concretely, a `Carrier` module is a module extending the `CarrierModule` class. If you review the `/classes/module/CarrierModule.php` file, you will see that it is a child class of `Module`, defining two abstract functions:

- `getOrderShippingCost($params, $shipping_cost)`
- `getOrderShippingCostExternal($params)`

As these are abstract, our main module class will have to implement them. We will see after our `Carrier` creation when these functions will be triggered depending on the chosen `Carrier` configuration for the current cart.

Before getting deeper into this notion, which requires a practical example in order to be understood, let's create the module structure necessary to have an efficient workflow.

Creating our module structure

As we are now well acquainted with creating modules, I'll let you create the /modules/ whrelaycarrier/ folder with the necessary files.

Our /modules/whrelaycarrier/whrelaycarrier.php main module class should look like this, following our module design:

```
class WHRelayCarrier extends CarrierModule
{
  private $relays = [['id_relay'=>1,'name'=>'Pickup point -
  Town hall - BUROS'],['id_relay'=>2,'name'=>'Pickup point
  - Post office - MORLAAS']];

  public function __construct()
  {
    $this->name = 'whrelaycarrier';
    $this->tab = 'shipping_logistics';
    $this->version = '1.0.0';
    $this->author = 'Web Helpers';
    $this->need_instance = 0;
    $this->ps_versions_compliancy = [
      'min' => '1.7.0',
      'max' => '8.99.99',
    ];
    $this->bootstrap = true;

    parent::__construct();

    $this->confirmUninstall = $this->l('Do you still you
    want to uninstall this module?');
    $this->description = $this->l('This module displays a
    new carrier');
    $this->displayName = $this->l('Drive relay delivery
    carrier');
  }

  public function install()
  {
    return parent::install()
      && $this->createTable()
      && $this->installCarrier()
      && $this->registerHook('actionCarrierUpdate')
      && $this->registerHook('displayAfterCarrier')
      && $this->registerHook('displayAdminOrderSideBottom')
      && $this->registerHook(
```

```
                'actionFrontControllerSetMedia');
        }
    }
```

First, we define the list of available pickup relay points in the `$relays` variable. It is an array of associative arrays. Each point is composed of the `id_relay` and `name` keys. We can add as many as we need. As you might expect, it can also be fetched from an external API directly in the constructor method.

Then let's study the `install()` function. It calls the following functions:

- `createTable()` is responsible, as usual, for creating the table and storing the `Carrier` id and `id_reference` in the `Configuration` variables

- `installCarrier()` creates the `Carrier` option corresponding to our drive delivery solution

- Hook registrations for the `actionCarrierUpdate`, `displayAfterCarrier`, `displayAdminOrderSideBottom`, and `actionFrontControllerSetMedia` hooks

Before defining the `createTable()` function, let's define which entities we need to create our module.

Creating a WHRelayCart entity to save our chosen relay points

We saw in a previous section that we decided to store the relay points data directly in the module's code. Even if it could have been stored in the database, it is much simpler to explain the other concepts of this module without putting too many entities inside it.

Let's focus on how to store the relay point corresponding to each cart/order. The best way to do it is by creating a new `Doctrine` entity named `WHRelayCart` made of three columns:

- `id_relay_cart` (index)

- `id_cart`

- `id_relay`

This will enable us to do the matching.

This entity can be created directly in the `/modules/whrelaycarrier/src/Entity/WHRelayCart.php` file containing the following code:

```php
<?php
namespace WebHelpers\WHRelayCarrier\Entity;
use Doctrine\ORM\Mapping as ORM;

/**
 * @ORM\Table(name="ps_whrelaycarrier_relay_cart")
```

```
 * @ORM\Entity(repositoryClass="WebHelpers\WHRelayCarrier\Repository\
WHRelayCartRepository")
 */
class WHRelayCart
{
  /**
   * @var int
   *
   * @ORM\Id
   * @ORM\Column(name="id_relay_cart", type="integer")
   * @ORM\GeneratedValue(strategy="AUTO")
   */
  private $id;

  /**
   * @var int
   *
   * @ORM\Column(name="id_relay", type="integer")
   */
  private $relay;

  /**
   * @var int
   *
   * @ORM\Column(name="id_cart", type="integer")
   */
  private $cart;

  /* ...Please find the getters and setter in the GitHub repository of
  this book... */
}
```

As you already know how to create the corresponding repository, you can create the `/modules/whrelaycarrier/src/Repository/WHRelayCartRepository.php` file and the `config/services.yml` files necessary for the following services calls if needed. Feel free to get them directly from the GitHub repository of this book.

You should also make sure that `composer.json` is available at the root of the module and that the `composer dumpautoload` command is executed in your **command-line interface** (CLI).

The resulting `createTable()` method of our main module class should finally contain the following necessary code to create the table in our database:

```
private function createTable()
{
  return Db::getInstance()->execute('
```

```
    CREATE TABLE IF NOT EXISTS `' . _DB_PREFIX_ .
  'whrelaycarrier_relay_cart` (
      `id_relay_cart` int(6) NOT NULL AUTO_INCREMENT,
      `id_relay` int(6) NOT NULL,
      `id_cart` int(6) NOT NULL,
      PRIMARY KEY(`id_relay_cart`)
  ) ENGINE=' . _MYSQL_ENGINE_ . ' default CHARSET=utf8');
}
```

As we should clean our table on uninstallation, we should add the following code to our main module class to clean the created table:

```
private function dropTable()
{
  Db::getInstance()->execute('DROP TABLE IF EXISTS ' .
  _DB_PREFIX_ . 'whrelaycarrier_relay_cart');
}
```

We will see later in the next section of this chapter how the preceding function is triggered by the uninstall() function.

Now that we have managed our data structure, let's see how to create Carrier programmatically to make our module directly install its linked Carrier.

Creating a Carrier programmatically

As seen in the previous sections, even if our Carrier module could simply manage an existing Carrier (created manually via the BO), we prefer to create our Carrier programmatically directly on install() via an installCarrier() method. It will enable us to have everything available.

Let's do it directly by explaining the following code of our installCarrier():

```
public function installCarrier()
{
  $carrier = new Carrier();
  $carrier->name = "Relay Carrier";
  $carrier->url = "https://www.domainname.ext/follow/@";
  $carrier->delay[Configuration::get('PS_LANG_DEFAULT')] =
    "24 hours";
  $carrier->is_free = false;
  $carrier->active = true;
  $carrier->deleted = false;
  $carrier->shipping_handling = false;
  //Highest defined range if false, true to disable
  $carrier->range_behavior = false;
```

```
$carrier->is_module = true;
//Computed by the module
$carrier->shipping_external = true;
$carrier->external_module_name = $this->name;
//Is it custom or range based?
$carrier->need_range = true;
$carrier->max_width = 0;
$carrier->max_height = 0;
$carrier->max_depth = 0;
$carrier->max_weight = 0;
//0 for longest, 9 for fastest
$carrier->grade = 8;
if ($carrier->add()) {
  $carrier->setGroups(Group::getAllGroupIds());
  Available from v.8.0 of PS
  /* --- For PS v1.7 only ---
  $groupsIds=[];
  foreach(Group::getGroups($this->context->language->id)
    as $group)
  {
    $groupsIds[]= $group['id_group'];
  }
  $carrier->setGroups($groupIds);
  --- For v1.7 only ---*/

  $rangeWeight = new RangeWeight();
  $rangeWeight->id_carrier = $carrier->id;
  $rangeWeight->delimiter1 = '0';
  $rangeWeight->delimiter2 = '1000000';
  $rangeWeight->add();

  $zones = Zone::getZones(true);
  foreach ($zones as $z) {
    $carrier->addZone((int) $z['id_zone']);
  }

  copy(dirname(__FILE__) . '/views/img/parcel.jpg',
    _PS_SHIP_IMG_DIR_ . '/' . (int) $carrier->id .
    '.jpg'); //assign carrier logo

  Configuration::updateValue('WHRELAYCARRIER_ID',
    $carrier->id);
  Configuration::updateValue('WHRELAYCARRIER_ID_REFERENCE
    ', $carrier->id);
```

```
    }
    return true;
}
```

In this code, we store a new instance of the `Carrier ObjectModel` in the `$carrier` variable. Then, we set the necessary parameters. Many of them are obvious; that's why we will only talk about the most important and/or most difficult to understand:

- `range_behavior`: This determines how the shipping cost is computed if the cart's total price or weight is out of the defined range:

  - If `true`, `Carrier` won't be available as the total weight/price is out of range

  - If `false`, the price of the highest range will be used instead

- `is_module`: This defines whether the carrier is linked to a module responsible for managing it.

- `shipping_external`: This defines whether the shipping costs are computed with the help of the module or only by the ranged price definitions.

- `external_module_name`: This sets the linked `Carrier` module name to link `Carrier` with the module.

- `need_range`: This defines whether the shipping cost for this `Carrier` must be computed with the weight/price ranges or without them:

  - If `false`, the linked shipping price will be returned by the `getOrderShippingCostExternal($params)` function of the main module class

  - If `true`, it will be computed by the `getOrderShippingCost($params, $shipping_cost)` function of the main module class

When `Carrier` is saved with the `add()` method, we define a simple `RangeWeight` to link it to `Carrier`. This range is defined between zero and one million kilograms (depending on your shop settings) to €0 (by default) for each available geographical zone.

Finally, we copy the icon of our carrier stored in the `/modules/whrelaycarrier/views/img/parcel.jpg` file to the standard shipping icon (45 **pixels (px)** by 45 **px**) location in the `/img/s/` folder with the name equal to the ID of the freshly created `Carrier`.

Then, we store the ID of the `Carrier` in the `WHRELAYCARRIER_ID` configuration variable and its reference in the `WHRELAYCARRIER_ID_REFERENCE` configuration variable.

> **Why store the ID of the Carrier and its reference?**
>
> As you may know, in PrestaShop, when a `Carrier` is edited or deleted, we keep all the information about it to make it possible to view old orders depending on old carriers. Practically, after the edition of a `Carrier`, its first instance is duplicated in the database by keeping the same `id_reference` but incrementing `id_carrier` and changing the other updated parameters. In our module, we will sometimes need to store the ID of the corresponding carrier in order to add JavaScript behaviors to the checkout page based on some classes using it.

This is now the best moment to define the shipping cost policy for our module. As we defined `$carrier->need_range` as `true` for our `Carrier`, we will implement our abstract functions responsible for it this way:

```
public function getOrderShippingCost($params, $shipping_cost)
{
    return $shipping_cost+2;
}
public function getOrderShippingCostExternal($params)
{
    return 2;
}
```

The only called function is `getOrderShippingCost()`. We will add €2 to the range-defined price corresponding to our cart weight. As it is always equal to zero initially for us in our range's definition, we will have a shipping cost always equal to €2.

Please note that if you add a definition of a `getPackageShippingCost($params, $shippingCost, $products)` method to our main module class, this method will be called instead. It enables you to compute the shipping costs by making selections based on the products array list provided as an argument. For example, we can add a different cost depending on the presence of a certain type of product in the cart.

We define the second `getOrderShippingCostExternal()` function, but it should never be called in our particular case.

As the `actionCarrierUpdate` hook is triggered on any carrier update, we need to use it to update our configuration variables by adding this code:

```
public function hookActionCarrierUpdate($params)
{
    if ($params['carrier']->id_reference ==
      Configuration::get('WHRELAYCARRIER_ID_REFERENCE')) {
      Configuration::updateValue('WHRELAYCARRIER_ID',
        $params['carrier']->id);
    }
}
```

This is also now the moment to define our `uninstall()` function, which takes care of cleaning our `Carrier` and dropping the created table:

```
public function uninstall()
{
  $id_carrier = Configuration::get('WHRELAYCARRIER_ID');
  $carrier = new Carrier($id_carrier);
  $carrier->delete();
  $this->dropTable();
  Configuration::deleteByName('WHRELAYCARRIER_ID');
  return parent::uninstall();
}
```

Now that we have created our `Carrier` and its shipping cost computation, if we leave it like this, the shipping option will be displayed in the shipping methods on the checkout page. But no pickup relay point will be displayed yet. Let's now display the relay pickup points on the checkout page.

Displaying the relay pickup points list during the checkout

As our module's aim is to make it possible for customers to choose a relay pickup point, we will use the `displayAfterCarrier` hook to create a modal `DIV` containing our relay points list on the checkout page, ready to show or hide whether our Carrier has been chosen or not.

The `hookDisplayAfterCarrier($params)` method uses this code:

```
public function hookDisplayAfterCarrier($params)
{
  $this->smarty->assign([
    'relays'=>$this->relays,
  ]);

  $relayCart = $this->findCheckoutRelayFromCart();
  if(!is_null($relayCart)){
    $this->smarty->assign([
      'id_relay_checked' => $relayCart->getRelay(),
    ]);
  }

  return $this->fetch(
    'module:whrelaycarrier/views/templates/hook
    /displayAfterCarrier.tpl');
}
```

It assigns the relays list to the view, retrieves any row containing the current `id_cart` for the `WHRelayCart` entity, and assigns the corresponding `id_relay` to the `id_relay_checked` Smarty variable if it exists.

The `findCheckoutRelayFromCart()` method can be coded this way:

```
private function findCheckoutRelayFromCart()
{
    $relayCartRepository = $this->get(
      'webhelpers.whrelaycarrier.repository
      .whrelaycart_repository');
    $id_cart = $this->context->cart->id;
    return $relayCartRepository
      ->findOneBy(['cart'=>$id_cart]);
}
```

It simply does the data retrieval business via `Doctrine`, nothing special there.

Let's continue by creating the `/modules/whrelaycarrier/views/templates/hook/displayAfterCarrier.tpl` template file this way:

```
<div id="whrelaycarrier_points">
  <div>
    <span>x</span>
    <h2>{l s="Relay points" d="Modules.Whrelaycarrier.Shop"}</h2>
    <ul>
    {foreach from=$relays item=relay}
      <li data-id-relay="{$relay["id_relay"]}" {if
      !empty($id_relay_checked) && $id_relay_checked ==
      $relay["id_relay"]}class="active"{
      /if}>{$relay["name"]}</li>
    {/foreach}
    </ul>
    <a id="whrelaycarrier_submit" class="btn
      btn-success">{l s="Save relay"
      d="Modules.Whrelaycarrier.Shop"}</a>
  </div>
</div>
```

This is a really simple modal `DIV` with a loop displaying all the relay points.

We then need to add CSS and JavaScript to manage the appearance and behavior of our modal box. As this book is not about CSS or JavaScript, we won't talk too much about assets.

Let's embed the CSS and JS files via the following hookActionFrontControllerSetMedia($params) definition:

```php
public function hookActionFrontControllerSetMedia($params)
{
  if($this->context->controller->page_name=="checkout")
  {
    $this->context->controller->registerStylesheet(
      'whrelaycarrier-style',
      $this->_path.'views/css/checkout.css',
      [
        'media' => 'all',
        'priority' => 999,
      ]
    );

    $this->context->controller->registerJavascript(
      'whrelaycarrier-checkout',
      $this->_path.'views/js/checkout.js',
      [
        'priority' => 999,
        'attribute' => 'async',
        'version' => '1.0'
      ]
    );

    $relayCart = $this->findCheckoutRelayFromCart();
    $id_relay = 0;
    if(!is_null($relayCart)){
      $id_relay = $relayCart->getRelay();
    }

    Media::addJsDef([
      'ajaxUrl' => $this->context->link->
        getModuleLink($this->name, 'ajax', ['ajax'=>true]),
      'id_cart' => $this->context->cart->id,
      'id_relay' => $id_relay,
      'id_carrier' =>
        Configuration::get('WHRELAYCARRIER_ID'),
    ]);
  }
}
```

There, we use the `registerStylesheet()` and `registerJavascript()` calls to embed the assets, then we retrieve the already registered matchings for the current `id_cart`, and use `Media::addJsDef()` to define the JavaScript global variables to pass data from the module to the JavaScript files:

- `ajaxUrl`: This contains the URL of the legacy FO controller that we will create later to handle Ajax calls to store the chosen relay pickup point
- `id_cart`: This contains the current cart ID
- `id_relay`: This contains the previously chosen `id_relay` if a relay has already been chosen before this visit
- `id_carrier`: This contains the current ID of our drive relay delivery module

For more information, the possible definitions for the `/modules/whrelaycarrier/views/css/checkout.css` and `/modules/whrelaycarrier/views/js/checkout.js` files can be found in the GitHub repository of this book. Feel free to adapt them to your theme!

As an Ajax call will be triggered by any relay point click, let's see how we can create a legacy FO controller acting in Ajax mode.

Handling a relay pickup point choice via an Ajax FO controller

Let's create a legacy controller in the `/modules/whrelaycarrier/controllers/front/ajax.php` file responsible for handling the Ajax calls to store matches between the current cart and the chosen pickup relay point. This will be the occasion for us to see how to use a FO controller as an Ajax handler. The definition for this class is as follows:

```php
<?php

use WebHelpers\WHRelayCarrier\Entity\WHRelayCart;

class WHRelayCarrierAjaxModuleFrontController extends
ModuleFrontController
{
  public function displayAjax()
  {
    $entityManager = $this->get(
      'doctrine.orm.entity_manager');
    $relayCartRepository = $this->get(
      'webhelpers.whrelaycarrier.repository
      .whrelaycart_repository');
```

```
$cart = Tools::getValue('cart');
$relay = Tools::getValue('relay');

if($relay==0){
  $relayCarts = $relayCartRepository->
    findBy(['cart'=>$cart]);
  foreach($relayCarts as $relayCart)
  {
    $entityManager->remove($relayCart);
  }
}else{
  $relayCart = $relayCartRepository->
    findOneBy(['cart'=>$cart]);
  $edition_mode = false;
  if(is_null($relayCart)){
    $relayCart = new WHRelayCart();
  }else{
    $edition_mode = true;
  }

  $relayCart->setRelay($relay);
  $relayCart->setCart($cart);

  if(!$edition_mode){
    $entityManager->persist($relayCart);
  }
}
$entityManager->flush();

$this->ajaxRender(json_encode(['return_code'=>'OK']));
  }
}
```

In this controller, we override the displayAjax() function responsible for handling the calls to the FO controller with the ajax GET variable equal to true. It simply updates the row with the id_cart equal to the current cart if it exists, or it inserts it via Doctrine. Then, it returns a JSON array using the ajaxRender($json) function.

Once this data storage is handled, everything is functional in our module. Our customers can validate their orders, and we have the necessary data to be able to display our pickup relay point in the BO order view pages.

Displaying the pickup point on the order view BO controller

Even if everything is done on the FO side, we need to make sure that the online seller can retrieve its data on the BO order view page to administrate the order and to make sure to dispatch the order's products to the corresponding pickup relay point.

This can easily be done with the help of the displayAdminOrderSideBottom hook. It enables you to add data to the left-hand column of the order view page in the BO.

The hookdisplayAdminOrderSideBottom($params) function can be implemented in the main module class with the following code:

```
private function findRelayNameById($id_relay)
{
  foreach($this->relays as $relay)
  {
    if($relay['id_relay']==$id_relay)
    {
      return $relay['name'];
    }
  }
  return false;
}

public function hookdisplayAdminOrderSideBottom($params)
{
  $order = new Order((int)$params['id_order']);
  if(!is_null($order) && !is_null($order->id_cart))
  {
    $entityManager = $this->
      get('doctrine.orm.entity_manager');
    $relayCartRepository = $this->
      get('webhelpers.whrelaycarrier.repository
      .whrelaycart_repository');
    $relayCart = $relayCartRepository->
      findOneBy(['cart'=>$order->id_cart]);
    if(!is_null($relayCart)){
      $this->smarty->assign([
        'relayName' => $this->
          findRelayNameById((int)$relayCart->getRelay())
      ]);
      return $this->fetch('module:
        whrelaycarrier/views/templates/hook/
        displayAdminOrderSideBottom.tpl');
```

```
        }else{
          return false;
        }
     }
  }
}
```

There, we retrieve the `id_order` of the order shown on the BO page and instantiate the `Order` object with the corresponding `id_order`. As an order contains the `id_cart` used before its creation, we retrieve it and use Doctrine to find the matching row containing the `id_cart` and the `id_relay` for the current order.

Once we have the `id_relay` for the corresponding `id_cart`, we assign the relay data to the /modules/ `whrelaycarrier/views/templates/hook/displayAdminOrderSideBottom.tpl` file. Its definition is simple, as seen here:

```
<div class="card mt-2" data-role="message-card">
  <div class="card-header">
    <div class="row">
      <div class="col-md-6">
        <h3 class="card-header-title">
          Pickup relay
        </h3>
      </div>
    </div>
  </div>
  <div class="card-body d-print-none">
    {if !empty($relayName)}
      {$relayName}
    {/if}
  </div>
</div>
```

With this, every order using `Carrier` shows the necessary information about the chosen relay point.

Finally, as we want our module to be able to promote the number of available relay points on the FO pages, instead of using hooks to display data on the FO, we will use a Widget.

Creating a Widget to promote our module anywhere on the FO

First, let's define what a widget is. From version 1.7 of PrestaShop, the new concept of widgets appeared. Any module can implement a widget interface by adding `use PrestaShop\PrestaShop\Core\ Module\WidgetInterface;` to its main module class and using `class ModuleClassName extends Module implements WidgetInterface` for the main module class definition.

Following this interface, we have to implement the two following functions:

```
public function renderWidget($hookName, array $configuration);
public function getWidgetVariables($hookName, array $configuration);
```

If we don't declare any `hookNameOfTheHook($params)` functions in our module, the `renderWidget()` function will be triggered by the hook's name provided via the `$hookName` argument. The `$configuration` argument will contain the params of the hook trigger.

The `getWidgetVariables()` function will be used to compute the data to assign to the template. It will have to be called in the assign call, usually done in the `renderWidget()` definition.

That all happens if a hook is called without any hook behavior definition available. But there is another way of using widgets on the front.

You can call a widget from anywhere in the FO templates by using this code in a Smarty template:

```
{widget name='mymodule' my_param_key='my_param_value'}.
```

This enables you to call it from anywhere without creating a custom hook. It renders the output of the `renderWidget()` function, as explained before with the hooks use case.

Let's apply it to our module by adding the definition of these two functions to comply with the interface:

```
public function renderWidget($hookName, array $configuration)
{
  $this->smarty->assign($this->
    getWidgetVariables($hookName, $configuration));
  return $this->fetch(
    'module:whrelaycarrier/views/templates
    /widget/whrelaycarrier.tpl');
}

public function getWidgetVariables($hookName , array $configuration)
{
  return [
    'numberRelays' => count($this->relays),
  ];
}
```

Then, we must create the `/modules/whrelaycarrier/views/templates/widget/whrelaycarrier.tpl` file containing the following code:

```
<div class="card-block">
  {l s="Pickup your order directly in one of our %s pickup relays"
  sprintf=[$numberRelays] d="Modules.Whrelaycarrier.Shop"}
</div>
```

That can be a quick and efficient way of displaying data anywhere on the BO.

Then, we can add `{widget name='whrelaycarrier'}` from anywhere in the theme to promote the number of relay pickup points available. Even if we only have two now, we can improve it by adding many relay points!

Let's now test our module.

Testing our module

Let's do the following actions to test our freshly created module:

1. We can now install our module via the BO modules manager controller.
2. Then, we can add products to our cart on the FO of PrestaShop
3. We can go to the checkout page. We can check the shipping method options and whether our `Relay carrier` module is available and displays the relay pickup points list when clicked on.
4. By choosing a pickup relay point, we can check in the BO order view when the order is confirmed whether the pickup point details are available.
5. We can add the widget to any FO smarty template and see whether it displays the relay pickup point promotion as planned.

Summary

In this chapter, we discovered what `Carrier` modules are and how to create an efficient drive relay delivery module. We saw how to create `Carriers` programmatically, how to add a modal box for choosing relay points on the checkout page, and how to display the choices on the BO order view pages. Finally, we learned how to use Widgets.

Now that we know most of what modules can do and how to create them, we can jump into the theming tasks such as the creation of a child theme to customize an existing theme without having to recode everything and benefit from any published updates.

Part 3 – Customizing Your Theme

In this last part, we will discover how to extend an existing theme by creating a child theme so as to make your e-commerce store look just like you need, from templating to assets management. Then, we will learn how to adapt module templates and assets to a specified theme so as to make it fit with the graphical context. Finally, we will discover the use of the Webpack bundler to simplify asset compiling.

This part has the following chapters:

- *Chapter 14, How to Create a Child Theme*
- *Chapter 15, Overriding Some Templates*
- *Chapter 16, Assets Compiling with Webpack*

14
How to Create a Child Theme

As online sellers or as e-commerce developers/maintainers, we sometimes need to buy themes from a marketplace, or we are simply provided with an existing theme for the website we are working on. Very often, we need to modify the theme template structure or some assets. A simple way to solve this would be to find the template responsible for what we have to modify and to change the code directly to obtain what we need. But this is not a best practice!

Indeed, our theme change would be completely overwritten by patch updates. We shouldn't act directly on a theme that is not ours; think about what would happen if no backups of the original theme were executed. The solution to this need for theme customization is the creation of child themes.

Let's learn how to create child themes by following these steps:

- Discovering what a child theme is
- Creating a child theme structure
- Installing and testing our child theme example

By the end of this chapter, we will understand what a child theme is, and how to create one.

Technical requirements

You will need the following elements to create our example child theme:

- Any PHP editor to code your child theme
- An (S)FTP client to browse your files and folders (only if you work on a remote server; it is not necessary if you work on a local server)
- A web browser to install and test our child theme
- A working PrestaShop installation (v1.7.x minimum) with the classic theme installed
- Access to the GitHub repository for this book to download the source code of our child theme example, available here: `https://github.com/PacktPublishing/Practical-Module-Development-for-Prestashop-8/tree/main/Chapter%2014`

Discovering what a child theme is

Working as a PrestaShop developer, you are likely to get some customers requesting things such as customizing an FO template structure, changing colors, CSS styles, or JavaScript scripts.

Some of your customers will have PrestaShop websites already working with an existing theme. Even if it would be quicker to locate the code responsible for what we need to change in the original theme and make our modifications to get the requested result, it is not recommended to change anything directly in a theme that is not ours.

First, it is dangerous to change something in an existing theme as, sometimes, it is not well backed up. Then, we don't really know the impact on a template or an asset change in terms of dependencies. Moreover, if our customer comes back to us by requesting to install the latest updates of their original theme, it will completely erase our previous changes. We will need to check all the modified files to merge our work with the new templates.

The best method for our customer's needs is to create another theme that will extend the original one. This theme will be called a **child theme**, exactly like we can create a child class in PHP by extending an existing one. This theme will be able to override or extend some parent templates. It will enable us to apply targeted changes without having to recode everything, and we won't change anything physically on the existing theme files.

> **This will ring a bell to WordPress developers!**
> If you also are a WordPress developer, you may have heard about child themes. That's good for you because it is exactly the same as doing a theme extension.

Let's follow our trip through theme customization by creating our first child theme.

Creating a child theme structure

Let's create our first child theme by following the present recipe:

1. The first thing before creating a child theme is to make sure that we have the technical name (folder name) of the original theme we want to use. As a practical example, we will work on the classic theme located in the `/themes/classic/` folder. Its technical name is `classic`. We will create a child theme of the `classic` theme, which we decided to name `childclassicwh`. So, let's create the `/themes/childclassicwh/` folder to store our child theme files.

2. The only mandatory files needed are the `/themes/childclassicwh/config/theme.yml` file to define the metadata necessary to describe our child theme, and the `/themes/childclassicwh/preview.png` file containing the thumb displayed on the theme's installation and settings BO pages.

3. Let's focus on the `/themes/childclassicwh/config/theme.yml` file first and see how to create it. Its mandatory properties will be the following ones:

   - `parent`: This is the technical name (folder name) of the parent theme

   - `name`: This is the technical name of our child theme

   - `display_name`: This is the name displayed on the **Design** | **Theme & Logo** BO page

   - `version`: This is the version number

4. Then, you can use all the optional properties that you can already put in the `config/theme.yml` file of a standard theme. Our child theme config file can be coded this way:

```
parent: classic
name: childclassicwh
display_name: Classic child theme WebHelpers
version: 1.0.0
author:
  name: "Web Helpers"
  email: louis@web-helpers.io
  url: https://www.web-helpers.io
assets:
  use_parent_assets: true
```

As you can see, it contains the mandatory parameters and the author subfields to present the creator's metadata.

You may have noticed that we added the `assets` field containing `use_parent_assets: true`. This enables us to reuse all the existing included assets from the parent theme.

From now, we can override any template file from the parent theme by adding the exact same folder structure and name from the theme root folder. We can do that too with the assets files (CSS and JS).

For example, if we want to override the original `/themes/classic/templates/index.tpl` file from the classic theme, we just have to create the `/themes/childclassicwh/templates/index.tpl`. In that case, the new file content will completely replace the original one on the FO index page.

Sometimes, as Smarty enables extending parent templates from a child theme template, we will be able to override one block from the original template files. The best way to do this would be to use the `parent:` prefix in the path of the file to extend. The extension would look like this:

```
{extends file='parent:path/to/parent/file.tpl'}
```

For the CSS or JavaScript original files, we can act the same way. For example, if we want to override the `/themes/classic/assets/css/theme.css` or `/themes/classic/assets/js/theme.js` files from our child theme, we can respectively create the `/themes/childclassicwh/assets/css/theme.css` or `/themes/childclassicwh/assets/js/theme.js` files.

Feel free to test these overrides by adding simple CSS code on the body selector for the `theme.css` file and an `alert(1);` for the `theme.js` file, for example. You will see how efficient it can be!

You will be able to find our child theme example in the GitHub repository for this book at this URL: `https://github.com/PacktPublishing/Practical-Module-Development-for-Prestashop-8/tree/main/Chapter%2014`.

This is all that we need to know for the moment in terms of child theme creation. Let's install and test our child theme.

Installing and testing our child theme example

Now that we have created a child theme to extend the classic theme, let's try it!

Just like all the themes, we can install and change the theme's settings via the **Design | Theme & Logo** BO page. If we go to this page from our BO, we should find this screen:

My theme for Test PS 8 shop

Classic Version 2.0.6
Designed by PrestaShop SA and Contributors

Classic child theme WebHelpers
Version 1.0.0
Designed by Web Helpers

Figure 14.1 – The theme installation interface

By clicking on the **Use this theme** button, it will activate our child theme. If we go to our FO index page after activating the child theme, nothing should have changed; it just displays all the content from the parent `Classic` theme.

To test the explained concepts presented in the last section of this chapter, please add the `/themes/childclassicwh/templates/index.tpl` file containing this code:

```
{extends file='parent:page.tpl'}
    {block name='page_content_container'}
      TEST
    {/block}
```

Please reload the index FO controller at the root of your website, which should then display something like the following screenshot:

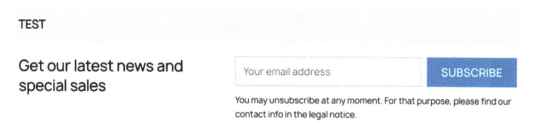

Figure 14.2 – The index.tpl file override in action!

As you can see, our child theme does what it is supposed to do. And we can do a lot more! Feel free to challenge yourself and modify some blocks of the FO of your shop.

Summary

In this chapter, we discovered what a child theme is. It enables us to customize an existing theme by keeping the ability to update the original theme. We saw the minimal structure required to create a standard child theme and tested it.

We will learn, in the next chapter, how to adapt module templates to our child theme in order to make them fit in to the graphical context of our shop.

15

Overriding Some Templates

Although we know how to create a child theme to extend an existing one, we would love to customize some of the installed modules' templates or assets to make them look like the rest of our child theme. As you can imagine, the best practice for this is certainly not to directly modify the modules' templates or assets in the module directories. We will learn, in this chapter, the most efficient and clean way to customize the assets and templates.

Let's follow these steps to discover the best practices for module template/asset overriding from a theme:

- Overriding a module template from a (child) theme
- Overriding a module CSS asset from a (child) theme
- Overriding a module JavaScript asset from a (child) theme

By the end of this chapter, we will know how to override any module template or asset in a clean and efficient way, so as to keep the module updatable and without having any impact on other themes.

Technical requirements

You will need the following elements to create our template and asset overrides:

- Any code editor to create our overrides
- An (S)FTP client to browse files and folders (only if you work on a remote server – not necessary if you work on a local server)
- A web browser to test our overrides
- A working PrestaShop installation (v1.7.x minimum) with a theme or a child theme active

> **Note**
> Before starting our explanations, all the examples presented in this chapter can be applied to a theme or a child theme. You can apply these principles if you create your own theme or also if you create a child theme. It will work in both cases.

The following information can be applied only to the FO templates and assets. It will be only used to customize the FO pages and make the modules look like the rest of the active theme or child theme.

Let's dive now into our practical example!

Imagine that you have installed the `whrelaycarrier` module presented in *Chapter 13, A Drive Delivery Module*, meaning that you should have the `/modules/whrelaycarrier/` folder available containing all your front templates and assets for the FO features provided by this module.

Let's complete our first challenge: a simple module template customization for the active (child) theme.

Overriding a module template from a (child) theme

If you remember our `whrelaycarrier` module, it adds a modal box that appears by choosing the **Relay Carrier** shipping option in the FO checkout controller. This modal box is provided by the `displayAfterCarrier` hook via the `/modules/whrelaycarrier/views/templates/hook/displayAfterCarrier.tpl` Smarty template file.

The modal box as designed in the original module looks as follows:

Figure 15.1 – The Relay points choice modal box provided by the original whrelaycarrier module

Our challenge here will be to add an H3 tag after the relay points H2 tag for the active (child) theme and not for others. This new tag will contain the `"Custom Line to add to our theme text"` text. The modal box should finally look like this:

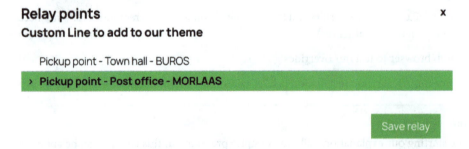

Figure 15.2 – The custom (child) theme relay points choice modal box with the new H3 tag

Let's suppose that the active theme is the child theme of the classic theme called `childclassicwh`, located in the `/themes/childclassicwh/` folder.

As explained before, the fastest way to complete our task could be to open the `/modules/whrelaycarrier/views/templates/hook/displayAfterCarrier.tpl` file and add the requested HTML H3 tag. It would work, but the constraint of being able to update our module without losing our customization wouldn't comply. Also, this code edition would be available for all the installed themes and not only for our `childclassicwh` child theme, which is not what we wanted. That's why this method is not the right one.

To solve this problem, the best practice is to create the `/themes/childclassicwh/modules/whrelaycarrier/views/templates/hook/displayAfterCarrier.tpl` file. Before displaying a module Smarty template, PrestaShop tests that the provided template is not overridden in the module's folder of the current theme (as implemented in the `_isTemplateOverloadedStatic()` method of the `Module` object).

The best way to know the path where to store the module FO template to override is to concatenate the desired theme folder path to the original template file path.

For us, the theme folder path is `/themes/childclassicwh/` and the module template path is `/modules/whrelaycarrier/views/templates/hook/displayAfterCarrier.tpl`. As a result, the template overriding our original one will be stored in the `/themes/childclassicwh/modules/whrelaycarrier/views/templates/hook/displayAfterCarrier.tpl` file.

To complete our challenge, we will add the `<h3>{l s="Custom Line to add to our theme" d="Modules.Whrelaycarrier.Shop"}</h3>` code after the existing H2 tag of the original template content. Then, we should have the following content in the `/themes/childclassicwh/modules/whrelaycarrier/views/templates/hook/displayAfterCarrier.tpl` file:

```
<div id="whrelaycarrier_points">
  <div>
    <span>x</span>
    <h2>{l s="Relay points"
      d="Modules.Whrelaycarrier.Shop"}</h2>
    <h3>{l s="Custom Line to add to our theme"
      d="Modules.Whrelaycarrier.Shop"}</h3>
    <ul>
    {foreach from=$relays item=relay}
      <li data-id-relay="{$relay["id_relay"]}" {if
        !empty($id_relay_checked) && $id_relay_checked ==
        $relay["id_relay"]}class="active"{
        /if}>{$relay["name"]}</li>
    {/foreach}
    </ul>
    <a id="whrelaycarrier_submit" class="btn
      btn-success">{l s="Save relay"
```

```
        d="Modules.Whrelaycarrier.Shop"}</a>
   </div>
</div>
```

Save this file and go to the shipping methods step of the checkout FO controller. If you click on the **Relay Carrier** option, the new modal box should look as expected in *Figure 15.2*.

As online sellers often want to get quick results, if you want to locate quickly which template has to be overridden, switch on the debug mode of PrestaShop and you will find comments providing the path of the displayed template in the HTML source code of the page.

It can be easily seen with the web inspector of your browser:

```
▼ <div id="hook-display-after-carrier">
    <!--begin module:whrelaycarrier/views/templates/hook/displayAfterCarrier.tpl-->
    <!--
    begin /Users/louisauthie/Documents/Apache/devps/PrestaShop/themes/childclassicwh/modules/whrelaycarrier
    /views/templates/hook/displayAfterCarrier.tpl
    -->
  ▶ <div id="whrelaycarrier_points" style="display: flex;"> ... </div> flex
    <!--
    end /Users/louisauthie/Documents/Apache/devps/PrestaShop/themes/childclassicwh/modules/whrelaycarrier
    /views/templates/hook/displayAfterCarrier.tpl
    -->
    <!--end module:whrelaycarrier/views/templates/hook/displayAfterCarrier.tpl-->
  </div>
  <div id="extra_carrier"></div>
```

Figure 15.3 – The Smarty comments providing the displayed templates paths

Let's see now how to customize the CSS code only for a specified (child) theme.

Overriding a module CSS asset from a (child) theme

Exactly as in the previous section of this chapter, still with the `whrelaycarrier` module, let's suppose that we would like to change the chosen relay point line background color from green to red in the modal box.

The expected output would look as follows:

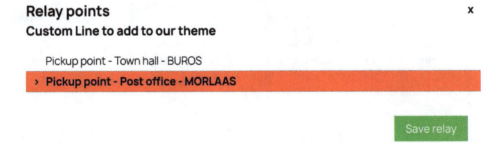

Figure 15.4 – The overridden modal box expected new look

For this modal box, the original CSS code is in the `/modules/whrelaycarrier/views/css/checkout.css` file. Following the same method as presented in the previous section for the templates, if we create a `/themes/childclassicwh/modules/whrelaycarrier/views/css/checkout.css` file, it will be applied instead of the original CSS for the current `childclassicwh` child theme.

Let's create this new file, copy and paste the content of the original CSS file, and replace the `#whrelaycarrier_points>div>ul>li.active` selector style with this one:

```
#whrelaycarrier_points>div>ul>li.active{
   font-weight: 700;
   background: #FF0000;
}
```

If you go to the pickup relay points choice modal box on the FO checkout controller, you will see that the color has changed as expected.

Let's now apply this method to the last asset type used in our module code, JavaScript.

Overriding a module JavaScript asset from a (child) theme

Still with the `whrelaycarrier` module, let's trigger an alert displaying the **Thanks for the choice!** message on a pickup relay line click, on the modal box. The expected behavior would look like this:

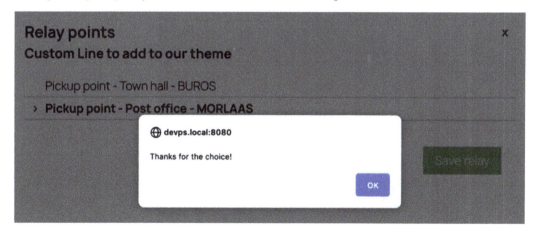

Figure 15.5 – The alert box displayed on a pickup point line click after the ajax process

As a reminder, the JavaScript code defining the modal box behavior can be found in the `/modules/whrelaycarrier/views/js/checkout.js` file.

By following the same method presented in the previous sections, for both templates and CSS file overrides, if we create a `/themes/childclassicwh/modules/whrelaycarrier/views/js/checkout.js` file, it will replace the original JavaScript file and will be executed instead.

So, let's do it and copy and paste the original JavaScript content and replace the `$('#whrelaycarrier_points>div>ul>li').click(function(){...})` selector event callback function with this one:

```
$('#whrelaycarrier_points>div>ul>li').click(function(){
  $('#whrelaycarrier_points>div>ul>li').removeClass('active');
    id_relay = $(this).data('id-relay');
    var itemSelected = $(this);
    if(id_relay!=0){
      $.ajax({
        method: "POST",
        url: ajaxUrl,
        data: { relay: id_relay, cart: id_cart },
        dataType: "json"
      })
      .done(function( jsonResponse ) {
        if(jsonResponse.return_code == 'OK'){
          itemSelected.addClass('active');
          alert("Thanks for the choice!");
        }
      });
    }
});
```

This should do the trick! The new alert message will now appear.

Feel free to apply it to any of your installed modules and see how things change in the corresponding FO parts of your shop!

Summary

In this chapter, we learned the best practices for the modules' template and CSS/JavaScript asset file overrides enabling us to keep the original content of the modules safe and updatable without changing other themes' appearances and behaviors.

In the next chapter, we will focus on how to set up the Webpack bundler to compile the assets of your modules and/or themes all at once, quickly and efficiently.

16

Assets Compiling with Webpack

With all the previous chapters, we know how the PrestaShop core works, how to build efficient modules, and how to customize our themes by using the best practices. Even if we can create our modules or theme assets directly by writing CSS and JavaScript code, most of us prefer using SASS to build stylesheets and to build JavaScript code with many third-party dependencies.

Instead of handling SASS compiling and embedding too many JavaScript files in the HTML code, leading to many HTTP requests, Webpack will help us manage all those tasks all at once.

Let's learn more about this useful bundler by following these steps:

- Understanding what Webpack does and its prerequisites
- Discovering the structure of a Webpack config file
- Building assets with Webpack

By the end of this chapter, we will know what Webpack does, how it works, and how to use it.

Technical requirements

You will need the following elements to learn how Webpack works and to test it:

- Any code editor to create our assets and configure Webpack
- An (S)FTP client to browse files and folders (only if you work on a remote server – not necessary if you work on a local server)
- A web browser to see the effect of our assets
- A terminal access to your web server with Node.js (v14.x or 16.x) and npm (v7.x or 8.x) installed and functional
- A working PrestaShop installation (v1.7.x minimum) with the classic theme installed and active

Understanding what Webpack does and its prerequisites

In a standard web project, we will often use CSS stylesheets, generated with/without preprocessors such as SASS. All the CSS files will be embedded into the web pages and each file will lead to an HTTP request/response. Very often, there can be repeats in the code that can be long, which leads to a slower user experience.

In the same way, for JavaScript scripts, we will often use many third-party libraries to benefit from ready-to-use functionalities and tools. As each library will have to be called and included in the web page to be executed by the client, this will make the page load slower.

What if we had a tool enabling us to compile the JavaScript code with all its libraries, the SASS code, and the CSS code all at once with one terminal command? This tool is Webpack, and it is a bundler. It enables bundling all the JavaScript and SCSS code in clean and minified output files.

The Webpack use is not mandatory in PrestaShop, and you can choose to use it or not in your modules or themes. The aim of this chapter is to make you understand how it works and show how it can be helpful. A good example of an efficient use of Webpack is the classic theme available from its GitHub repository: `https://github.com/PrestaShop/classic-theme`. Here are the steps for setting up Webpack:

1. First, if you want to use Webpack somewhere, you will need to install **Node.js** (version 14.x or 16.x) and its **npm** tool (version 7.x or 8.x). **Node Version Manager** (**NVM**) is also a great tool to make sure that you install the right versions.

> **Note**
>
> If you work in a (child) theme, please create a `_dev/` folder at the root of your theme, if it still doesn't exist. Then, you can put or modify all the (S)CSS files in the `_dev/css/` folder and the JavaScript scripts in the `_dev/js/` folder.
>
> If the `_dev/package.json` and `_dev/webpack.config.js` files don't exist, to avoid recoding everything, please download them from the classic theme example at this URL: `https://github.com/PrestaShop/classic-theme/tree/develop/_dev`.

2. Open the `_dev/package.json` file and replace the `name` and `description` fields to customize it. Beware that the `name` field must be lowercase, one word, and may contain hyphens and underscores.

3. Then, you can execute the `npm install` command in the terminal directly in the `_dev/` folder. It will install the necessary packages to run the Webpack compiling commands correctly.

Before running the commands, let's discover the structure of the `webpack.config.js` file in order to understand where to put the input and where the output files will be delivered.

Discovering the structure of a Webpack config file

If we want to use Webpack correctly, we need to understand the structure of the `webpack.config.js` file, which will set the behavior of Webpack executions.

Let's open the `_dev/webpack.config.js` file and see how it works. By going through it line by line, we will first find the required JavaScript libraries block calls. We can find the following requirements:

- `Path`: provides a way of working with directories and file paths

- `MiniCssExtractPlugin`: enables creating a separate CSS file if an SCSS or a CSS is in the entry list or in a file

- `Terser`: enables minifying/minimizing the JavaScript scripts

- `CSSO`: enables cleaning and minifying CSS code

- `LicensePlugin`: cleans the license code from plugins and stores it in the same file instead

Then, let's see how the `entry` field is defined and what it stands for:

```
entry: {
    theme: ['./js/theme.js', './css/theme.scss'],
    error: ['./css/error.scss'],
},
```

This field defines a group of entries per key defined. Here, we have two keys – `theme` and `error` – defining two entries, one containing a JavaScript file and an SCSS file, and the other an SCSS file only.

With the `output` field defined as follows, we defined where and how the output files will be stored:

```
output: {
    path: path.resolve(__dirname, '../assets/js'),
    filename: '[name].js',
},
```

This code defines that we will save two output files: `assets/js/theme.js` and `assets/js/error.js`.

We will see later in the rules how the SCSS will be processed! Be patient!

With the following code, Webpack is set to prefer to resolve module requests as relative requests instead of using modules from `node_modules` directories:

```
resolve: {
    preferRelative: true,
},
```

Finally, the rules are set this way:

```
module: {
    rules: [
        {
            test: /\.js/,
            loader: 'esbuild-loader',
        },
        {
            test: /\.scss$/,
            use: [
                MiniCssExtractPlugin.loader,
                'css-loader',
                'postcss-loader',
                'sass-loader',
            ],
        },
        {
            test: /.(png|woff(2)?|eot|otf|ttf|svg|gif)
            (\?[a-z0-9=\.]+)?$/,
            type: 'asset/resource',
            generator: {
              filename: '../css/[hash][ext]',
            },
        },
        {
            test: /\.css$/,
            use: [MiniCssExtractPlugin.loader, 'style-loader',
            'css-loader', 'postcss-loader'],
        },
    ],
},
```

The first rule tells Webpack to use esbuild-loader for all the JavaScript files to load. It's a plugin that uses the esbuild library to improve the performance of the builds. It speeds up the bundling process. If not used, it will become slower.

Then, the second rule, applied to the SCSS files, tells Webpack to use MiniCssExtractPlugin.loader to create a separate file for the SCSS files present in the entries files lists. sass-loader loads the SASS code and translates it to CSS, css-loader loads the CSS code and cleans it, and postcss adds a post-treatment to the loaded code.

If you look at the plugins definition field present in this file, there is the new MiniCssExtractPlugin({filename: path.join('..', 'css', '[name].css')}) line, telling the plugin to store the SASS compiled code in the assets/css/theme.css and assets/css/error.css files.

With the third rule, Webpack will store all the image and font files in the `assets/css` folder by renaming them with a hash as the name and keeping the extension.

Then, with the final fourth rule, Webpack will do the same as for the SCSS files, but without the SASS compiling!

With the following code, Webpack avoids the multiple imports of the `prestashop` and `jquery` libraries and does it only once:

```
externals: {
    prestashop: 'prestashop',
    $: '$',
    jquery: 'jQuery',
},
```

As the rest is pretty obvious, we now know how everything will behave.

If you want to learn more about Webpack and get advanced concepts, feel free to visit the official documentation via this URL: `https://webpack.js.org/concepts/`.

Keep in mind that we should only have to modify the `entry` field to update the input files and `entry` keys to fit our needs.

Let's now test a compilation. First, let's have a quick look at the `_dev/package.json` file. There, we can see in the `script` field what will happen if we use the `npm run` command to use scripts:

```
"scripts": {
    "build": "NODE_ENV=production webpack --progress",
    "watch": "webpack --progress --watch",
    ...
},
```

Focusing on these two scripts, we see that if we execute the `npm run build` command in the `_dev/` folder, we will compile the assets with the `NODE_ENV` variable set to `production` once, and it will minify and clean the code as much as possible.

If we execute the `npm run watch` command in the `_dev/` folder, we will compile the assets each time one entry asset is saved. The command will be watching the code changes and will not stop until we stop the command in the terminal.

The best way to see how this works is to try a real building process. Let's do it together.

Building assets with Webpack

Here are the steps for building a process with Webpack:

1. Please empty the `/themes/classic/assets/css/` and `/themes/classic/assets/js/` folders to make sure that the output files will be generated by us.

2. From the `/themes/classic/_dev/` folder, please execute the `npm run build` command.

3. If you go to the `/themes/classic/assets/` folder, you will find the compiled CSS and images/fonts in the `/themes/classic/assets/css/` folder and the compiled JavaScript in the `/themes/classic/assets/js/` folder. That works and saves us a lot of compiling commands!

4. In the same way, if we execute the `npm run watch` command, it does the same thing, but we see that it repeats the process when an entry file is saved. That will enable us to code and preview without having to retype the compiling command all the time. It's a nice tool during long coding tasks.

Feel free to test it again with our *Customer Callback Request* module available at this URL: `https://github.com/PacktPublishing/Practical-Module-Development-for-Prestashop-8/tree/main/Chapter%209/whcallback/views`.

Summary

In this final chapter, we discovered Webpack – what it does, how to initialize it, how to configure it, and how to test its behavior. We saw that it could make us save lots of commands to compile JS or SASS/CSS assets. Even if we used it in the themes' context, as is the case with the classic theme provided by PrestaShop, we can use the same process in the modules by changing the configuration file and setting the appropriate output path and entries.

In conclusion, we now understand how PrestaShop's core works with Symfony and the old legacy libraries. This knowledge of the full environment helped us to understand how modules could embed and add new features into our system without disrupting the life cycle of Prestashop. Our multiple examples and use cases enable us to apply modern design patterns to our module projects. Finally, the last chapters about theme customization and asset bundling showed us how to make our shop look the way we prefer, fitting with a trademark platform.

We are now able to provide great solutions to online merchants in order to make them succeed!

Appendix – Module Upgrade, The Hooks Discovery Tool, and Multi-Store Functions

Getting the hook parameters quickly

Even if we presented methods to find which hooks to use in our modules multiple times, we haven't yet presented the **Hooks** tool in the Symfony profiler toolbar visible in the BO Symfony-based controllers.

If you connect to your BO, and go to a Symfony-based controller in debug mode, you will find, in the profiler toolbar at the bottom of the page, the new **Hooks** tool:

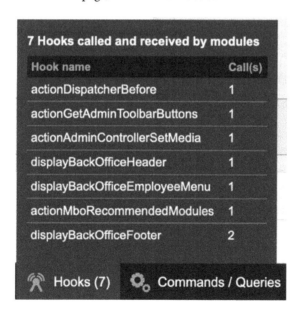

Figure A.1 – The Hooks profiler tool

It will give you a shortlist of triggered hooks registered to modules. But if you click on the **Hooks** tab in the profiler, you will access the full list of hooks present and called on this page, whether they are received by module classes or not.

If you want to know more about a `hook` parameter, you can browse the code of PrestaShop to reach the Hook call definition and see which parameters are sent.

Another great tool offered by the PrestaShop open source developer documentation is the **hook list**, which is accessible by going via this URL: `https://devdocs.prestashop-project.org/8/ modules/concepts/hooks/list-of-hooks/`. You will get all the necessary information on a hook by searching for it in the list. That can be a great shortcut!

Making a module multistore-compliant

As you may have seen how multistore worked in the BO controllers, PrestaShop can contain multiple shops, each shop can present some of the items of the catalog, and some categories can contain a separate inventory. A shop is a sub-member of a shop group, which enables us to share data with other shops.

The general idea if you use multistore features is that your database tables and entities must contain the `id_shop` and `id_shop_group` attributes, even if you are in localized tables. As you now know how to handle the `Lang` entities for your entities objects, you should be able to add the necessary `shop` attributes in the same way.

The necessary information about the multistore status, such as which shop and shop group are selected, is available via the `multistore` feature adapter. You can retrieve this service like this:

```
$multistoreFeature = $this->get('prestashop.adapter.feature.
multistore');
```

And the shop context adapter is accessible this way:

```
$shopContext = $this->get('prestashop.adapter.shop.context');
```

All the important functions available to get enough information are well presented in the official developer documentation at this URL: `https://devdocs.prestashop-project.org/8/ development/multistore/shop-context/`.

Let's talk about the `Configuration` variables stored in the `prefix_configuration` table. If you browse the database, going to the corresponding table, you may see that the `id_shop` and `id_shop_group` columns are present:

- If both are set to `NULL`, then the configuration data is shop- and shop-group-independent. It is global.
- If `id_shop_group` is set to `INT` and if `id_shop` is set to `NULL`, then the variable is shop-group-dependent but not shop-dependent.
- Otherwise, if both are set with `INT` values, the corresponding variable is shop- and shop-group-dependent.

Programmatically, from anywhere in a Symfony controller or in a module class, you can use the Configuration adapter and get the corresponding values with this code:

```
$configuration = $container->get('prestashop.adapter.legacy.
configuration');

$shopConstraint = new ShopConstraint(
   (int) $id_shop,
   (int) $id_shop_group
);

$variableValue = (int) $configuration->get('PS_CONFIGURATION_NAME',
null, $shopConstraint);
```

In this code, we first retrieve the configuration service, then we instantiate a `PrestaShop\PrestaShop\Core\Domain\Shop\ValueObject\ShopConstraint` object and provide it with `id_shop` and `id_shop_group`, depending on the needed scope. Then, we call the `get()` method to retrieve our data.

Upgrading a module

Imagine that we have a module in version *1.0.0* and that we want to change its version to *1.0.1*. In the first version, we missed a column in a table, and we decided to add it in the new version. How can we do it without obliging our users to reset the module and lose the data? That's what upgrades are for!

Let's say that our initial table was the `ps_testmodule_item` table and that we want to add a `position` integer column to it in the new version.

First, we can add an `upgrade/` folder to our module root folder. And let's add a new `upgrade/upgrade-1.0.1.php` file to it. It will contain the function that will be called on upgrading to the `1.0.1` version of the current module. There, we will be able to execute our table column changes.

On upgrading, the called function will be `upgrade_module_1_0_1($module)`.

In our example, our `upgrade/upgrade-1.0.1.php` file will contain the following code:

```php
<?php
function upgrade_module_1_0_1($module)
{
$db = Db::getInstance();
$db->execute("ALTER TABLE `"._DB_PREFIX_."testmodule_item` ADD COLUMN
`position` INT(1) NOT NULL AFTER `id_item`");
//Here you can choose to register or unregister a list of hooks
//$module->registerHook('hookName');

return true;
}
```

If there had been many version upgrades, the system would have executed all the upgrade files and functions from the current version installed to the newest one, one by one, to apply all the migration scripts.

This way, you will give the best upgrade experience to your customers without losing data.

Index

Other Books You May Enjoy

If you enjoyed this book, you may be interested in these other books by Packt:

Joomla! 4 Masterclass

Luca Marzo

ISBN: 9781803238975

- Build your websites using Joomla 4's enhanced features

- Explore advanced content-handling features like scheduled publishing options, custom fields, and the workflow feature

- Discover the search engine optimization features included in Joomla 4

- Set up your website to handle multiple languages and structure the navigation system

- Understand the customization features provided by Joomla -- templates, overrides, and child templates

- Find out how to use CLI to operate without accessing the CMS backend

- Design tailor-made graphics by customizing Joomla templates

Drupal 10 Development Cookbook - Third Edition

Matt Glaman, Kevin Quillen

ISBN: 9781803234960

- Create and manage a Drupal site's codebase
- Design tailored content creator experiences
- Leverage Drupal by creating customized pages and plugins
- Turn Drupal into an API platform for exposing content to consumers
- Import data into Drupal using the data migration APIs
- Advance your Drupal site with modern frontend tools using Laravel Mix

Packt is searching for authors like you

If you're interested in becoming an author for Packt, please visit authors.packtpub.com and apply today. We have worked with thousands of developers and tech professionals, just like you, to help them share their insight with the global tech community. You can make a general application, apply for a specific hot topic that we are recruiting an author for, or submit your own idea.

Share Your Thoughts

Now you've finished *Practical Module Development for Prestashop 8*, we'd love to hear your thoughts! Scan the QR code below to go straight to the Amazon review page for this book and share your feedback or leave a review on the site that you purchased it from.

https://packt.link/r/1-837-63596-X

Your review is important to us and the tech community and will help us make sure we're delivering excellent quality content.

Download a free PDF copy of this book

Thanks for purchasing this book!

Do you like to read on the go but are unable to carry your print books everywhere?

Is your eBook purchase not compatible with the device of your choice?

Don't worry, now with every Packt book you get a DRM-free PDF version of that book at no cost.

Read anywhere, any place, on any device. Search, copy, and paste code from your favorite technical books directly into your application.

The perks don't stop there, you can get exclusive access to discounts, newsletters, and great free content in your inbox daily

Follow these simple steps to get the benefits:

1. Scan the QR code or visit the link below

https://packt.link/free-ebook/9781837635962

2. Submit your proof of purchase
3. That's it! We'll send your free PDF and other benefits to your email directly